Oct 23, 1998

Mindsets

Dear [name],

Keep smiling with
the right "mindset"
and attitude.
It is much appreciated

E Ping

Mindsets grow companies.

Roger Enrico
Chairman and
Chief Executive Officer,
Pepsico Inc.

Mindsets

Mental Health:
The Ultimate Productivity Weapon

A Report and Commentary
First of Two Parts

Edgardo Pérez, M.D.
&
Bill Wilkerson

The Homewood Centre for Organizational Health at Riverslea
1998

Canadian Cataloguing in Publication Data

Wilkerson, Bill, 1942–
    Mindsets: Mental health, the ultimate productivity weapon

ISBN 1-894083-04-0

    1. Employees—Mental health. 2. Job stress. 3. Labour productivity
I. Pérez, Edgardo, 1951–
II. Homewood Centre for Organizational Health at Riverslea.
III. Title

RC967.5P47 1998   658.3'82   C98-901143-7

Published by

The Homewood Centre for Organizational Health at Riverslea
150 Delhi Street
Guelph, Ontario
Canada
N1E 6K9

For author inquiries, call Bill Wilkerson at Homewood, (519) 824–1010.
For copies of this book, write or call Carol O'Brian atHomewood,
(519) 824–1010.

Editing and design by

Fomorian Press
471 Athlone Avenue
Ottawa, Ontario
Canada
K1Z 5M9

        613.728.5587
        613.728.9754
        baddog@cyberus.ca

Table of Contents

Dedication

To those who suffer a hand dealt by fate — and who play that hand with courage and resolve in their return to health and to the productive lives they were born to enjoy. God bless them.

About the Authors

DR. EDGARDO PÉREZ IS CHIEF EXECUTIVE OFFICER AND MEDICAL CHIEF of Staff of the Homewood Health Centre in Guelph, Ontario. He is also Co-Director of the Centre for Organizational Health at Riverslea, located on Homewood's historic grounds, CEO of the Homewood Behavioural Health Corporation and Vice-President of the Homewood Corporation.

Dr. Pérez is a graduate of Cornell University; the State University of New York Health Science Centre, where he received his medical degree; Harvard University, where he studied health services administration and behavioural sciences, receiving a Master's Degree in Public Health; and the University of Ottawa Medical School, where he received his diploma in psychiatry in 1979.

He is a professor of psychiatry at the University of Ottawa and McMaster University, as well as professor of both psychiatry and health administration at the University of Toronto. Dr. Pérez's areas of academic interest are management and organizational health, health services research and health care quality assessment.

Dr. Pérez is also a surveyor, consultant and trainer for the Canadian Council on Health Services Accreditation, an organization that focuses on developing standards and assessing quality of healthcare.

Bill Wilkerson is Co-Director of the Homewood Centre for Organizational Health at Riverslea, Special Advisor to the Homewood Health Group, President of the Canadian Business and Economic Roundtable on Mental Health and Vice-Chairman of the Mayors' National Initiative on World Mental Health Day in Canada. Mr. Wilkerson served as "the transformational president" of Liberty Health, the successor company to Ontario Blue Cross — this, after 30 years in fields as diverse as broadcasting, banking, education, major league sports, politics, government and large multinational corporations.

For 10 years, Mr. Wilkerson was co-owner of a successful consulting business that continues today, The CorpWorld Group, with Mr. Fraser Kelly, formerly one of Canada's leading journalists. Mr. Wilkerson is a veteran of service in senior positions at all three levels of government in Canada, and, in his corporate career, has served in and advised organizations such as ITT, Royal Bank, the University of Toronto, Canadian Broadcasting Corporation, CTV Television, The Sports Network, Shell Canada, the EdperBrascan Corporation, Skydome Corporation, Stelco, BCE, INCO, George Weston Limited, the National Hockey League and the Canadian Football League.

Mr. Wilkerson served as an Adjunct Professor at the University of Western Ontario Graduate School of Journalism, and was selected for the prestigious Wharton School of Business-ITT Executive Seminar on Financial Management and Control at the University of Pennsylvania, under the leadership of Wharton School Dean D.C. Carroll and Assistant Dean Jules Schwartz.

About this Report

THIS COMMENTARY IS BEING PUBLISHED BY THE HOMEWOOD CENTRE FOR Organizational Health at Riverslea, created in 1998.

Riverslea is a place, a grand old mansion reflecting the early part of this century, which Homewood preserved for its history, and adapted for its own purpose. Riverslea is located on the lovely perimeter of the gracious Homewood grounds, a sentinel overlooking the Speed River, which flows, rises and falls in consonance with the advent and retreat of each season.

The Centre for Organizational Health at Riverslea is affiliated with the Homewood Health Centre, and to the best of our knowledge, it is the first of its kind directly associated with a psychiatric hospital.

Homewood Health Centre is a specialist provider of mental health services. The Centre for Organizational Health is designed to identify, and interpret those non-medical determinants of mental health which affect human productivity and economic performance.

The genesis of this Report occurred in October 1997. At that time, an experiment of sorts took place. A number of very senior business executives, physicians and psychiatrists were brought together privately to discuss the topic of depression and work. The result demonstrated two things — one) these two categories of leaders had a lot to talk about, and two) it was generally agreed that, yes, depression was a business issue.

Two people in particular were instrumental in making that meeting happen.

One was Tim Price, Chairman of the Board of the Trilon Financial Corporation, and the other was the Honourable William G. Davis, former Premier of Ontario and now Counsel to the very distinguished law firm of Tory, Tory, Deslauriers & Binnington.

In the course of that meeting, Mr. Price spoke definitively: "Depression is a business issue that we simply must know more about." Mr. Davis explored a telling point. He observed, in effect, that some time ago, persons with physical disabilities had difficulty gaining acceptance. Times and things change. Today, the Special Olympics is recognized as an authentic sports event aside from its humanitarian purposes, and buildings are now commonly equipped with access for those with physical disabilities.

Could not we aspire to, and attain a similar standard of acceptance, understanding and observation, Mr. Davis asked, for those with mental disabilities?

Could we not indeed.

Earlier this year, the Homewood Centre for Organizational Health launched two initiatives. One was the *Dr. Stephen Lett Lecture Series* — named after Homewood's first medical superintendent who held office nearly a century and a fifth ago — aimed at exploring the connections between the way communities and organizations function, and how mental health is preserved or fractured. Dr. Heather Munroe-Blum, Vice-President of Research and International Relations at the University of Toronto, and a prominent epidemiologist, helped launch the series and did so in a provocative and thoughtful way.

The other was the *Homewood Letter* to discuss mental health in an economic context. The first edition considered the mind-body connection and discussed mental illness from the perspective of how physical wellbeing and performance are influenced — so fundamentally — by mental wellbeing.

References and Interviews
Mindsets is based upon our review and analysis of thousands of technical papers, medical and business journals, corporate strategy documents, health studies, newspapers and newsmagazine stories, television documentaries, polling and survey reports and specialized medical research data.

We conducted scores of interviews, held plenary discussions among clinicians, and examined in detail the landmark studies by Harvard University on two significant fronts — the global burden of disease and mental illness worldwide. These stupendous initiatives by Harvard were undertaken in concert with the World Bank and the World Health Organization. We are grateful for access to the materials and their authors.

Over the past year, we have explored the business-health theme reflected in this report with a number of accomplished Canadian business and health leaders. Their influence is reflected in this report.

On questions relating to depression and heart disease, a prominent theme of this book, our thanks go to Dr. Robert Swenson of the Ottawa Heart Institute, Dr. Francois Lespérance of the Montreal Heart Institute, Dr. Susan Abbey of Toronto Hospital, and Dr. Paul Dorian of the Terrence Donnelly Heart Centre at St. Michael's Hospital in Toronto.

To Dr. Walter Rosser, Chairman of the Department of Family and Community Medicine at the University of Toronto, our thanks for his support and interest in our discussion of the relevance of mental health to physical wellbeing and vice versa.

To Dr. Barbara Dorian, Psychiatrist-in-Chief at Women's College Hospital, our thanks for several fruitful discussions on the gender dimension of mental health.

To Dr. Pierre Beauséjour, President of the Canadian Psychiatric Association, and to Dr. Rodrigo Muñoz, President of the American Psychiatric Association, our most genuine thanks for your interest in this project and its related work.

To Dr. Beth Reade of the Homewood Health Centre, our thanks for her dedication and judgment in reviewing and sourcing an invaluable range of medical literature, which we drew upon extensively.

Our thanks to Dr. Harvey Skinner, Chair of the Department of Public Health Sciences at the University of Toronto, and his colleagues Dr. Irv Rootman and Dr. Martin Shain for their insight into questions of organizational and population health and the re-engagement of that discipline with the healthcare field.

To Dr. Jacques Bradwejn, Chairman of Psychiatry at the University of Ottawa, and Dr. Russell Joffe, Dean of Health Sciences at McMaster University for their interest in and contribution to our broader efforts to merge business and health into a defined policy unit.

To Dr. Paul Garfinkel, President and Chief Executive of the Centre for Addiction and Mental Health in Toronto and Chairman of Psychiatry at the University of Toronto, our thanks more generally for his visionary leadership in the mental health field and support of projects related to this report.

To Ed Pennington, Executive Director of the Canadian Mental Health Association for his splendid stewardship of the community-based mental health movement in Canada and support of our work.

To Dr. Ruth Berman, Executive Director of the Ontario Psychological Association, our thanks for her forthright and telling contribution to our thinking on the subjects discussed here.

To Helen Bozinovski and her colleagues at the Heart and Stroke Foundation of Ontario for their timely and influential expression of interest in this project.

To Dr. Jane England and her colleagues at the Washington Business Group on Health for access to their meetings and their rich assessment of health questions in a business context.

Our best wishes to Dr. Lisa Doupe, co-founder of the Canadian Business Group on Health and Productivity. We had an informative dialogue and are grateful for it.

We thank Dr. Bruce Rowat, a physician-educator who teaches at the University of Toronto and serves as medical director and advisor to both Sun Life and the Bank of Montreal for his broad view and regular input to our work.

We wish to thank two outstanding Bank of Montreal executives for their collaborative interest in, and support of our work. Maria Gonzalez, Vice-President of Strategic Initiatives for the Bank of Montreal and Tom Reynolds, BMO's International Director for Employee Assistance Plans.

Our appreciation, as well, to Dr. Earl Berger, Managing Director of Canada Health Monitor, who saw our initiative in its earliest stages and gave us valuable and timely support.

Special Friends

There are some we consider special friends of this project. To them a particular word of thanks.

Olga Cwiek, former broadcast executive and recently-elected member of the Board of Directors of the Homewood Corporation and Homewood Health Centre — for her tireless editorial oversight.

Neil Seeman, a lawyer, writer and now a member of the editorial board of Southam's new national newspaper, *The National Post*, who influenced the direction of this initiative at an early time.

Dr. Peggy Leatt, Chair of the Department of Health Administration at the University of Toronto, will wonder why she is mentioned here. The answer is found in our gratitude for access to her writings — and herself — in the earliest stage of this report.

Marilou McPhedran, lawyer, health advocate, Member of the Order of Canada, for sharing with us, in an ongoing way, her knowledge and insight on many of the most sensitive issues facing business and health leaders today, prominently those affecting women.

And Sherry Stein, who was indefatigable in her skillful assembly of this report.

World Mental Health Day in Canada

THE AUTHORS OF THIS REPORT AND COMMENTARY WISH TO ACKNOWLEDGE the World Federation for Mental Health, the Pan American Health Organization and the World Health Organization for their leadership in advancing the interests of all peoples through education, service and enlightenment in the field of mental health.

We also wish to salute the splendid work of Harvard University and particularly Dr. Christopher Murray and his associates at the Harvard Center for Population and Development Studies for their milestone work in the analysis of the global burden of disease. Their herculean volumes helped inspire our "modest by comparison" effort.

Public leadership is a staple of democratic life. In that context, we believe His Worship Don Cousens, Mayor of the Town of Markham, Ontario, has exemplified leadership in its truest sense by launching the Canadian Mayors' National Initiative on Mental Health as the vehicle for bringing World Mental Health Day to Canada for the first time in 1998.

Mayor Cousens' initiative has drawn a remarkable response. Mayors across the country have come together in recognizing World Mental Health Day in their communities, more than 40 in all, representing every province and both territories of Canada, from the largest metropolis and cities, to local rural communities. Every capital city in Canada is part of this initiative.

A Mayors' National Proclamation on World Mental Health Day in Canada will be presented to all Canadians through Her Excellency Diana Fowler LeBlanc, wife of the Governor-General of Canada, and as such, our nation's First Lady.

Notably, the Honourary Chairs of World Mental Health Day in Canada symbolize the business-health partnership that Canada's inaugural World Mental Health Day is designed to foster. We wish to acknowledge Dr. Paul Garfinkel, President and Chief Executive of the Centre for Addiction and Mental Health in Toronto, and Tim Price, Chairman of Trilon Financial Corporation. Dr. Garfinkel is also Chairman of the Department of Psychiatry at the University of Toronto, and Mr. Price is Inaugural Chairman of the newly-formed Canadian Business and Economic Roundtable on Mental Health. Both are outstanding examples of leadership in their respective fields as well as the wider community where otherwise divergent interests embrace.

A number of people — as is always the case — were instrumental in bringing World Mental Health Day to Canada.

We applaud Ed Pennington, Executive Director of the Canadian Mental Health Association, and Dr. Pierre Beauséjour, President of the Canadian Psychiatric Association. Both greeted the concept warmly and decisively. Event Co-ordinator Donna Montgomery has been pivotal. Homewood's Ric Ament has been an able overseer of the project and Barbara Nanninga, Executive Assistant to Mayor Cousens has been solid and committed.

And to Richard Hunter, Deputy Secretary General of the World Federation for Mental Health, our most genuine thanks.

The Business-Health Axis

FOR YEARS, BUSINESS EXECUTIVES, MANAGERS AND EMPLOYEES HAVE GIVEN of themselves in one form or another, to the cause of mental health. They have participated in local committees, hospital boards, fund-raising campaigns and special community initiatives. In these terms, the heart of business has been worn on the sleeves of millions of business people.

In 1998, a new level of business interest in mental health was expressed by a diverse range of senior executives — CEOs, corporate directors, vice-presidents of various rank — to form the Canadian Business and Economic Roundtable on Mental Health.

The Roundtable is designed to make mental illness more intelligible as a business issue; to seek ways to modify the non-medical forces in the workplace that contribute to mental and emotional disorders; and to put a definition, for business-health purposes, around the impact of mental illness in the workplace when it is co-morbid (co-present) with chronic physical disorders.

The Canadian Business and Economic Roundtable on Mental Health does not consist of business people alone. Leading Canadian psychiatrists, researchers, medical doctors, psychologists and health educators provide the other half of the business-health partnership embodied by the Roundtable. It is the axis created by this partnership that gives the initiative an important strategic purpose in merging a wide range of medical and non-medical issues into a single composition or agenda for action.

The Homewood Centre for Organizational Health at Riverslea has dedicated a considerable part of its analytical and communications mandate to the work of the Canadian Business and Economic Roundtable on Mental Health.

The authors are pleased to play personal roles in the start-up and furtherance of the Roundtable and wish to acknowledge the personal leadership of Tim Price, a partner in the EdperBrascan Corporation and Chairman of the company's financial services affiliate, Trilon Financial Corporation.

Mr. Price is serving as the inaugural Chairman of the Roundtable and in remarks videotaped for the XVI Congress of the World Association of Social Psychiatry in Vancouver, B.C., he went right to the point: "Mental illness *is* a business issue and we simply must know more about it."

In Brief

IN INTERVIEWS FOR MINDSETS, LEADING FIGURES IN BUSINESS AND MEDICINE
commented on the symmetry of the mind and body that bridges human
health and the productive performance of individuals and the organizations of which they are a part.

"Physicians must treat the soul and not just the body."

> Dr. Albert Cheskes,
> leading Canadian eye surgeon
> Toronto

"Superstars in hockey play at a level that other players can't even
aspire to, because of their intellect more so than their physical skills."

> Glen Sather,
> President and General Manager of
> the Edmonton Oilers of
> the National Hockey League and
> Wayne Gretzky's former coach

"In the end, everything, including the intangible worth of people, is
or must be reflected in share value."

> Gwyn Paul Williams,
> corporate strategist and
> governance expert,
> Toronto

"Depression is clearly a business issue we've got to get a handle on."
Tim Price,
Chairman of the Board,
Trilon Financial Corporation,
an EdperBrascan company

"Absolutely, the mind and body are two sides of the same coin and the education and practices of physicians must increasingly reflect that fact."
Dr. Walter Rosser,
Chair of the Department of
Family and Community Medicine
at the University of Toronto

"Depression can be and often is triggered by today's lifestyles."
Dr. Barbara Dorian
Psychiatrist-in-Chief ,
Women's College Hospital,
Toronto

The First Word

THIS REPORT AND COMMENTARY BEGAN AS A MEMO, PROVING HOW RIGHT the man was who said it was easier to write long than short.

Mindsets — Mental Health: the Ultimate Productivity Weapon is an attempt to create a context in which to consider mental illness and economic performance as a significant public issue in the early 21st Century.

This is the first of two parts. The second will be published next year. In either case, the authors fully appreciate we are exploring, not defining the topic.

We found a surging growth in mental disorders worldwide. Mental disability affects — and in may cases grips — the lives of a quarter of a billion people on the planet.

We found that advanced economies are more likely than developing ones to produce the conditions which breed mental disability, specifically depression.

We found that depression is increasingly a disease of the young. It kills and it maims. And it cruelly targets women.

We found that 30–40 million women in North America alone are afflicted by this satanic disorder. Depression will rob more working people of more productive working years than any of the big-name killers, cancer, heart disease, AIDS, violence or war.

Yet four out of five people who suffer from depression are neither treated nor even diagnosed. What we know, then, about the impact of this disease is only partial and even in those terms, it represents a goliath among destructive health and economic forces stalking our global, national and local communities. *Mindsets* found that mental illness extends in every direction.

We found that life expectancy is an incomplete measure of the health of populations. Disability has an enormous and generally unrecognized impact, according to studies we reviewed. And once taken into account, the surging growth and impact of mental disorders come into view.

We found that psychiatric disorders are growing faster than cardiovascular disease as a percentage of the global burden of disease. Mental and behavioural disability is destroying the quality of life for more people than any other disease or disorder.

We found that the co-morbidity of mental and physical illness represents a public health risk that is becoming better understood by medical science but remains by and large a virtual mystery to the general public.

In many respects, we found the term "mental illness" to be obsolete and not suitably descriptive. One might argue, for example, that depression is as much a physical disorder as a mental one.

We discuss in this report the powerful alliance between depression and heart disease as a source of death and disability. We discuss it extensively. Through the report, the reader will find:

- Our examination of mental disorders as the source of escalating economic and business costs.
- A detailed appraisal of human capital as an instrument of corporate productivity and human health in the face of an unheralded crisis in mental illness worldwide.
- An evaluation of the impact of information technology on the perceptions and behaviours of people.
- A review of the health and business implications of the world's transition from an industrial to an information economy.
- A survey of health care reform as background for our discussion of mental health as the ultimate productivity weapon.
- A detailed review of mental illness as a medical issue, the history of psychiatry and the non-medical forces undermining the mental health and resilience of working people.
- A detailed discussion of efforts by some corporations to use human health as a competitive edge in the world economy.
- Discussion of the fundamental change now occurring in the relationship between machines and workers. People are winning. Mental health has enormous asset value in this context.
- A weighting of the stakes involved in efforts to contain the spreading effects of mental disability. This is a "billions and millions" issue. Billions of dollars and millions of people.

- And recommendations or interpretations as to where our response to these issues will take us.

If anything, we have attempted to capture the magnitude of the challenge facing the post-deficit society — a challenge shaped by the convergence of mental health and economic performance as a powerful axis of opportunity and controversy in the setting of public and corporate policy.

If our commentary on the following pages encourages a greater recognition of what those stakes are — and the clouds of uncertainty which engulf them — then the authors feel we will have contributed something useful to the state of public information on the influence of mental illness on all our lives.

Part I

A Society Rattled
by Change

❦ 1 ❧
A Passage Begins

LIKE EVERYTHING CANADIAN, OUR HEALTH CARE SYSTEM HAS EVOLVED against the political, social and emotional backdrop of the American experience, defining a fundamental difference between the cultures of our two nations.

The feared devolution of Canadian Medicare into a two-tier system — one for the rich and one for the poor — has haunted the debate about what it means to be Canadian. Our trembling seems unwarranted. Canada *does* have a distinctive North American face, culture and values, expressed by universal access to physician care and hospital services. There's no political will or need to upset that.

Healthcare is a deeply personal matter and a very public issue. Our country has one of the most admired and efficient healthcare systems in the world. But an aging population, biomedical advances, declining social networks, changing values, and, most of all, the burden of government debt have generated pressure for reform.

Healthcare: Cost or Investment?
Until now, healthcare reform has pivoted mainly on the question of who pays. That's fair enough — as far as it goes. But the concept of "payer" is inherently self-limiting.

To visualize health as an investment seems more fruitful, and in the information age, the return on investment in the health of individuals or populations might well take the form of a more resilient, productive workforce. In a way, this defines human capital. Which is more than an incidental consideration.

The World Bank says human capital will have a lot more influence on the future performance of the knowledge economy than financial capital.

In those *terms*, and in these *times*, an investment in human health produces economic benefits particular to the nature of a global world immersed in an information revolution. In that vastly-changed world, the generation of human capital is essential to promoting the sustainable health of the workforce and the economy. In this light, the destiny of people living through what University of Toronto Vice-President Heather Munroe-Blum describes as one of the greatest social transformations in several hundred years — that is, from one kind of machine age to another — is forged by a new strategic connection between human health and economic performance.

A New Machine Age

The industrial age was about machines that ruled people. The information age is about machines ruled by people. The industrial age was about automation and mass production. The information age is about mass customization.

The industrial age was about bosses and hierarchies. The information age is about workplace trust, flexible work arrangements, "work-life" strategies and empathetic leadership in corporations and government departments where downsizing has flattened the layers of the managerial pyramid.

The industrial age was about capital investment in things. The information age will capitalize human intelligence and place economic value on investing in people. In this new world, thinking, creating and feeling will replace repetitive work and emotional non-involvement. Workforces will give way to skillforces.

The industrial age made a lot of people sick at work. The information age will prosper only if it doesn't.

The machine age was about industrial relations. The information age is about human relations. Empathy is not just for softies in the 21st Century. It is the only kind of leadership that is likely to pay off. Empathy-based leadership sustains the resilience of working people. In this context, health becomes a business strategy and *healthcare* an important management tool.

Medicare: A Brief History

Universal Medicare, a comprehensive system of public health insurance in Canada administered by government, is quite a departure from the country's earlier history on the subject.

At one time, healthcare services in Canada were mostly a private matter. It took economic distress to help change our minds: the Great Depression. Now, as the 21st Century dawns, health and economic concerns are being drawn together once more as constituent parts of the same social, economic and political fabric. The past is prologue.

In 1915, one of the first government health initiatives was the introduction of a workers' compensation system in Ontario. But over the ensuing 70 years, this "health initiative" became a huge political football. Workers' Compensation devolved into an expensive extension of Canada's social service system and was notoriously ineffectual in the rehabilitation of its clientele. Unfunded liabilities finally drove reforms that began to unshackle the system. The unshackling process has continued ever since.

Universal health insurance was first proposed by Mackenzie King in 1919. It didn't take. In the years following the Depression, Saskatchewan and Newfoundland (before its entry into Confederation) introduced tax measures to finance physician and hospital services. A federal role did not emerge until 1934.

World War II had a defining effect. Canadians drew insight about the state of Canada's health by discovering how many would-be soldiers were rejected for military service on health grounds. At the same time, Canadians confronted distressing rates of infant and maternal mortality.

By 1945, the Government of Canada was ready to act, introducing unilaterally provincial grants to stimulate hospital construction. The federal healthcare funding envelope was born.

Later, the provinces got into the act, legislating public health insurance. In 1962, Saskatchewan moved to cover all medically necessary services inside or outside a hospital. The medical profession strongly opposed the initiative, but the historic die was cast. A landmark in Canadian health history was reached.

Four years later, in 1966, Ottawa offered the provinces money for healthcare. Those who accepted it had to run non-profit publicly-administered services covering all residents of Canada regardless of where they came from or the province in which they received medical care. Thus the advent of two basic principles of today's system — universality and portability as defining characteristics of a system where all Canadians had a right of citizenship to "medically necessary" physician services.

Fast-forward a decade or so. Medicare's national roots grew deeper in the soil of Canadian consciousness. In 1979, the famed Hall Commission affirmed the principle of universal access, condemning "extra billing" by physicians as a threat to its basic axioms.

In 1984, the *Canada Health Act* stipulated that Canadians must have "reasonable access to health services without financial or other barriers." Hall had only criticized physician's extra billing five years earlier. The government banned it outright.

It must be recalled, despite all of this, that the Canadian healthcare system — inside and outside the Medicare frame — remains not a unitary social model but a mix of public and private services for which Canadians spend upwards of $70 billion a year. About two thirds of that amount is covered by tax dollars and one third by private insurance and out-of-pocket spending by individuals and families. Notably, private insurance plans cover the fastest growing element of healthcare costs — prescription drugs, currently increasing at an annual rate of nearly 15%.

Healthcare and the Public Debt

The ink on the landmark 1984 legislation — the *Canada Health Act* — was barely dry when Canadians began to feel the impact of a dramatic economic downturn in the late eighties and early nineties — matched by the deadening weight of public debt that had accumulated over the past two and a half decades. The suffocating impact of government deficits began to tighten around the necks of Canadians and their elected representatives. Ultimately, federal cash contributions to provincial health care systems were first capped, then cut.

Health services in Canada were reorganized. Hospital restructurings were protested. Talk accelerated about new, more efficient ways of managing the public health care system. Terms like service integration, outcomes measurement, evidence-based decision-making all became part of the administrative and political lexicon. Hospitals and clinics, even practitioners no longer had patients, they had clients. The language of business took hold.

The goal was to weather the storm of health spending reductions and stem the tide of year-over-year budget increases. Canada had become the second heaviest spender of healthcare dollars among all 23 member countries in the Organization for Economic Co-operation and Development. Not all of that, though, came through tax revenues. Prescription drugs, funded mainly through private insurance and consumer payments, was the fastest growing of all. Governments everywhere began to seek to reduce the demand for healthcare services. The objective: simply to make the system more affordable. And, presumably more effective. For good reason. The link between healthcare spending and good health is tenuous. The National Forum on Health tells us that higher levels of spending on healthcare do not necessarily gain more health for people. Or even more health services. The more we spend, it seems, the more unit costs go up.

Spending Our Healthcare Dollars More Effectively

Common sense tells us that spending $70 billion a year on healthcare services would seem to be enough to get *a* job done.

The real question is *what* job do we want those dollars to do and what works or doesn't work in keeping people healthy or getting them well?

Pretty basic stuff. And that is exactly what Canada and countries the world over are trying to figure out after years of lavish spending on assumptions that health is found strictly within the four walls of a hospital room, doctor's office or operating theatre. When, in fact, health is found in the jobs we do, the lives we lead and the societies we build, an ancient truth that Western civilizations somehow lost track of.

Health is a desired *end state*. Healthcare is one *means* to that end. But there are others.

Wealth and poverty, violence and abuse, employment and unemployment, economic wellbeing and economic hardship, being white or being aboriginal, being a man or being a woman, being rich or being poor, all influence the status of health of our population, some argue, more than healthcare itself.

These are 'non-medical' or 'social' determinants of health. They demand our attention. Again. Hospitals, doctors, nurses, pharmacists and therapists cannot alone do what's needed to protect, let alone enrich, the health of Canadians at a time of immense social and economic change.

Putting Medical Care in Context

We need non-medical strategies to tackle the social, economic and institutional conditions that breed physical and mental disease, which returns us to the question of 'payer' versus 'investor' in the funding of health services.

The notion of payer is about hospitals fighting for scarce operating dollars, governments struggling with doctors' fees, and politicians vowing to preserve services with funds they can't easily come up with.

The concept of "payer" caters to short-term thinking, annual budgets declining from year to year. The tyranny of fiscal planning one year at a time. Till now, we have not had ways to measure the return on investing in the health of people.

Historically, healthcare has been seen as an operating cost to control, not a strategic investment to make.

The investment concept — in this or any other context — demands two questions: Invest in what? And at what rate of return? What defines our nation's human capital? What is the investment needed to preserve and build on reserves of human capital? What is the investment needed to help people live full, creative, productive, healthy lives?

The questions reach polar extremes in probing the interests of the very young and the very old in our society as well as those of working families, the working poor, the disabled, the indigent, the powerful and the less powerful.

The return on this kind of investment — the obvious answer — is an enhanced asset in the form of resilient people; in the form of productive, healthy communities and workplaces; in the form of safe and secure families; in the form of less vulnerable children and the aged being protected and cared for.

The return on this form of investment, in these terms, is measurable and visible. The concept of human capital — in a world of information technology and knowledge work — thus becomes a bridge between human health and economic performance as a matter of national strategic interest.

The Cost War

The war on dollar costs was declared by governments and business in the face of three emerging conditions. *One condition was the recession of the late 80's and early 90's,* complete with a collapse of the world real estate market; an implosion of leveraged corporate debt which shook the financial markets; plunging share values; and now out-of-place cost structures which paralyzed scores of large corporations that suddenly faced smaller, flexible and quick-footed competition.

Meantime, the borrowing powers of government in the international community were threatened by shortfalls in revenue versus costs. Taxpayers were fast becoming a credit risk.

The second condition was the *information revolution* itself. It facilitated globalization. It became a vehicle with which to eliminate a range of traditional expenses and staff. It was a new world of fast decision-making and customer immediacy. The industrial age gave way to the information age.

As a result, competition intensified on a global footing. The advent of microprocessing spawned the concept of mass customization. Customers, righter than they ever were, demanded more quality, and value and spot-on service.

The third condition was born of the first two. Massive downsizing. The end of the era of corporate diversification, and the beginning of large scale industrial consolidation.

Governments faced the music composed by excessive spending in the past — deficits — by embarking upon several remedial strategies: budget cuts, deregulation, and, in some cases, privatization of government agencies and services.

Meanwhile, the global economy was forming like a giant constellation, a new critical mass, bloc economies created by the imperatives of simpler and freer trade. All born on the wing of new information technology. The Communist world disintegrated. And a billion new consumers were born.

The information revolution literally pushed the industrial age aside at a scale and pace no one could have imagined.

As a result, society finds itself frontally exposed to the future. The sensation is a peculiar and unnerving one, sort of like travelling in a car at accelerating speeds toward a brick wall that seems to be moving toward us at the same time.

Information technology seemed to appear out of the blue — IBM blue originally — and began to re-write every rule we live by. How we work, how employable we are, what we expect of each other, and what each of us must learn just to stay employed.

'Middle age' was no longer a stationary target 10 or 20 years away. It was creeping down the corporate ladder to claim 20-year company veterans in their late 40's. Their future was suddenly unclear. The givens of job security and retirement were shaken. Powerful change from an assortment of sources and for a variety of reasons converged in their lives with thunderclap immediacy. New rules of work were being written, single-spaced, ever faster, on ever cheaper personal computers.

Merger Wave

In 1997, a record $1 trillion in mergers took place involving U.S. companies. Given their interests and subsidiaries in Canada, Europe and Asia, this statistic has enormous global implications. *The New York Times*: "Not since the wave of industrial takeovers created the great oil, steel and auto companies at the beginning of the century has corporate America been reshaped by a sweep of merger activity as broad as the one taking place today."

Industries from telecommunications to banking, tofood products, to aerospace and financial services are involved in consolidations that will create blocs of competitive strength. The Chairman of the U.S. Federal Trade Commission, which regulates mergers in that country, calls it "an astonishing merger wave".

The forces propelling this trend include the expansion of financial capital and the birth of the new, post-communism consumer markets of Eastern Europe. Combined with the birth of the information revolution, merger mania is both a product and creator of the global economy. *The New York Times* once again:

> What is happening at the end of the 20th Century is a *reprise* of the industrial upheavals that took place at the beginning of the century, when more than two dozen auto companies merged in 1908 to form General Motors, and J.P. Morgan paid $1.4 billion in 1901 to acquire Carnegie Steel and dozens of others to create U.S. Steel.

The whole private sector has undergone a truly unbelievable transformation. Companies have decided either to go for scale or to target niche sectors. There seems to be no middle ground.

The 20th Century opened with a wave of consolidation, the *Times* noted, but these were aimed at forming domestic monopolies. "Today's mergers are driven by a desire to gain global reach." In the 1980's, many of the mergers were hostile and financed through debt. Today's version are being financed largely through corporate stock, not borrowed money.

The Top Line
In this competitive global world, the search is on for new forms of productivity and for a whole new approach to creating value and profitability.
Business is returning to the top line, revenue growth, not just strong bottom lines through cost reduction.

For stressed-out employees, the top line is a more hopeful place, but also more demanding. Top-line growth puts the pressure on managers to become leaders and leaders to get creative. Growing profits is harder than cutting costs. "Unlike raising profits by striking down expenses," one economist noted, "growing revenues through product innovation, or geographic expansion requires managers to have a point of view about the future."

Top-line growth in the post-deficit era will require resilient, motivated, skilled and healthy workers, the occupants of what AT&T CEO Michael Armstrong calls a "commitment culture." *Fortune Magazine:*

> Without doubt, it's easier to get a dollar of profit growth by cutting costs than by raising revenues. But investors, the final arbiters of value, will know that those two dollars are very unlike in terms of the futures they presage for companies.

A study by William Mercer and Company in the United States neatly quantifies the difference.

> The compound annual growth rate in the market value of the companies that achieved higher-than-average profit growth but lower revenue growth than their industry's average — the cost-cutters — was less than 12% between the years of 1989 and 1992.

> By contrast, the companies that achieved their higher-than-average profits as a result of higher-than-average revenue growth saw their market value jump at an annual rate of nearly 24%. Double the cost cutters.

Mercer concludes: "The market looks forward with wise eyes." There is a stubborn problem in all of this, however.

Current accounting practices can not yet quantify the human factor, the key element in a top line growth strategy and productivity initiatives centred on employee health. At the same time, the accounting profession in the United States is accelerating an examination of ways to report on "intangible assets."

Nonetheless, as the 1998 "Health Agenda" Conference of the Washington Business Group on Health clearly illustrated, the search for a health-based model of productivity is on in earnest.

Barriers to productivity that this search must scale include work-family conflicts — juggling priorities, feelings spilling over, being mentally in two places at once. These sensations "contribute significantly to turnover and related business costs."

Data of this nature will be examined later in this report. For the moment, let it be said that **new incentives are needed to stimulate productivity based on human health.** This is, in effect, a quest for new forms of competitive advantage in a global economy where companies can no longer achieve a competitive advantage simply by offsetting costs. ❧

◦ 2 ◦
The Paradox of Prosperity

SOCIETY'S RUSH TO A DEADLINE — ANY DEADLINE — IS ON. THE GLOBAL economy knows and respects no borders; it is a networked world where intellectual capital — the brainpower and skills of people — will increasingly drive industrial performance.

It is a world where the number of people employed to produce goods has gone down steadily while the number providing services has gone up by 15% the past six years. It is a world where technology is decentralizing and diversifying the source and power of information. Orwell was wrong. 1984 has not happened. (*Illustrating the point: an underground network of video cassettes facilitated the liberation of Poland. China recognizes the danger to their autocratic society posed by the expanding role and influence of the World Wide Web.*)

Keeping a tight lid on information was easy until the late 20th century. The march of technology has become a dictator's nightmare. As a political tool or threat, the Internet is unsurpassed by anything in history.

Meanwhile, society has entered a time in which public opinion shifts are increasingly volatile. This reflects deeper changes occurring in the values of Canadians. Author Michael Adams says Canadians are "reinventing what it means to be human."

Society today worries and hurries a lot and not surprisingly, stress and anxiety are escalating. Work-related uncertainty gnaws at the peace of mind of breadwinners. *Maclean's* Business Editor Deirdre McMurdy says this uncertainty stems, among other things, from "several key economic areas in which Canadians have seen control slip away."

More than 9% of the population is unemployed — and often desperate. Even more alarming, almost 17% of people between the ages of 15 and 24 are unemployed. Statistics Canada reports that in 1996, one in five people under 25 had no job experience, twice the 1989 figure. A transportation company advertises its ability to meet impossible deadlines. Today's customer can't wait. A "Genius Reading" service trains people to "read a novel over lunch" or a computer manual in one evening.

University of Toronto Professor Mark Kingwell describes this late 90s phenomenon as "our high-speed chase to nowhere." He explores the matter in *Harper's Magazine*. We listen in:

Speed is a drug, and not just the old-time hep cat high of Dexedrine or bennies ... the experience of speed releases into the biochemical soup of our heads and a cascade of naturally occurring drugs, not the least of which are ... the hormones that course through the brain in the bone-melting, stomach-clenching high of sexual attraction.

On the perception of slow and fast in a changing world of technology:
I have my laptop open to take notes ... this machine was considered pretty fast when I bought it eighteen months ago ... but now it feels slow because I know there are so many faster machines out there. In fact, my 5300 has been placed in the "discontinued archive," destined for quick-time oblivion.

On a world of instant forgetting:
There is a secret bond between slowness and memory, between speed and forgetting [quoting a novel by Milan Kundera called Slowness*]. In a world forever overseen by television cameras, a world of instant forgetting... the most successful performer is not the person with the truth but the one with the sharpest tongue and the handiest numbers.*

On modern machines and speed:
... buried deep in the logic of speed (are) machines (which) not only go faster with each generation but also move from generation to generation at a brisker pace. The speed of personal computers, dutifully conforming to Moore's Law, now doubles in eighteen months or less ... technology's genius is that it plots its upgrade ambition on this striving curve, carrying us ever and ever more sharply upward.

(This reminds us of Stephen Hawking's "big bang" theory according to which critical mass expands to the point where it falls in

on itself. The fate of post-modern technology?)
When it comes to our (information) machines, nobody has to plan obsolescence. It just happens.

On the globalization factor:
We confront now, a new topology, a world of instant and direct contact between every point on the globe. The world's business, the total globalization project, takes place at the speed of light, the speed accommodated by fibre-optic cable. Today, there are 228,958 miles of such cable on the ocean floor ... (and) by the end of the century that number will almost double.

On the social contracts between an accelerating world and the standstill effects of moving through it:
Extreme speeds are not available to most of us (who experience) the frenetic plodding of the urban landscape. Sitting in traffic these days, watching the dollars count themselves off (on) the taxi's meter as helicopters take off from distant buildings.

On human perception of the hurried and worried society:
We feel we should resist speed by engaging in activities, like reading or gardening or ambling, that are perforce slower. Indeed, there is an underground of this resistance in the culture, a theme of sundial slowness set against the overarching digital quickness of life — themes that grow obvious and somehow more frenzied as we near the socially constructed limit of the millennium.

And finally:
Faster and faster can only mean, in the end, stasis ... what is the point of being able to read a page every three seconds? To read every book ever written? Then what? Meanwhile, the vehicles of our speed ruin the planet as fast as we move around it.

Finally, finally:
Ours is a crash culture [quoting political scientist Arthur Kroker], in which we are always speeding up to a standstill, a spasm of useless speed ... [not] pure speed worship anymore but rather a curious post-modern double movement of velocity and lethargy.

The Insecurity of Work
Job security is becoming obsolete. The definition of work is changing.

Employment in the future will increasingly mean part-time and contract jobs, employees working for many different companies throughout their working lives, sometimes more than one at a time. Training and upgrading one's skills will be a way of life. As of now, *most of the new jobs being created in the United States are part-time.* Toronto has the single largest concentration of lower paying part-time jobs in Canada. Through it all, income polarization is widening in Canada and the U.S. both.

We have entered a global world. Jobs, goods and services are produced for a global market with less and less concern for national boundaries. We may still have company towns but we have fewer 'company nations.'

In seeking to better understand the implications of the 'global world' in terms of what we might call *humanomics* — a mix of health, employment, family-security and personal wellbeing issues caught up in a blender of rapid change — we must come to terms with one of the most powerful influences of all: modern technology.

If society is sailing a turbulent ocean of exponential change, the growth in computer technology is one of the mightiest waves of all. *Moore's Law,* the axiom of the co-founder of Intel Corporation, says that computer power will double and the price of computers will halve every 18 months. This touches all of us — regardless of where or how we live, and whether we own or operate a personal computer or take refuge in pen and ink.

At the tail end of this tumultuous century the digital revolution is transforming the world just as the industrial revolution did a century earlier.

The Internet has become indispensable to universities and libraries and the power of this revolution is in a microchip. The global world is driven by an engine of information. *For the first time, the world's corporations are spending more on telecommunications than oil.*

The power of information as a commodity — more particularly, its infusion into the workings of institutions, commerce, work, entertainment and international exchange markets — inherently places a premium on human behaviour and knowledge as factors in the successful performance of institutions and economies.

Computer technology is the thread of globalization. Business leaders foresee commercial applications unforseen a decade or so ago. The chairman of the Alliance of Manufacturers of Canada, William McLean, says "we are entering a whole new era" where computer technology will soon allow customers to help design products to their own requirement "rather," he says, "than settling for one that is the least inappropriate."

New Forms of Perception

The computer on a chip, microprocessing, is re-shaping our perception and use of information. With biotechnology, it has come to represent a profoundly influential means to deepen our understanding of human consciousness itself.

Imaging technology is changing how we perceive ourselves. Brain research is penetrating one of the great mysteries of the ages. Scientists can see the brain reacting to forces stimulating it. Neuroscience is beginning to answer questions about human instincts inherited from our stone-age ancestors — and reigning ever since over our emotions and capacity to reason. The inquiries of ancient philosophers and theologians are finding their place on the agenda of contemporary science.

When we first entered the 20th century, we became aware of the mechanical functions of things. This drove the industrial age. As we prepare to leave it, our fix is on the mechanics and mysteries of being human. With some luck, this will define the information age.

Microsoft founder Bill Gates believes the computer revolution (which he has helped lead) will improve human understanding. In fact, it is already changing the way people relate to each other.

Cyber space and time simulate human experience and *actual* reality. They spawn new forms of perception, awareness and possibilities. Perhaps even new kinds of relationships. Virtual sex is a protective alternative to the real thing in the expanding AIDS era. Virtual pets are now available for children, but are not selling well. This is one aspect of the virtual world that has not replaced the real thing. Kittens and puppies are safe. Perhaps we are not ready for virtual affection.

"Fictional" television recently foresaw criminals housed in virtual prisons of their mind as an alternative to the bricks, mortar and steel of high walls and cell doors. The distance we must travel in cyberspace to align fiction with fact is an ethical question of our time.

Author Michael Adams tells us we have become more self-focused and less secure. We walk in a Dickensian forest of times best and worst. And if there are defining figures moving anxiously through that forest, it is that of a hurried and worried single parent, or a working couple trying harder than ever to support their family, care for an aging parent, and juggle two jobs.

In them, we see the struggle of the "sandwich generation" — wives, husbands, mothers and fathers juggling the intensifying obligations of work and home. More than before, women are working in demanding and stressful senior executive and professional positions. More than men, they are squeezed by the sandwiching effect of simultaneous obligations.

Society has been "rattled by change." Everyone is hip-deep in being busy. In one survey, a respondent anguished over the question "How are you?" After some thought, her all-inclusive answer was "Busy." All of us have been swept up into a generalized state of distraction and deadlines. How could it be otherwise with the 24-hour virtual workday. Fax machines are always on. E-mails stockpile overnight. This is the "enslaving power" of electronic office communication.

In his book *Sex in the Snow,* author Adams says Canadians are becoming more intent on instant gratification, more impatient, wanting things here and now. We are the "customer who won't wait." Technology is helping to facilitate this kind of immediacy. A chartered bank appropriately proclaims its ability to serve consumers "at the speed of life."

In turn, the "speed of life" is fuelled and pumped by information from concurrent sources in incessant flows at constant rates. Information overload is weighing down the capacity of people to react. More information, it seems, is not producing a more informed society. Software companies, sensing the "overload" factor, are advertising software options that differentiate between tons of junk e-mail and tons of essential information.

Meanwhile, Adams notes a steep decline in Canadian's acceptance of institutions — churches, legislatures, lawyers, doctors, the clergy, the legitimacy of established authority. Canadians are more individualistic, a characteristic of diversity, and embrace what Adams calls "an incredible range of values, configurations and lifestyle choices."

Adams foresees no early return to economic or social traditionalism. Demographics no longer reliably tell us what's going to happen in the future — forces such as feminism, the mass media, globalization and technology are largely independent of demographics and are influenced by behavioural forces we have yet to fully understand. One thing we do understand is the degree to which this country has bought into the world of information technology.

A Wired Nation
Canadians are probably the most wired people in the world. Between

1981 and 1994, the sale of computers in Canada grew faster than all consumer products and at twice the rate of audio-visual electronics. Spending on new cars, movies, tobacco and alcohol, meanwhile, actually declined. For the size of our population, there is more television cable buried in Canada than anywhere else in the world. More personal home computers and more than three million cell phones, many equipped with "silent ringing" vibrators so people can reach us in church or at the opera without disturbing the congregation, or audience, the mindset of a hurried society.

Canadians and Americans have the highest rate of Internet access at home. In 1995, the smallish population of British Columbia (small compared to the city of New York) requested as many sites as the whole of Manhattan.

But for millions, the computer age means much more than cell phones that ring noiselessly in church. *It means a new way of thinking.*

The information age means re-learning how to manage ideas and new information. Through digitization, data can be connected, disconnected and reconnected a gazillion different ways. *Linear thinking is headed for obsolescence.*

In this kind of future, the model for organizing jobs and skills may mimic the art of making a movie more than running a production plant. It will have a vision component. A concept component. Like a movie, it will not have the characteristics of conventional sequencing as in the count of numbers. Movies are shot out of sequence. The actors know their own part but often have no idea what the final product will look like. Nonetheless, the leader — the director — must still motivate the cast around a shared vision. This is the essence of empathetic leadership.

The marvelous and maddening realm of digitization is changing how we approach business. Meetings and memos one day will become analogues of the past. Through enhanced nanotechnologies, human thought may eventually interact directly with a microprocessor — the organic tissue of the brain "backing and forthing" with the machinery of a computer.

The Internet is an expanding marketplace. Companies are able to sell direct, presumably saving significant sums of money previously spent on packaging and distribution and the jobs that go with them.

The transaction value of goods and services bought and sold on the Internet was $100 million (U.S.) in 1995. Experts think that figure will reach $186 *billion* early in the new century.

"Halve that figure, or quarter it, and this is an opportunity without equal," Microsoft's Bill Gates says. His statement begs a question. An opportunity for whom? Likely not for retail workers shut out of the cyberstores and electronic malls of the future.

The information technology revolution is penetrating our work and personal lives at skyrocket speeds. "Collaboration software" allows people to work simultaneously on projects and documents — without regard to distance. E-mail transmitted over the Internet, according to Gates and others, already rivals the telephone as a common means of communication. The challenge is to find ways to make sure people are not overwhelmed. Nonetheless, on the Internet, the pace of innovation continues to accelerate.

BCE Inc. CEO Jean Monty says the Internet has "profoundly and forever" changed the way business functions. He cautions us, however — electronic commerce will succeed only if consumers trust the technology. As a result, he calls the retail dimension of the Internet a "work in progress."

The Euphoria Gap

Our society has been rattled by change. According to Charles Handy in his 1990 Harvard bestseller, *The Age of Unreason*, "changes are different this time; they are discontinuous and not part of a pattern." He says such discontinuity happens from time to time in history, "although it is confusing and disturbing, particularly to those in power. It is the changes in the way our work is organized which will make the biggest difference to the way we all live."

The discontinuity that Handy talks about is the face of a world which seems to be colliding with its future. Society is certainly in a rush to get somewhere. And technology is helping to get us there. But where *are* we going?

These are economic good times. But according to the National Opinion Research Centre at the University of Chicago "there is not a lot of euphoria out there." More than three quarters of all Americans are worried about job security.

Deirdre McMurdy of *Maclean's*:

Despite rosy economic forecasts, despite the constant assurances that we are on the cusp of renewed prosperity, many Canadians are contending with declining real incomes, record personal debts and insecure employment.

Author John Dalla Costa, in a *Financial Post* meditation entitled "Managing the Profit Stream": "What should be a time of back-slapping economic celebration in Canada remains, instead, a period of uneasy questioning."

The indicators for the economy are overwhelmingly positive, yet the mood among average Canadians is cautious bordering on pessimistic. Their apprehension straddles a fault line of uncertainty portending — emotionally if not economically — another downturn or downsizing just around the corner? Writer Dalla Costa describes the national psyche as "sombre." *(A diagnosis that recent Statistics Canada data might dispute. Depression rates in Canada have dipped slightly. By that measure, the national mood may be lifting slightly.)*

Nonetheless, research tells us people are "bone-tired, drained by both the angst of not having enough disposable income and the personal burden of having to realize higher productivity at work."

The paradox of modern prosperity shows up in family earnings. In Canada, 52% of individual workers and 13% of families earn less than $20,000 a year. The United Way of Greater Toronto published findings of "one-in-five" child poverty in Toronto. The news hit hard at the conscience of Canada's biggest and richest city.

In a special edition on jobs, *Maclean's* says the "world of work has so wholly changed that the word *job* has become indefinable." Twenty years ago, job layoffs were temporary and part of an up-turn cycle. Not any more. John Challenger, a New York City-based consultant, who tallies layoff data, says the United States has suffered more than three million permanent layoffs in the past six years. *Maclean's'* Deirdre McMurdy once again:

> While freer trade and information technology have brought benefit to the domestic economy, they have also extracted a high price. Corporations, more intent than ever on gaining a competitive advantage, have laid off thousands and shifted to low-cost labour offshore.

"That has overturned the implicit bargain between labour and management," she says, reprising the melancholy theme struck earlier in this report.

> There may be progress to laud in the current economic situation — but Canadians do not grasp that; rather, there is a widespread feeling, both individually and nationally, that things are out of control.

The *Globe and Mail* also writes in an editorial: "Things are better than they were, but not nearly as good as they need to be." The newspaper cites the ill effects of lagging productivity in Canada, by world standards at least. And relatively, a falling standard of living for Canadians. Here we find another face of the paradox of prosperity in the late 1990's.

"Canadians have exhausted every source of cash in their struggle to keep up their standard of living," the *Globe* says. Saving rates dropped from 12% to 2% of average incomes between 1989 and 1997. Less heavily taxed Americans have held firm at 5%. A decade ago, Canadians' savings were proportionally more than twice those of Americans. Now the reverse is true. It was calculated then that the difference in savings represented the high cost of chronic medical care in the U.S. The decline in Canada is thus greater than would first appear, since we still have most of our Medicare.

In a "Temp World"

In the face of increased uncertainty and sweeping change, *New York Times* columnist, psychologist and author Daniel Goleman says adolescents are more troubled now than ever. Surveys in the United States found that "job satisfaction, financial satisfaction and overall happiness are now lower than at any time in the past 20 years."

In Canada, anxiety levels are climbing. Some experts are assessing the impact of the economic uncertainty of parents on the mental stability of children. The discontinuity of the times is producing a sense of lost control for families and workers of all stripes, the point made earlier by columnist McMurdy. In the U.S., employees work 160 hours more each year than they did 20 years ago. Work-related stress has increased to the point where five-minute back rub stores in New York have become a niche enterprise.

The work force has undergone permanent change in the wake of massive economic restructuring over the past decade, as mentioned earlier. Emerging is a "temp world" of part-time unemployment. A study two years ago by the Canadian Council on Social Development says that the number of temporary jobs in Canada rose by 21% in the five years leading to 1994. As of 1996, one in every ten employed Canadians is part of the temporary work force.

The author of the report, Chris Clark, a policy analyst at the Council, said the study points up a "trend toward other forms of non-standard employment, which now make up about a third of all jobs." Three-quarters of all temporary workers fill jobs that last less than six months.

In periods of economic adjustment and dislocation, it is predictable that public attention is fixed on the process of organizational downsizing. The "unemploying" of people. *The fact is that corporations have also been creating employment during the difficult times:* growth opportunities for thousands of small and medium-size suppliers. There has emerged a synergy between large corporations and small businesses as one driving force of economic growth. Direct job creation in the small-business sector is stimulated by big business customers. More than one million jobs were created in Canada between 1990 and 1997. More than 60% were self-employed. But they too depend on a growing private sector to prosper. At the same time, while 95,000 public sector jobs were eliminated, business created nearly five times that number of new jobs.

Nonetheless, uncertainty in the workplace has been characterized by what some sociologists call the "rust-out syndrome," a phenomenon that occurs after significant change has been introduced within an organization.

In one case we looked at, an "earthquake" at work took the form of the announcement of a departmental reorganization. Flex hours. Early retirement options as a prelude to overall job cuts representing 10% of the work force. Aftershocks, uncertainty, mistrust, acts of self-preservation at the same time as "team mandates" were unveiled as part of the restructuring plan.

A corrosive, rusting period set in. People's priority was about how they would survive, not growing in their jobs or finding ways to develop new skills. Next, confusion set in. And then a kind of mass paralysis.

For some employees, truth at work just flew out the window. More management decisions were made and announced and then things changed again. Employees started feeling that superiors knew more than they were telling. Bonds between employees and the company disintegrated.

Employees became more concerned with self. They began to network. Résumés were updated just in case there was another round of layoffs. Distraction. Political behaviour, rumoring-mongering and a terrific sense of isolation.

The "rust-out syndrome" is fairly common in today's restructured organizations. Unless those experiencing it make a conscious decision to move through change, and not become paralyzed by it, uncertainty and mistrust are inevitable. This is where management can reach out. Where discontinuity need not be a crippling phenomenon.

Where the nurturing of employee resilience becomes all-important.

Rage in a Hurried Society

The hurried society is a faster, less patient, even angrier world. Road rage and urban anger are the scar tissue of unemployment, personal distress, disorienting social change and pervasive uncertainty in the lives of millions.

On the streets and highways of big-city life in Toronto, New York and other large cities, aggressive driving has reached epidemic proportions. *Time Magazine* called it "America's sickness *du jour,*" and wondered if there was a cure for thinking everyone else on the road is an idiot?

Sixty-four per cent of respondents to a national survey in that country say people are driving less courteously and more dangerously than they were five years ago. Among 60,000 people who received speeding tickets, the most common excuse, *Time* reports, was "I'm late."

Not only are roads crowded, but crowded with drivers who are rushed, vulnerable to flashpoint reactions. In the Toronto region, a decade of road construction and suffocating traffic congestion, spring to winter, year after year, has loaded the gun that road rage triggers.

Road rage can be unlearned. The principles of emotional intelligence are one means. Driver education is another — the kind that teaches cooperation and promotes the acceptance of driver diversity on the road. It should start a lot earlier than the legal driving age. Perhaps another solution might rest with the actual planning process for providing services to taxpayers.

In a hurried and distracted society, over-reaction is a symptom. Behaviour such as tailgating on Highway 401, Canada's busiest, is a virus. It produces emotional heat and represents physical danger.

The cell phone, eating "on the run" behind the wheel of a the car, lane-surfing, driving too slowly, failing to yield. The features of a hurried society. Stress is the face of a worried society.

Quoting one psychologist, the *Toronto Sun:* "Highway hostility is a natural extension of growing pressure and frustration." One youth service leader says the condition reflects a decline of community spirit. "Everyone is out for themselves, sensing that everyone else is a competitor, or worse yet, an enemy." An ethos permeating the large urban centres.

The "speed of life" has become a fatal lure for a distressingly high number of snowmobilers. In one 10-day period in 1998, seven people were killed in snowmobile accidents near Toronto. Speed was the principal factor, sometimes in combination with alcohol. But the essential motivation, in the words of one snowmobiler, "It's the rush, man. It's the rush."

Protracted Uncertainty

According to Dr. Barbara Dorian, Psychiatrist-in-Chief at the University of Toronto-affiliated Women's College Hospital, depression is triggered by "today's frantic lifestyles."

Growing social isolation and violence are a breeding ground for depression, premature death and disability in the world today. Women are the most vulnerable, for one thing, because of the pressure of the multiple roles they play as breadwinner, mother, wife, and more often than men, caregiver to an elderly parent, pressures and stresses that their male counterparts experience less often.

The pace and volume of work in the downsized economy have generated a sense of being overwhelmed for many people. Even with the mastery of new technology, allowing them to manage huge quantities of data electronically, getting routine things done is not nearly as routine as it once was. Direct contact between human beings is giving way to "data relationships" and the stockpiling of things to do.

Meanwhile, the restructuring of North America — has it worked? Are downsized companies more competitive, given that downsizings are urgent remedies to sudden threats more than a strategic response to the future? In effect, they are the past (excess industrial capacity) in violent collision with the future (lower prices, tougher competition).

One corporate leader says companies that got "leaner and meaner" actually became "smaller and angrier." *One study of 4,000 downsized companies in the U.S. showed that only 20 per cent actually gained a competitive advantage.*

We live in transitional times. The family norm is becoming two breadwinners, not one — where there *are* two parents. The "dual economy" — well paid professionals on one side, and less skilled workers on the other. The transition from an industrial to an information-based knowledge economy.

A transition that has destroyed "the company as family" according to the *New York Times* in its series "The Downsizing of America." *The Times* chronicled evidence of "primal anger" expressed by employees in the United States as one lay-off became another, and another one after that.

Writer John Dalla Costa says "one of the darkest legacies of the 1980's boom was that questions of structure and social justice were largely ignored" in public debates about economic performance and business profitability — topics, he says, which are "dense with complexity and emotion." He adds:

> Now that the economy is performing so well, whatever our beliefs regarding profits and the role of business, one thing is clear: neither the economy nor society can afford another such myopic lapse.

There is room for optimism, though. The CIBC's chief economist, Joshua Mendelsohn, says businesses are getting better at focusing on their core businesses and "costs have been largely wrung out of operations." If so, for downsizing, past need not be prologue.

But how safe is that bet? The *Wall Street Journal* reports that the "psychology of overcapacity" may be taking hold once again in North American industry — a phenomenon which one steel executive calls "the law of the jungle" and one of the core reasons for massive cuts in employment through the late 80s and early 90s.

Some companies, the *Journal* tells us, "play mind games with capacity" — hoping that announcing expansion plans will scatter the competition. "Ego also plays a role. CEOs are, by and large, used to winning, and the fight for market share is an extension of that."

Galloping Just To Keep Up

Whether or not we must brace ourselves for another bout of expansion and retraction along these lines, time will tell. Meanwhile, the stress of Christmas Past is still affecting a substantial minority of the North American population. For example, one third of Canadians say the are "constantly under stress" and one in four considers himself or herself a workaholic. The rush to get ahead in the 70s has become, in the 90s, an all-out gallop just to keep up.

The majority of respondents to a Canadian Mental Health Association survey said work-related stress was a principal demotivator in their life. Over four in 10 say that work-related stress impacts their performance on the job. The emotional outlaws stealing Canadians' sense of well-being have familiar names — family finances, problems at work, relationships, marriage.

That being the case, one quarter of Canada's working population is apparently prepared to work fewer hours for less money so they can escape deadline-type pressures of the "hurried and worried post-modern world." The Canadian Federal Advisory Committee on the Changing Workplace describes the modern workplace as an "environment of great insecurity."

Job-sharing today is a fact of life for a growing number of working people. And the experience is not altogether a bad one. In 1995, 8% of the part-time workforce in Canada was involved in job sharing — the vast majority of them being women over 35 with college or university degrees. Statistics show that employers find higher than average productivity among those sharing a job. They also discover evidence of innovation, better organization, more commitment and enthusiasm.

Between 1986 and 1993, the number of collective bargaining agreements in Canada which contained job-sharing provisions, quadrupled. As the face of work and the workplace change, things associated with permanent employment change along with them.

Many of the life stages that Canadians once took for granted — like health benefits at work — will no longer be a given unless the "temp world" is re-designed with these features built-in. In fact, the Parliamentary Committee on the Changing Workplace has recommended new forms of compensation for part-time and contract workers to counter such underlying insecurity. ❧

❧ 3 ❧
The Globalization of Work

TORONTO STAR COLUMNIST DAVID CRANE — A THOUGHTFUL OBSERVER of economic matters on an international level — notes that globalization is a source of painful change. Quoting World Trade Organization sources, he says in a recent column that:

> for workers who lose their job in traditional industries, the shift is not just from textiles to automobiles, it is from one world to another in which there is a different culture and a different educational requirement.

Globalization is creating several billion new consumers worldwide. Every time mankind has been confronted with major change, there have been uncertainties, and what we are confronted with now is not just change, but revolution.

The World Trade Organization makes this seminal point: Globalization is not just a process that involves free trade and capital movements — more and more it touches human nature. So we have the globalization of hopes, globalization of career and the globalization of work.

U.S. Federal Reserve Chairman Greenspan adds this: There will be early in the new century a global labour shortage of the kind of 'knowledge skilled workers' who will be needed for competitive success in the 21st Century.

Author Michael Adams makes the "globalization point" differently when he discounts the primacy of demographics as an indicator of the future. Our kids, thanks to technology, may have more in common with other kids in Kiev than they do with their own parents.

As Canadians look ahead seven or eight years, what will we be most preoccupied with? In a national survey, *Maclean's Magazine* found that most fears centre on the prospect of never again finding full-time work, the Canada Pension Plan going bankrupt, not being able to retire at age 65, charities taking over social services, having to work longer for less. These concerns are the worry lines on the face of the post-deficit society.

Futurist Peter Drucker says that "if history is any guide, the economic transformation we are navigating will not be completed until the year 2020." Coincidentally or not, this time line parallels the projected surge of depression as a leading cause of workdays lost through disability and premature death. Change has a cost.

Drucker coined the terms "knowledge economy" and "knowledge worker," and says that in this new world, commercial value will be created by productivity and innovation. Which, in the "knowledge economy" are the output of human intelligence and imagination. Both, he says, are the result of applying knowledge — a human asset — to the process of work where information is a commercial commodity in its own right.

Those who work most effectively in this milieu will know how to allocate knowledge just as traditional "capitalists" know how to allocate money. Thus is born the concept of human capital. "In this new era," Drucker says, "knowledge becomes a utility, a means to obtain economic and social results." Knowledge has become *the* economic resource of the day, not one among many, as defined by the axiomatic importance it has in advancing economic progress.

"This," Drucker says, "will change the structure of society." He adds: "Knowledge now means information in action. Information focused on results — results measured in terms of the advancement of knowledge itself."

Thomas Malone, a professor at the Sloan School of Management at MIT says that in performing "the old work", information was very expensive, so we managed with relatively small amounts of it; we developed organizations that could work in what he called "an information desert."

"We are now in something of an information jungle and survival techniques that worked in deserts won't be as effective."

An "infoglut" has developed among companies all over North America, according to author Thomas Stewart, in his book, "*Intellec-*

tual Capital: The New Wealth of Organizations." At Sun Microsystems, for example, this infoglut:

> represents a hundred year flood — 120 internal messages, per day, per employee, which translates into a million and a half internal messages transmitted every day in the same company.
>
> There's no way to turn it off, and the dangers are obvious — the *urgent* drives out the important, others impose on your time, everyone's a critic, especially the uninformed.

FYI's and "comments please" reach mountainous proportions, Stewart writes. "Information overload is an all-too-real phenomenon pointing to a real challenge in managing intellectual capital."

Sociologists Sara Keisler and Lee Sproull, in their book about electronic methods, *Connections*, say companies and individuals consistently over-invest in forms of gathering and communicating information — referring to studies that gather dust, annual reports and employee attitude surveys seldom consulted again.

In this context, the knowledge economy is not about how much information you pile on, it is about applying that information productively. Author Thomas Stewart: "wealth is the product of knowledge — knowledge and information are the primary new materials and a company's most important products."

Scarce Human Capital

Time Magazine describes the global information economy as "specialized." Dr. Peter Drucker estimates that knowledge workers will:

> account for one third of the total work force of most developed countries. Skilled service workers will represent the next largest portion of the workforce, with the remainder made up of imperiled 'industrial age' workers.
>
> The machine once decided not only what we did but how we did it on the plant floor.

In the knowledge economy, according to Drucker, we will need a machine, whether a computer or an ultrasound analyzer, but neither will tell the knowledge worker what to do because a "knowledge machine" is unproductive without the knowledge of the operator.

Dr. Drucker says the world is entering on an employee society — "where the employee and his or her tools (knowledge and service) are interdependent." He says "capital in the 21st Century must now serve the employee. Previously, the employee served the capital."

Human capital becomes a public asset, renewable, unlike a harvested forest to be cut down and replanted but more like a great river whose continuity and replenishment are a source of strength. Where production technology has displaced workers in the performance of repetitive, sequential, linear tasks and functions, information technology poses a different challenge. *Part of that challenge centres on the clash between data and voice systems.* Voice mails, e-mails, the interconnection of voice data modems are an alternative to actually talking to people during day-to-day business. Entire phone exchanges, like bank transactions can be entirely electronic. Call forwarding to numbers and voices that aren't there when your call is urgent or you do, in fact, need to speak to a person, is a feature of voice transmission that mocks its basic intent — facilitating communication.

Nortel, Canada's leading telecommunications company, has seen a dramatic jump in voice transmission products and service compared to data. We are not talking to each other as much anymore. While turning off the voice mail system is not the best solution (although Toronto Mayor Mel Lastman strongly believes in it), the self-absorption of many callers needs to be corralled to modify the number of working people intruding indiscriminately on each other's time at epidemic levels. We will return to this point. Meanwhile, Thomas Stewart:

> Knowledge has become the single most important factor of production and managing intellectual assets has become the single most important task of business.

Columnist David Crane:

> Human capital is the most important form of capital in the world today, more important than money. Knowledge and ideas now have a bigger part to play in economic affairs than monetary capital.
>
> Human capital is fundamental to economic growth. The advancement of knowledge and the education of people affect all dimensions of our lives — from healthy people and healthy communities to artistic expression and a wider search for truth.

One might supplement Mr. Crane's observation: *human capital not only influences human health, its productive use depends on it.* This is the link between health and economic performance in a global world where knowledge and ideas are "as important as money."

Three decades ago, Buckminster Fuller found that the best way to measure economic activity at the start of the 20th century was the use of raw materials. By 1940, the critical measure was our consumption of pure energy.

Citibank Chairman Walter Wriston recalls that when he began his banking career, the key economic indicator was freight car loading. Today "it is the knowledge we bring to the work we do."

Sylvia Ostry, a distinguished Canadian economist and former Chairwoman of the Economic Council of Canada, says globalization has placed a new emphasis on the development of human resources — and needs to foster the capacity of people to do productive work creatively.

Where Mr. Crane says human capital is more important than money, the World Bank's Chief Economist goes a step further. Joseph Stigetz says access to funds needed to develop human capital is now as important to the future of developing societies as their access to oil and natural resources in the industrial era.

Mr. Stigetz says countries will realize prosperity as much on the strength of knowledge as they will on the strength of capital and industrial output. "Human capital" defines workers as a valued asset in the new global economy and provides a basis or metric for investing in human health for sound business and economic reasons.

The World Bank tells us that *human capital is formed through education, health and social development. As such, it is becoming the most important tie among nations in a global economy.* The World Bank believes it must be built into any future measure of economic output. It will serve as a "genuine progress indicator."

Author Thomas Stewart says, "knowledge is more important than raw materials, often more important than money, and more important than automobiles, oil and steel, or any of the products of the industrial age."

If that's true, then one can also presume that our economic and financial investment in the temple of that knowledge — the human person — should become an obvious economic priority. On the altar of this logic, non-medical investments to foster resilience and good health among working people is an easy-to-claim complement to the billions we spend on medical services, and could in fact reduce the cost of healthcare.

The Self-Universe of Healthcare

There is no doubt that the doctors and nurses who serve within the healthcare system are dedicated and selfless in what they do. But the system itself has expanded as the centre of its own universe, and has been funded primarily around its own needs. What has become apparent, however, is that the work and research of health professionals is not enough to protect the status of the health of our population, working and otherwise.

Health practitioners, alone, cannot heal all of the wounds that society inflicts upon itself. The expenditure of healthcare dollars alone will not produce more and better health. There is a huge non-medical world populated by business people, government officials, university presidents, school teachers, and a plethora of others who have an enormous non-medical influence on our health.

Even if health practitioners doubled or tripled their efforts, quadrupled their numbers and multiplied their dedicated spirit beyond human limits, it would not be enough.

Well beyond the reach of any physician or caring nurse, one employer, supervisor, or organization can protect or damage the health of working people by the decisions they make, supervision they provide, dreams they encourage, hopes they allow, recognition they give and relationships they foster.

The Minister of Finance has as much to do with the health status of Canadians as does the Minister of Health, through the fiscal decisions he makes. Unemployment is a social determinant of health. The way organizations are set up can create negative stress or foster a healthy working environment. Both impact the physical and mental well-being of working people and their superiors. (As a society, we have yet to fathom the casualty toll of office politics. That topic will be explored later in this report.)

Society has been forced by fiscal realities to look hard at the role of healthcare and at the health needs of families that go beyond the system itself. Healthcare must be weighed in broader strategic terms — in matters concerning the economy and social justice. This is an essential point of convergence between economic interests and human health.

Author Thomas Stewart says the downsizing of America is secondary to the "real story" of the information age. The "reinvention of business and economic life."

Knowledge is at the heart of the reinvention process. It has become the primary ingredient of what we make, do, buy and sell — building or growing information is the most important economic task of individuals, businesses and nations.

Laptop computers are part of the knowledge tools of everyday life. New airliners have now been designed entirely on computers without paper drawings. A typical automobile, powered by gasoline, has more microchips than spark plugs. A car's electronics cost more than the steel in it. Even the physical part of steel is now less important than the information that goes into its production.

Formerly, it took three or four hours of workto make a ton of steel. With computers, that has been reduced to 45 minutes per ton. The steel in steelmaking has shrunk while the intellectual component has grown. In fact, it has been said microchips have a greater aggregate value than steel itself in the global information economy.

What gives microchips value? Certainly not their physical composition. They are mainly silicon. It is the discrete, intellectual capacity of the human beings who invented, designed and refined it.

Drucker's words resonate. We will always need machines of some sort. But now machines — computers — will depend on people as instruments of economic performance, not *vice versa*.

Shaping History
Charles Handy believes small changes shape history. The chimney probably caused more social change than war. It allowed the common huddling of people around a central fire to be replaced by private, independent huddling. "The cohesion of the tribe," he says, "slipped away in winter."

Cohesion, however, is what's needed to manage the information economy, if not in a tribal sense, certainly in a broader social sense. "The essential requirement facing workers of the knowledge economy is to read, interpret and fit together the elements of this new currency (information). That is a skill of the brain." Brawn is being replaced by the brain as the key instrument of a common day's work. And while the transition from back to brain is vexing and hard, it is laden with hope and possibilities.

In this spirit, Charles Handy strikes a chord for organizations that treat people as assets requiring maintenance, love and investment, and that behave quite differently from the organization that looks upon them as costs, to be reduced whenever possible." ❧

❧ 4 ❧
The Surging Human Factor

UNIVERSITY OF MICHIGAN PROFESSOR DAVID ULRICH SAYS:

"From now on, successful companies will be the ones that are the most adept at attracting, developing and retaining individuals who can make a global organization responsive to customer needs and to opportunities associated with burgeoning technology."

And, he says:

"In the new economy, winning will spin from organizational capabilities — speed, responsiveness, agility, learning capacity and employee competence."

Human issues all. Advocating a bold new role for human resource professionals, he also cites the relevance of employee morale at a time of stunning change, a point worth underlining in the face of merger mania.

Employee communication and motivation are defining issues of the late 90s.

GE Capital in the United States has created a post-merger/acquisition "integration unit," a team of people acutely expert in human relations. One theme has emerged from their experience: learn to "restructure with respect" once the acquisition is done.

It is critical to treat those individuals who will be negatively affected with dignity, respect and support — not only is this the right thing to do, it is also a powerful way to show those who remain what kind of company they (now) work for.

This is good advice. There is no sign merger mania is letting up.

Nineteen ninety-seven was the third consecutive record year of mergers and acquisitions around the world, with transaction values climbing to $1.63 trillion, up 48% over 1996.

As powerful changes rumble across the economic landscape, we are reminded by writer John Dalla Costa that "Canada is not alone in searching for new business solutions while soul-searching for new social ones."

No country seems to have escaped this search. Bell Canada CEO John McLennan notes that "the rate of technological change is faster and the implications of globalization more demanding than anyone could have anticipated." Naturally, profit is still "primary" and "growth is co-primary." Both sharpen the focus on the need for effective human resource management strategies. Both underscore the importance of health-based productivity models as a competitive advantage in the face of cost-cutting exhaustion.

At the centre of the vision of health-based productivity is the concept of human capital, the key to future success in the global knowledge economy. "More important than money," was the way columnist David Crane put it.

We revisit author Thomas Stewart, a member of board of *Fortune Magazine*, who says that companies make two basic kinds of expenditures — one is capital spending and investment in fixed assets or research, whose return on investments is earned over a period of time. The other is day-to-day operating expenses.

"The information age has drastically changed both kinds of expenditure," Mr. Stewart says. For one thing, industrial-age capital (machinery and equipment for metalworking purposes or material handling) has held steady for more than 15 years at about $110 billion a year. Meanwhile, capital spending for "information machines" has ballooned.

By this measure, the information age was born in 1991, the year that spending for production technology dropped below spending levels for information technology — $107 billion as against $112 billion.

Wal-Mart has spent more than a billion dollars on information technology — but in Mr. Stewart's powerful analysis, a "corporation becomes a true knowledge company when it reaches a deeper level where information technology is used for its own intrinsic value and not just simply to automate or report on other activities." The concept of human capital flows from this point. And it goes to the question of creating market and shareholder value.

People are Assets — Not Costs

For example, as of November, 1996, IBM's total market capitalization was $85.5 billion worth of property, plant and equipment. Microsoft's net fixed assets totalled just $930 million. "Put another way," Mr. Stewart says, "every $100 socked into IBM buys $23 worth of fixed assets, while the same $100 investment in Microsoft buys fixed assets worth just over a dollar." The question, therefore, is what has value in the information age?

Obviously, the definition of assets in the two companies differs dramatically. And as trends carry us further into new territory and the human factor assumes greater intrinsic, productive value, we will find that a dollar invested in a corporation is buying value defined differently than it once was.

Inherently, the difference is found largely in the fact that "knowledge and knowledge assets now have a reality of their own." Knowledge-intensive companies — those that have 40% or more knowledge workers — now account for only 28% of total U.S. employment. But, in the past five years, they produced fully 43% of new employment growth.

One of the ironic problems with human capital is that accountants and tax lawyers don't yet know how to count it. Up to now, human resources have been solely an expense and are accounted for as such. Judy Lewent, the Chief Financial Officer of Merck & Co. offers this: "The accounting system doesn't really capture anything inside a knowledge-based company."

Edmund Jenkins, a partner in the accounting firm Arthur Andersen, also quoted in Thomas Stewart's book, says one reason for this is the nature of the old (current) accounting system "which tells us the cost of material and labour." This no longer applies. "The components of cost in a product today are largely R & D, intellectual assets and service." Michael Brown, Microsoft CFO:

Ideas have power by themselves in contrast to machinery and money, which must be animated by the purposes of people using them. [Netscape, a Microsoft competitor] concentrated an enormous amount of intellectual capital that assumed scarcely any physical or institutional form until it was released into the market as an initial public offering in 1995. At that point, the intellectual capital took on financial form — to the tune of $2 billion.

Yale University's Robert Stiller estimates that 72% of U.S. household wealth is in human capital, which he defines in Thomas Stewart's book as "the present value of expected lifetime wages."

As assets, rather than costs, employees can appreciate in their dollar-value to the company. When an entrepreneur starts his or her own company, the lesson is fast and sharp about human assets and the need for value appreciation. In the consulting business, the age-old observation that "the assets ride the elevator to and from the office each day" is literally true. The concept of human capital is not a foreign one. It simply lacks stature as an expression of asset value, and is missed by conventional accounting doctrine.

The fact is that human assets, like machines and equipment, must be maintained, supported and generally kept up. In the case of human beings, the process of doing so is complex and unique, yet the principle is the same.

Human Capital Write-Off

The economic implications of the human capital concept show up in this analysis of probably the single biggest downsizing in corporate history. When AT&T announced it was reducing its work force by 40,000 people, the action amounted to a $4 to $8 billion-dollar human capital write-off — "equivalent," author Thomas Stewart says, "to wiping out more than a third of the company's stock of property, plant and equipment."

One U.S. study showed that, *on average, a 10% increase in employee education produced an 8.6% gain in productivity. By comparison, a 10% gain in capital stock (which values fixed assets) produced a productivity gain of just 3.4%.* "Put another way, the marginal value of investing in human capital is about three times greater than the value of investing in machinery." One of the conundrums facing business people is how to separaate "paying" people to do a job, and accounting for investment in their growth and development.

Nonetheless, **the ingredients that constitute a healthy and growing person can make a sizable contribution to the balance sheet, including top line growth and cash flow.**

Simplistically, a balance sheet shows liabilities and assets. According to present accounting rules, people are liabilities and are expensed. Machines are assets and are capitalized. The latter has favorable tax implications.

Intrinsic human values, if marshalled and protected and fostered, can flower in many forms. Thomas Stewart:

Money talks but it doesn't think; machines perform but don't invent.

The question for companies is how to acquire as much human capital as they profitably can. If the primary purpose of human capital is innovation, then human capital is formed and deployed when more of the time and talent of the people who work in a company are devoted to activities that result in innovation.

...Human capital grows two ways: when the organization uses more of what people know, and when more people know more that is useful to the organization.

General Electric CEO Jack Welch supports the view that business cannot afford to use human capital inefficiently — "[in the search for the best ideas] we have to get everybody in the organization involved. If you do that right, the best ideas will rise to the top."

Canadian corporate strategist Gwyn Paul Williams said innovation is the process of improving what a company does well already. It should not be confused with invention.

Mr. Williams, an expert in corporate governance, believes that personal honour and corporate integrity "have a place in the valuation — and values — of companies." Corporations which are honorable about employees and suppliers, and which have a responsible board providing the proper kind of management oversight, "tend to do well." He says, "all non-financial things are reflected in that company's rate of return which, in turn, reflects how a company behaves."

People count. Hardly a new idea. It is new to say — and companies are saying it — that people doing productive work count for more of a company's wealth prospects than its physical plant or financial capital.

In this, there are two ironies, and a paradox. Just as many employers have strained the security and trust of their employees, they now depend more than ever on them — as human capital.

The creation of a health-based model of productivity, in this light, becomes not only possible but necessary, as cost advantages wane as an expression of corporate or comparative advantage.

The human asset is getting its sea legs in economic and business terms. It is also standing on wobbly pins because of the pace and intensity of change over the past several years. Resiliency, surely a jewel in the crown of employee health, is under attack. ❧

₰5 ₰
A More
Melancholy World

"IN A UNIVERSE OF VINDICATED HOPE" (THE POETRY OF *ATLANTIC MONTHLY* senior editor Jack Beatty) the values of Canadians are changing. We are questioning loyalties and relationships. We are reassessing what's important, and what's not important.

Sociologist and opinion researcher Michael Adams is the founder of one of Canada's leading opinion research firms, Environics. He tells us that in the closing hours of this decade, the disposition of Canadians is centered on issues such as personal autonomy, pleasure and spiritual fulfillment. Immediate gratification has become a "social characteristic" of Canadians.

We are engaged in a quiet social revolution. Adams foresees psychographics — mindsets, experience and cultures — replacing demographics as the most reliable predictor of Canadian behaviour and preferences. He sees a deepening of the Canadian personality. Character and motivation for people of different ages, or the same age, are beginning to define a new kind of diversity within the population of this expansive, horizontal land.

Canadians will experience "mood swings" due to an increasingly arbitrary collective outlook. A fact which politicians and marketers may have to contend with in polling of the future. Canadians, it seems, are going through a "character evolution" paralleling the country's shift from an industrial to a post-industrial, post-modern information base.

Adams sees breathtaking social change in a single generation and a national personality growing from one dimension to many. Canadians may well be shedding our dull maple brown image.

Historically, the two solitudes of Canadian life have been the founding peoples of French and English Canada. In a way, *these are being superseded by other solitudes — the young and old, and the cultures of "before and now."* Adams says Canadians' quest for immediate gratification is expressed in the search for personal empowerment and a growing need to be connected. *Social isolation will increasingly become a darker state removed from the healing light of human relationships.* It is a breeding ground for emotional disorders.

The deepening emphasis Canadians are placing on immediate gratification is sowing the seeds of what Adams describes as an addiction to speed (the time kind, not the drug kind), intense impatience and more immediate demands on each other.

Canadians, it seems, are re-examining what it means to be Canadian. One wonders if the Quebec question seems less relevant today in the minds of many Canadians, at least in the constitutional context, not because we care less, but because *we are looking in other directions for answers to other questions.*

Spiritual Unity
Spiritual unity is "very much of this world," according to Jay Conger, associate professor of organizational behaviour at McGill University, and may be one of those new directions:

In the truest sense, spirituality gives expression to the being that is in us; it has to do with feelings, with the power that comes from within, with knowing what is sacred to us.

This might explain Michael Adams's observation that we are becoming more "self-focused." If that's the case, it is no wonder we are less attentive to constitutional and political rhetoric.

In this frame of mind, for people who are re-thinking their values, who are getting acquainted with a world quite a bit different from the one we've known up to now, who value home and community but who, in the same instance, are redefining their own interpretation of self, it is not surprising we are less concerned about the details of any one political arrangement, and more concerned about the net effect of all such arrangements.

What is prompting Canadians to become more self-focused, to seek out, in effect, a new friend within? Perhaps we hear, in the near distance, the drums of the 21st Century sounding a challenge of furious change, danger and magnificent opportunity. Our caution may well be an act of protection *against*, as well as preparation *for*, the future. It is not hard to understand why.

Unheralded Crisis

In the face of unprecedented change, the globe sits on the precipice of what the Harvard School of Public Health describes as a "largely unheralded mental health crisis." In its landmark analysis, the *Global Burden of Disease*, done in association with the World Health Organization and the World Bank, Harvard calls upon health professionals, business leaders, educators and the world's media to mount the research, education and public awareness that will be needed to contain a number of trends threatening the health and well-being of millions of people.

After two years of momentous work taking their analysts to 30 countries, Harvard this past year completed the first systematic survey of disease and suffering from all sources. Having completed this most significant work, Harvard then urged the United Nations to designate a mental health decade in order to stimulate research, education and public awareness.

The Harvard analysis determined that *mental health problems alone make up over **eight per cent** of the global burden of disease. Worldwide, depressive and anxiety disorders account for about one quarter to one third of all visits by individuals to primary-care physicians.*

Mental, neurological and behavioural disorders are, in total, the single largest cause of quality years lost through disability and death. Around the world, **300 million people,** equal to the populations of the U.S. and Canada, suffer from such disorders.

In established market economies alone, fully one fourth of all years lost to disability and injury result from neuropsychiatric conditions. At this moment, alcohol-related disease affects an estimated five per cent to 10% of all people on earth. This alcohol statistic is deadly. The risk of suicide among those who abuse alcohol is 50 to 100 times greater than that of the population at large.

In its analysis, Harvard demonstrated that the number of work years lost to neuropsychiatric conditions will, by the year 2020, increase by 50%, as a proportion of the global burden of disease, outpacing even cardiovascular disease as an indiscriminate killer and disabler of human beings in terms of work years lost.

By the year 2020, according to Harvard's projections, heart disease, depression and road traffic accidents will constitute the three primary causes of work years lost to early death and disability among all sources of sickness and injury. AIDS will rank 10th, violence, 12th and self-inflicted injuries, 14th.

More than one third of the global burden of disease could be prevented by modifications in human behaviour, including the reduction of violence and prevention of motor vehicle accidents.

In a report on the global burden of disease study in the *Harvard Public Health Review*, we are told that "despite fears of an infectious disease comeback," the Harvard analysis predicts that the toll from non-communicable deaths will climb from 28.1 million deaths a year (1990) to nearly 50 million in the year 2020. The *Harvard Review* says:

Of course, death tolls are only one measure of a nation's health — and a relatively crude one at that. One of the unique features of the *Global Burden of Disease* study is its estimate of the toll of non-fatal diseases, such as diabetes, osteo-arthritis and depression.

Because they affect large numbers of people, particularly young adults, these diseases exert a heavy burden on society that doesn't show up in death counts.

Psychiatric Diseases Rise

The three main causes of disease burden in 1990, respiratory disorders, diarrheal disorders and perinatal conditions, won't even be in the top five 25 years from now, being displaced by ischemic heart disease, unipolar major depression and road injuries.

The Harvard research team, led by Dr. Christopher Murray, developed a calculation to measure the global burden of disease, the disability-adjusted life year (DALY), described by the *Harvard Public Health Review* as both innovative and controversial.

According to this measure, the share of the global burden of disease due to neuropsychiatric conditions, will increase from 10.5% to 14% in the year 2020, outpacing even cardiovascular disease. Both unintentional and intentional injuries will increase as a share of global DALYs from 11% to 13%.

Overall, Harvard found a major shift in the expected age pattern of mortality from younger to older ages. The HIV epidemic is projected to increase sharply, causing some 1.7 million deaths in the year 2006. This epidemic underscores the potential for other new diseases to emerge or for known diseases to radically alter patterns.

Harvard also found that largely because of the demographic transition brought about by declining fertility rates, the number of individuals 15 to 59 is likely to increase by 52% between 1990 and 2020. As a result, the burden of some neuropsychiatric conditions will increase as noted.

The study predicts deaths from chronic respiratory disease will double. By 2020, the annual death toll from lung cancer will more than double, mainly for males in developing nations.

Smoking is at the heart of the matter. Harvard co-author Dr. Alan Lopez describes a "tobacco epidemic" that will account for just under 9% of the total disease burden by 2020. "Not only is tobacco killing people," Dr. Lopez said, "but it's causing a tremendous amount of disability."

A significant feature of this massive work is the light it sheds on the scope and severity of disability as a health issue. It changes common perceptions enormously, especially on the global effect of mental illness. The *Harvard Public Health Review:*

To understand how (the disability measure) works, compare two very different diseases: unipolar major depression and prostate cancer. As a cause of death, prostate cancer outranks depression. Yet because it generally occurs late in life, it causes less disability over a lifetime than depression.

Indeed, the *Global Burden of Disease* found that in 1990, unipolar major depression ranked as one of the leading causes of disability worldwide, despite its comparatively low mortality.

The *Harvard Public Health Review* concludes:

This has enormous implications for the health adviser who needs to determine where to spend money on intervention. If mortality statistics alone were considered, the adviser would likely overlook depression as a significant health priority.

Vicious Maze

Among mental disorders worldwide, Harvard found "an almost impenetrable maze of causes and effects, vicious spirals of mental illness and social pathology, self-perpetuating and producing human suffering on a mass scale." The study finds mental health in the midst of interconnecting forces — many of which do not appear to be psychiatric in nature at first glance.

As noted earlier, Harvard created the DALY (=disability-adjusted life-years) formula during its analysis. In effect, the formula combines the years lost through premature death and years lived with disability, calculating an impact of the two.

As a public policy tool, DALYs will, for the first time, give health and business policymakers a means to compare the status of health statistically across a wide spectrum of economies and health systems around the world, comparable, potentially, to the development of the national income and product accounts in the 1930's that shaped economic analysis ever since allowing for the advent of standardized constructs for the management of income, output, investment and consumption.

Weighing the global burden of disease, Harvard sees a world in transition. Human resilience is increasingly under severe duress. The emergence of the knowledge economy underscores — it doesn't diminish — the inherent value of the human factor, both human capital and health capital. Both constitute a new order of economic values to be considered in the face of what Harvard calls an "unheralded crisis" in mental illness.

Harvard cites a worldwide "epidemiological transition" from communicable (infectious) disease to non-communicable disease as the main cause of death, despite the AIDS epidemic.

As noted above, neuropsychiatric disorders will grow as a proportion of the global burden of disease by nearly 50 %. Such disorders now represent fully 22% of all workdays lost in the developed countries of the world. Meanwhile, the rise in cardiovascular diseases will slow slightly. The HIV epidemic is unprecedented as a reversal of progress in human health.

Fully 18% of all deaths in children under the age of 15 now occur in developing countries. Will globalization, a determinant of health and death, reverse this cruel fact?

At home, Health Canada puts a dollar figure on the economic burden of illness in Canada, telling us that the **total cost of illness in 1993 was $157 billion, more than half in indirect costs associated with lost productivity.** This means that preventive and non-medical investments in health will attack the largest part of the disease cost burden. In pure dollar terms, the indirect cost of bad health represents an issue of greater magnitude than that of spending on the healthcare system itself.

Mental illness represents at least $8 billion a year in lost productivity in Canada, likely a conservative estimate. Health Canada says the extent and severity of disability due to mental illness has been severely underestimated.

In 1993, the costs of mental illness represented 14% of all hospital charges; 8.5% of all drug charges and nearly 8.0% of all physician charges. The missing estimate thus materializes.

The Cost of Mental Illness
The National Association of Psychiatric Health Systems tells us that in any given year, mental disorders in the U.S. affect 22% of that

country's adult population. For comparison purposes, respiratory problems affect about half of all American adults, and cardiovascular disease, one in five in any given year.

Conservative estimates indicate that 12% of children in the United States — or nearly eight million youngsters under the age of 18 — require mental health services and at least three million children are seriously mentally ill.

In 1990, the direct cost of treating all mental disorders in the United States was $67 billion. This represented 10% of what that nation spent for all forms of healthcare. When indirect costs such as lost productivity, death, lost employment, vehicular accidents, crime and social welfare are included in this breathtaking calculation, **the total cost of all mental-related disorders in the United States neared $150 billion that year.**

Compare that to the total costs of cardiovascular system diseases in the U.S. in 1990: $159 billion. *When you include alcohol and drug abuse in the direct and indirect costs associated with mental impairment, the bill for emotional disorders soars to $275 billion.*

It is believed that mental illness imposes more limits on the ability of people to function in a normal way than all other disabling diseases except cancer and stroke. Limitation is defined as impairment of the ability to perform a major daily activity. When that limitation grows into a disability in the performance of work, mental illness is, in fact, the most limiting disease of all.

When we consider the importance of early intervention in the treatment of mental illness, as is the case with all other diseases, we come face to face with this financial fact. *The social and economic costs of mental illness and chemical dependencies are three times the actual cost of treatment.*

Studies in the United States show that when mental illnesses are properly diagnosed and treated, the cost of treating "medical" illnesses goes down. Problem drinkers, for example, generally use medical services eight times more than non-abusers of alcohol. Early intervention and effective treatment in these cases reduced the use of other medical care in 10 of 13 case studies.

The cost of neglect in the management of mental illness materializes in other ways. Data produced by the National Institute of Mental Health in the U.S. found that 72% of people suffering from mental or addictive illnesses, or both, received no treatment, whatsoever, for their disorders.

Dr. Graeme Cunningham, Director of Homewood's Addiction

Division and President of Canada's first Institute for Addiction Medicine, an initiative of Homewood and McMaster University, presents the "neglect" issue this way:

- Five per cent of daily visits to family physicians in Canada are made by active alcoholics and drug addicts who are neither diagnosed nor offered treatment for their addiction.

- Thirty per cent of hospital beds in Ontario and other Canadian provinces are, at any given time, filled with active alcoholics and drug addicts, and again none are diagnosed or treated for their addiction.

It is believed that effective mental health treatment has the potential of reducing the overall use of the healthcare system by 50% to 85%. Even if these estimates were only two-thirds or half true, the positive cost impact of *not neglecting mental illness* is dramatic. In linking mental illness and general mental care in terms of overlapping costs and service utilization rates, these statistics underscore the importance of a closer partnership between psychiatrists and primary-care physicians.

The National Foundation for Depressive Illness in New York says depressed people see primary-care doctors up to 16 times more often than non-depressed people or those whose depression is being properly treated.

Dr. Walter Rosser, Chair of the Department of Family and Community Medicine at the University of Toronto, says that primary-care physicians see patients with low-grade depression three or four times per 1,000 visits, much oftener than patients whose condition formally qualifies for referral to a psychiatrist. In either case, early recognition of the symptoms of this destructive disease can prevent a full- blown major depressive episode.

Human Natural Resources
The human mind, the essence of human capital, and the principal natural resource of the burgeoning information age, is under duress. Some might say attack — even siege. But not all of us believe the assault to be real.

There is a great stigma attached to mental disease. A 1989 study in the United States showed that large segments of the public viewed chemical imbalance as a possible cause of mental illness; about the same number believed stress to be a possible cause. But a smaller but notable number stubbornly believed that mental illness may be caused by a lack of self-discipline.

A recent study by the Lou Harris polling organization in the United States found that only one in five of those surveyed felt "comfortable" being with someone they knew to be mentally ill. In the mind of one psychiatrist, distinctions between mental and physical illness are pointless. A bipolar disorder and a myocardial infarction (heart attack) are acute illnesses. Both require care. Both affect work and health. Both have emotional and physical dimensions. Both should be recognized by insurance companies as authentic illnesses requiring treatment.

In one case study in the United States, psychiatric hospital admissions among Chrysler's employees actually went down 12% from one year to the next and the length of stay in mental health facilities dropped 22%. The dollar savings, Chrysler reports, stem from the introduction of new psychiatric benefits, and employees and health professionals doing a better job of matching patients to the kinds of treatment needed.

At Chrysler, the average cost for mental health and substance abuse benefit coverage dropped 30% through 1991. Patient surveys found high satisfaction with treatment and providers.

The economic quantification of health costs is an imperfect science so far. Nonetheless, costs associated with depression are believed to exceed $43 billion annually in the United States. The weightiest portion of this burden is indirect, that is, a cost to the economy and to the wider community, including $7.5 billion in pay-outs resulting from employee suicide.

The expanse of mental illness — as a "presence" in our lives — is visible from another perspective. A quarter of all medical outpatients in the United States, and between one third to more than half of hospital inpatients suffer from significant emotional disorders. This is some 40% of all in-hospital days in the U.S.

Mental impairment often wears a mask. The symptoms of panic disorders can be confused with heart or brain problems. Eating disorders can appear as a chronic "something else" and are often linked to depression. Depression itself is two to three times commoner in general medical patients than in the community at large.

Reality bites. With these words, *Time Magazine* summed up the sharp edge of 1997 — a year in which U.S. journalists and social observers sensed a "strong current of melancholy seeking to express itself." This is part of the paradox of prosperity in the 1990's. One observer said high-profile tragedy in 1997 and the continued decline of "security" for ordinary people at home and work created a state he described as "the presence of absence."

Depression and the Young

For many, it is the price of isolation in a crowded city. One TVcommentator, on the death of Princess Diana, suggested that it was hard to tell why so many wept so hard — yet they did. Dr. Paul Grof, in the *Canadian Journal of Psychiatry*, wondered if the joltingly high rates of major depression among young people and those born after World War II meant that "the world has entered the age of melancholy." Michael Adams warned earlier about the mood shifts Canadians will experience: mood disorders, and the disabilities they cause will be part of the tapestry of the early years of the 21st Century. Good times, it seems are not necessarily good times any longer, at least in ways we recognize.

Canada and other Western countries seem to be experiencing something between the blahs and outright despair. One of Canada's leading epidemiologists, Dr. Roger Bland, set out to determine how many in the Canadian population experienced abnormal moods. He found, for one thing, that *depression is increasingly a disease of the young.* There are more depressed adolescents and young adults in Canada than ever before.

In Edmonton, Alberta, among both sexes, the cumulative rate of depression among individuals born after 1945 was nine times higher than for those born prior to 1925. Analyses also showed gradual but steady increases in the rate of depression among teenagers between the ages 15 and 19.

Depression is hitting the younger, earlier. Studies reviewed by Dr. Bland revealed a mean age of 27 for the onset of depression while 40% of all lifetime cases, in his analysis, reported an onset of the disease prior to age 20. A study in Zurich, Switzerland says *depression is a recurrent disorder.* Only 11% of the cases over 25 years were one-time events. The Edmonton study concluded that only one in four were single episodes.

Affective disorders are on the rise. The growth of depression is spurred by increasing numbers, long duration, high likelihood of recurrence, long delays in seeking or receiving treatment, diagnostic deficiencies, and inadequate treatment and follow-up.

More than 18,000 deaths were attributable to affective disorders in the United States in 1990, representing 60% of all suicides recorded in that country that year. Mental illness is killing younger adults at a dismaying rate: 37% of deaths in the U.S. attributable to affective disorders occurred in 25 to 44 year-olds.

Dr. Bland: "Affective disorders represent a major public health challenge that requires changes in public awareness and attitudes as well as improved diagnosis and treatment." He calls for specific preventive health goals. Notably, the United Kingdom set a specific target to reduce its suicide rate by 15% by the year 2000. Mental illness accounted for more than 18,000 deaths in England in 1991, 5,500 of them attributed to suicide.

In the U.K., suicide has risen 75% since 1982 among young men between the ages of 15 and 24 years. In England, suicide is the second most common cause of death for males between 15 and 34. Canadian rates in this age group are also high.

The British government, in turn, made what Dr. Bland describes as a "clear commitment" to mental health by designating it one of five key (health) goals. At the same time, a Swedish study demonstrated significant reductions in hospitalization and suicide rates in response to an educational program for general practitioners (physicians) in the management of mental illness.

Affective disorders are common in all countries, of course. They constitute a major health problem. But why are they accelerating? The "main jump", according to Dr. Grof, occurred in the 1970's, likely because methods of diagnosis improved. Beyond that, there is only conjecture and anecdotal evidence.

Among other things, the evidence points to *the intensification of cumulative or negative stress,* flowing like a great electrical current from the transformation of industry and fragmentation of social structures into the viscera of millions of people worldwide.

Born to Suffer
Another issue is genetic predisposition. Major scientific advances in the next three to five years are expected to clarify how far our genes contribute to affective disorders. The question is, are some of us born to suffer mental illness?

Newsweek Magazine answered part of the question in its cover story "Are We All a Little Bit Crazy?" by quoting researchers who are "finding genes that seem to increase the risk of particular mental illnesses." For example, the abnormal version of one gene was found more often in heroin addicts than in non-addicts.

The Biology of Despair

Neurologists, psychiatrists and biologists are closing in on the physical determinants of mental disorders. In one recent study, it was found that middle-aged men who feel hopeless and see themselves as failures may develop narrowing of the arteries. *Despairing people have a 20% greater chance of developing the conditions that lead to stroke and heart disease.*

Research shows that babies feel pain — longer lasting, more widespread pain — and may suffer after-effects later in life. Pain unleashes a cascade of stress hormones that can weaken the immune system, making the heart rate and blood pressure soar.

Decreased levels of brain chemicals called neurotransmitters are biological evidence of the presence of depression, the effects of which are spreading worldwide like an *invited* epidemic — *invited* because depression *can* be successfully treated if diagnosed early. Unhappily, that is not the case most of the time.

Technical imaging of the brains of people suffering depression reveals a lowered blood flow to the cerebral cortex, the area of the brain that psychiatrists at the Homewood Health Centre describe as the executive centre of the brain, the frontal lobes. Depression interferes with the immune system. Sleep is hijacked. Hypothyroidism, a common under-activity of the thyroid, can cause depression, as can some medications and other illnesses.

Whether society is entering an "age of misery or melancholy," or suffering a bout of the 20th-Century blues, the stuff of mental illness is often found in our genes, materializing in a compound of social, economic, biochemical and experiential properties.

Dr. Paul Garfinkel, President and CEO of the Centre for Addiction and Mental Health in Toronto, says of depression:

It isn't a moral weakness, as we were all brought up to believe: it is an illness. Not merely an illness about brain chemistry as some people are saying these days. Rather it is an illness that involves the whole person in a sense of hopelessness and lost meaning.

It is an illness that affects the biological, the psychological, the interpersonal and the spiritual components of any individual. And it is an illness that can strike any one of us because it is the product of an interplay in genetic, constitutional and experiential factors. Anyone can become depressed. Where we differ is in how much stress it takes to precipitate it.

Dr. Beth Reade, once a family doctor, now practising psychiatry at the Homewood Health Centre, says it is unclear whether fluctuating serotonin levels are an effect of depression or a cause of the disease. External factors, such as stress, are all part of the same event. "Unlike pure science, you can't take it apart."

Nonetheless, **depression, the cause of 12% of human disability worldwide,** according to the World Health Organization, is a huge burden to our society and overwhelmingly the chief cause of suicide in this country.

Facts like these stare at us like the glowing eyes of a panther in the dark. There are unknowns in the darkness. But we are aware of at least one presence. We do know that the mental capacity of people is inextricably linked to the physical compositions of the body. They cause and implicate each other. We do not always know how or why. These are the looming mysteries.

Mental health has a biology. Our emotional experience has a biology. In the reverse, physical trauma, disease and suffering have a psychological dimension. Heart disease and depression are joined by more than fate. Dr. Garfinkel once again: "Depression is particularly lethal when it is co-morbid with other states." **The likelihood of dying from a heart attack is increased five times when depressive and cardiac states co-exist.**

Back pain illustrates the point of connection between the mind and body. Dr. Richard Gillette of Northeastern Ohio University's College of Medicine says in a recent paper that "there is mounting evidence to suggest that chronic back pain is a multifaceted biopsychosocial disorder" in which the patients' perception of pain and suffering is influenced by factors ranging from the personal support they receive to stress in their life and their own personality, mood and beliefs.

"For instance," Dr. Gillette says, "patients who are depressed or lack confidence may feel overwhelmed by physical discomfort or stresses that more self-assured patients would take in stride."

In all of this, there seems to be an emerging view that the term "mental health" seems obsolete. Dr. Robert Swenson, Professor of Psychiatry at the University of Ottawa, who treats depressed heart patients at the Ottawa Heart Institute, agrees it is "certainly obsolete to separate mental illness from physical illness. They are intimately connected."

Canadian Business Magazine, in a cover story "Rewiring the Brain", places "the physical self" in intimate proximity with our behavioural and perceptual side. The magazine told of the experience of one Ada Vernon who suffered brain trauma as a result of a stroke in 1991 at age 68:

> The trauma altered her perception of things quite fundamentally. She insisted that her left side wasn't paralyzed (it was) but also that her left arm and leg weren't actually hers.
> "Whose hand is this?" Dr. Marika Holol asked her.
> "I don't know," Ada replied.
> "Any idea?" the doctor pressed gently.
> Ada thought for a moment and replied: "People have told me it's my left hand but it doesn't feel like it's mine at all."
> "Is this your wedding band?"
> "No, but it looks very much like my own."

Ada wasn't crazy or suffering some kind of elusive psychosis. She suffered from a rare condition called "asomatognosia" which, as *Canadian Business* reported, is often accompanied by the two syndromes she exhibited — a denial of paralysis and ignoring everything on one side of her field of vision, even though her eyesight was perfect.

"Not long ago, the best explanation medical science could have offered was a purely psychological one: Ada was in denial," Dr. Sandra Black, Ada's neurologist, said. "Her syndrome, however, has nothing to do with her psychological make-up, with personality, intelligence, emotional profile, age or gender."

"Ada's condition," Dr. Black said, "will appear in anyone who has sustained enough damage to specific areas of the right hemisphere of the brain."

The *Report on Business* commentary adds this: "Like so much else we believed about the brain, the old explanation is wrong, but we don't have a new one to replace it — not a complete one anyway."

The Creativity of Isolation

The frontiers of self-discovery are being pushed back as the investigative, scientific human mind wades into the "chemical soup" of the brain. Writer Robert Hercz:

> In the four centuries since the scientific revolution began, our understanding of practically everything else in the universe, from the origins of life to the four-dimensional space/time continuum grew. But the 1.3 kilograms of dense, pinkish-white tissue within each of our skulls has remained an almost total mystery.

[He adds:] But new discoveries about the brain are piling up so fast that scientists are confident the wait won't be long.

Richard Murphy, director of the Montreal Neurological Institute, says "we have learned more [in our time] about how the brain works than in the whole previous history of mankind."

The history of mankind is a long one. Like so much of history, a lot of it — especially in terms of scientific advancement — was written in the last 15 or 20 years of the 20th Century.

While often perceived as a passionateless pursuit, science and technology have enormous implications that inflame human passions. *The essence of being human becomes more, not less relevant in the face of scientific discovery.*

The role of "feelings," a specific function unique to humans, was definitively raised as a public issue in the wake of the death of Princess Diana. Strong emotions leave vivid memories but also project lucid pictures of what might have been. The English Rose will rival Camelot in the mists of lost possibility.

Intellectual memory is routed through one part of the brain, gut level memories are involuntarily revived with terrible clarity by abnormal activity in another part called the amygdala. This is an essential finding for the development of the concept known as emotional intelligence, and insight into treatment of trauma.

Once again we come upon a link between mental health and biology. Severe stress, we know now, can change the way the brain functions biologically. Isolation will do the same. Unless the brain receives information it needs, it will make things up and produce physical reactions of its own isolated making.

Therefore, when people are alone or isolated by physical fact or social condition, their brain will create reactions to fill in the blanks caused by the very experience of that isolation. The singular, distinct and lonely world of the isolated person begins to take shape by way of this inventive neural response.

Stress and Disease

Scientists know that stress can reduce the effectiveness of the body's "disease-fighting immune system," as the *Globe and Mail* called it, "leaving healthy people more susceptible to colds and infections." A new study at Ohio State University, reported by the *Journal of the National Cancer Institute*, shows that stress has the same effect on cancer patients.

"The findings by no means prove that stress causes cancer or makes cancer worse," Sheldon Cohen, a psychologist at Carnegie Mellon University and an expert on the relationship between stress and disease, said in the news account. "Nor do they mean that reducing stress necessarily will help cure a cancer patient."

Nonetheless, medical researchers have been intrigued with the notion that reducing stress can improve a cancer patient's prognosis since psychologist David Spiegel of the University of California made a surprising observation, first reported in 1989.

According to the *Globe and Mail*, Dr. Spiegel had conducted a study using stress-reduction techniques in breast-cancer patients. The idea was that they would feel better. Years later he realized that patients who had the stress-reduction counselling were outliving those who had not.

A subsequent study by investigators at the University of California at Los Angeles showed that stress-reduction techniques had improved the immune systems of patients with melanoma, a deadly skin cancer. But that study failed to show that the more active immune systems had any effect on the outcome of the disease.

The Ohio State study, headed by clinical psychologist Barbara Andersen, is one of several attempts to duplicate the Spiegel study while making measurements of immune system activity. Ms. Andersen and her colleagues found that the women under the greatest stress had lower levels of natural disease-killing cells, and their immune systems responded more slowly than those of participants who suffered less stress. Statistical analyses were performed to rule out the possibility that the differences were affected by age, the extent of the disease or the stress of surgery.

"The effects of stress on the immune system of healthy people is better known," Dr. Rabin said. "When the brain registers stress it causes hormones to be dumped into the bloodstream. Immune system cells undergo a change in function."

Insecure Hearts

Meanwhile, the *Journal of the American Heart Association* reports, Belgian researchers found that negative, insecure and anxious patients who had difficulty expressing their emotions were three times more likely to suffer a repeat heart attack than patients with sunnier, more sociable personalities. The findings were published in the *Journal of the American Heart Association*.

Emotion can save your life. That's the view of Dr. Dean Ornish, author of *The Scientific Basis for the Healing Power of Intimacy*. After his own mid-life crisis, he began to concentrate on the connection between the physical and mental processes of life. *People Magazine* — not a scientific journal — reported his findings, noting that physicians "who are used to separating the processes of the mind and body will not find Dr. Ornish's prescriptions easy to follow."

Essentially, he believes love can extend a person's life, noting: most of us don't realize that people who feel isolated have three to five times the rate of premature death. When we're lonely, we tend to overeat, work too hard, drink too much and engage in self-destructive behaviours.

·ᴫ6ᴪ·
The Depression
of Productivity

DESTRUCTIVE CHANGE IS CHARACTERIZED BY UNPREDICTABLE WAVES OF UN-certainty, isolation and dislocation washing over the prospects and plans of people. Change, in this sense, carries a trailer that reads "no end in sight." It becomes, to people on the receiving end without the control to direct or temper it, an endurance test of sorts. The drop-ping of "the other shoe" at work (more job revisions, next/new priori-ties, headcount cuts) is expected but when and where is unknown and not forecastable. This disrupts our sense of who and what we are. Our equilibrium is tested.

Such is the storm that everyday Canadians and Americans have weathered, or tried to. It is the storm of change that has pounded away at the workplace and the resilience of individuals working there. *Work and health are intimates in the human community.* The intimacy of work and health is illustrated by the connection between depression and productivity.

In October of 1997, a group of business executives, physicians and health academic leaders, met in Toronto for a private discussion of issues connecting business interests to health — and, specifically, to the economic impact of depression, as a clinical disease. Hosted by Tim Price, Chairman of Trilon Financial Corporation, an affiliate of the EdperBrascan Corporation, the executives and physicians arrived at a consensus on at least one point.

Depression is a "business issue" that business people do not know enough about.

The group agreed on a second point: the impact and growth of depression need to be quantified as a source of disability and prevent-able dollar loss. What kind of workplace stress is healthy? What is not? How can business managers know the difference?

Stress can trigger depression and people have different capacities to absorb and handle it. Depression is an illness, not a character flaw, "an interplay of genetic, constitutional and experiential factors." If depression and stress go hand-in-hand, which they do, the challenge is to find ways to modulate the stress for those vulnerable to it.

Deadlines Stacked Up

For this, understanding the non-medical forces that create stress is key. For example, "stacking up" deadlines on employees, without relief, can stimulate a sense of limitless pressure and lack of control. As television personality Paul Reiser might say, "deadlines that are reasonable, good! Deadlines that are not, bad!"

In the business-physician meeting, one business participant said, "a large segment of our society probably accepts stress at home or work as normal, rightly or wrongly, and as a result, may not take depression seriously, having dealt with their own stress reactions. They may look upon others as weaker and not worthy of redemptive consideration."

These views were expressed by an executive with a strong social conscience, and an equally strong belief that depression and mental illness are business issues. He felt public and executive education was key.

Because of the chemical imbalance aspect of depression, another executive wondered, how does business approach the question of managing stress? We will examine this question later.

Stress in the workplace is natural, and necessary. Where is the line however, between stress that has negative implications, and stress that motivates people to get things done?

"Certainly in the business environment some stress is needed for good performance," according to Dr. Diane Whitney, then a Homewood psychiatrist, and now at Women's College Hospital. "The problem is when the stress is excessive or the coping patterns are maladaptive (such as drinking too much). But no one should tell business leaders they can't create stress."

The question revolves around the degree and nature of stress and one's personal predisposition and capacity to manage it.

The Homewood Health Centre has identified 10 principal sources of workplace (and work life) stress. At the top of the list is too much to do in too little time, and a lack of involvement by employees in decisions and problem-solving at work.

The lack of two-way communication between senior management and support staff, the sense of being unappreciated, the absence of performance management policies and practices, all give employees a sense of inequity and drift.

In the same light, intrusive stress streams from ambiguity on various points, including one's career. The absence of future direction — and therefore, of hope — in terms of growth and promotion can also contribute to conditions that produce stress.

Uncertainty, doubt, and random interruptions all gather as sources of stress that working people manage according to individual instincts and predisposition.

Overarching all these points of derivative stress is the "treadmill syndrome" evident in today's consolidated and downsized global economy, the sense among surviving workers of doing more with less. The sense, and the pressure of deadlines which multiply and bunch up. The sense and reality of being confined by the obligations of work and home in a fast-paced post-modern world.

One CEO participant in the executive-physician meeting referred to the need for business people to be more aware of the links between depression and the workplace. The education process needs to start at the top — "in the executive suite" — "but I wonder if it is misguided to believe we can manage a business by maintaining certain levels of stress?" Here again, as Dr. Garfinkel noted, people's capacity to handle stress differs greatly.

Homewood's Dr. Beth Reade tells us that "stress in day-to-day life activates depression, and the increase of stress in one's life increases the odds of depression." Dr. Wilson Lit says clinical evidence at Homewood points to the impact that economic uncertainty and job insecurity are having on the resilience and mental health of breadwinners, parents and their families.

The body chemical serotonin, is a "cause or reflection" of depression, medical science isn't sure which. Homewood Corporation Chairman Ken Murray says that "people expect a certain amount of stress in an organization — the question is how much stress, and what form is too much or too much of the wrong kind. Can that be determined?" He says research is needed to produce data defining the links between depression and work in these terms.

In response to that very point — raised by several of the business people present — the Homewood Centre for Organizational Health at Riverslea was created as a vehicle for analysis of this nature.

Stress is also linked to a multitude of health and behavioural issues such as high blood pressure, accelerated heart rates and plunging morale. Chronic pain, a physical experience, produces emotional responses — such as desperation and hostility — which, in turn, trigger bio-chemical reactions.

Research Urgently Needed

Dr. Garfinkel underscored the urgency of research on this , stating that stress claims by working Canadians will increase over 50% in the next 30 years. He told the group that the risk of disability skyrockets when depression co-exists with cardiovascular problems.

A CEO participant called for case studies to establish an information base from which to design workplace programs aimed at increasing executive awareness. Early diagnosis and treatment of depression will produce a successful outcome eight times out of 10. Conversely, failure to diagnose and treat depression like other dangerous diseases puts the sufferer in an unforgiving vice which can maim and kill the human spirit and body.

Earl Berger, Managing Director of the *Canada Health Monitor*, said surveys:

consistently find the public's strongest affiliation is with the workplace, but it is also one of the places most likely to make them sick.

...fully 15% of mental and emotional strain among Canadians is caused by the working conditions in which they are employed. This represents millions of people.

A study conducted by *Canada Health Monitor* for the Homewood Centre for Organizational Health, found that *Canadian workers are now more than twice as likely to report work-related stress, mental or emotional health problems as they are to report work-related physical illness or injury.* Many workers with job-related stress problems reported receiving workers' compensation, even though stress problems are not eligible for benefits in most provinces.

A quarter of Canadian workers canvassed in the study reported work-related stress or mental or emotional health problems in the previous year, compared to nine per cent who reported work-related physical illness, and nine per cent who suffered injuries.

A quarter of those with work-related stress problems reported taking time off work, the study found, and in all, seven per cent of Canadian workers were absent from their jobs in the previous year because of work-related stress. Half of them reported being absent 13 days or more, or did not return to that job.

Stress is not exclusively an executive condition as perceptions commonly hold. In fact, blue-collar workers are almost as likely to report stress-related conditions as are white-collar workers: 30% of white-collar workers and 25% of blue-collar. The latter were more likely to report absence from work and to stay away longer. Among blue-collar workers with stress-related health problems, 37% reported being absent and 59% were absent 13 days or more, or did not return. By comparison, 24% of white-collar workers with stress-related health problems were absent from work and 35% were absent 13 days or more.

It is apparent from these numbers alone that *workplace stress is growing as a threat to workplace health, but is often overlooked as a driver of provincial health costs and a drag on corporate productivity.*

It is also apparent from this analysis that treating stressed workers in a purely clinical or medical manner is inadequate.

Organizations that emphasize superior performance must actively support their workers' mental and emotional well-being. Otherwise performance lags. An investment in an employee's potential is a non-medical investment in health.

A 1996 Ontario Institute of Work and Health study said that negative energy at work puts the health of employees at risk if it creates "the stress of being unable to relax at home after work," not being able to "leave the job" behind at the end of the work day. This differentiates the stress that goes naturally with the job from a kind that is most likely to have destructive consequences.

Organizational Health
This harmful form of stress often flows from things that reflect the status of the health of the organization itself — that is, excessive office politics, the failure to recognize honest effort, unclear job mandates, ambiguous direction-setting by those in senior management, frequent changes in priorities and intrusive interruptions and distractions in the performance of daily work, excessively long, poorly run and unproductive meetings, lack of trust, an atmosphere of suspicion and poor communications and, as other studies show, the wear-down effects of unmanaged electronic communications inside the office, described by one researcher as "enslaving e-mail."

Organizational health is an authentic employee health issue. One participant at the meeting of executives and physicians described it as "fundamental to the sustainable performance" of the businesses around which the organization is built.

Trilon Chairman Tim Price noted that depression affects one in every 10 families in Canada and according to data published recently by Harvard University, "heart disease and depression will be one-two as the world's leading sources of workdays lost through premature death and disability inside the next years."

"A scary trend," Mr. Price said, "one that we should try to understand and do something about."

As a "business issue," depression is tied to workplace stress and business performance. The business participants in the health discussion called for a quantification of its "spreading effects" as a source of preventable business dollar losses.

Depression is a disease of the body, and not just of the mind. Let us examine this third dimension through the eyes of a young psychiatrist, Dr. Bob Swenson.

♪7♪
The Place of Usefulness

WORK IS AN EXPRESSION OF LIFE. "ALL OF US HAVE A BASIC DRIVE ABOUT work and love. In fact, even those who are chronically ill and have never worked for most or all of their life, mourn the fact they can't work," says Dr. Bob Swenson, an assistant professor of psychiatry at the University of Ottawa who practices at the Ottawa General Hospital and Ottawa Heart Institute.

The need for self-esteem is central to the drawing power of work. The need to be useful. The need to secure a place of usefulness we can claim in our lives. "Few of us do not want to work."

Dr. Swenson, who treats heart patients who suffer from depression, believes strongly that "it is human nature to want to be productive in life, to be recognized for that productivity, as family members, as community members, as a working people."

He decries rigidity in systems of disability compensation and management that prevent people from returning to work when they have the capability to be productive even if their disability prevents them from doing their normal job. "This is when job and work modification become such a valuable thing."

"Most of the time, in such cases, an appointment with another doctor won't help get people back to work," he says. Businesses, medical doctors and insurance companies create disability systems to manage injury and chronic ailments such as heart disease. "But do they know that their employees can become cardiac cripples because of a mental disorder?"

Occupational mental health is "dangerously less well advanced" in the growing disability management community populated by unions, physicians, health benefits consultants, various kinds of therapists and pain managers, health promotion people, academics, drug specialists and company human resource managers.

"Functionality" — the medical and business term — involves the physical and psychological dimension of being human. Human capital is formed from the functional health of skilled, working people. Function, then, is a bridge between human health and economic performance, and, more specifically, business productivity.

Homewood's Dr. Beth Reade says "enhancing functional performance, not symptom reduction, must become the driving force in the resolution of mental disability."

Enhancing function becomes the essential plank in a health-based productivity model. That, in turn, depends on greater recognition in the workplace of the "holistic nature" of the things that allow people to work effectively — or prevent them.

The Canadian Medical Association reported in November 1996 that: occupational medicine is facing an unprecedented and increasingly complicated series of challenges created by the converging forces of downsizing, economic globalization, rising healthcare costs and the emergence of new diseases.

Dr. Neva Hilliard, a former director of the British Columbia Workers' Compensation Board, cites workplace stress as a rising contributor to disability as "we enter the era of the white-collar knowledge worker."

She noted that today most injured workers are absent from work longer, and the cost of caring for them "has risen dramatically." Reported WCB claims in British Columbia were down 35% over a five year period, while the cost of claims has soared 264%. The duration of claims and illness or injury has replaced frequency as the principal issue — a finding of the 1995 study entitled *Unfolding Change* led by a co-author of this report.

Dr. Hilliard also cited **the rise of newly recognized illnesses and disorders,** *chronic fatigue syndrome* among them. The Homewood Health Centre would add *traumatic stress syndrome,* which, as noted earlier in this report, has been validated by brain imaging as an "authentic" neurological disorder.

Dr. Swenson would "put *co-morbidity* on the list" — the destructive and sometimes lethal combination of disorders that implicate, among other things, the human neuro-immune, nervous and cardiac systems. Depression and heart disease are discussed extensively in this report.

Dr. Hilliard calls for new lines of inquiry to deal with economics, technology, physiology, psychology and social factors. "It's no longer gross trauma we are dealing with," she says, referring to occupational injuries. "We are dealing with many, many issues that relate to health and ill health in the workplace." On this note, Dr. Hilliard focuses more tightly around health and corporate productivity, and, beyond that, around the role of work and the workplace as a determinant of the health and wellbeing of people.

Earlier in this report, we referred to a paper published by the Ontario Institute for Work and Health in Toronto. A further examination of this study has merit within the context established by Dr. Hilliard's comments.

Psychological Demands of Work
The Institute finds that the social and psychological demands of work are becoming more important. Once again, contrast this theme with traditional occupational health, safety and health-promotion issues, specifically the elimination of the physical hazards of heavy industrial work, the reduction of toxic work environments, the reduction of high absenteeism, employee wellness through fitness, and lifestyle and education initiatives, to name some.

All vital, but these are an incomplete reflection of the factors affecting work and health, or sustainable performance of either.

The Ontario Institute of Work and Health calls for a new approach to tackle "workplace determinants of health:"

Despite perhaps a decade of repeated calls [on industry and health leaders] to address organizational effects on workplace health …workplace health promotion in small and large workplaces remains primarily focused on changing individual workers' lifestyles, with little consideration of the conditions that shape behaviours.

Most health indicators (absenteeism, sick leave, and usage of health benefits) are not pure indicators of worker health since they also reflect non-worksite factors such as life stresses on employees, or disease trends in the community.

Further, the Institute notes, traditional health promotion efforts tend to produce some health improvements and employer cost savings but there has been a lack of clinical research reaching beyond anecdotal evidence. As well, changes in the behaviours of employees — relating to lifestyle concerns, for example — tend to be short-term or transient and don't change the social and cultural factors influencing employee health in and out the workplace.

The Institute reports that in one company 90% of smokers who quit smoking resumed within a year; in another only 10% of employees who learned stress management skills actually used them over the long-term. In a third, weight loss rates remained low despite a conscious investment by the employer in promoting it:

> One of the most rigorous of behavioural change programs in the U.S., the Multiple Risk Factor Intervention Trial, achieved no significant improvement in cardiovascular outcomes despite highly motivated participants, a well designed plan, very generous resources and excellent staffing.
>
> Clearly, [the Institute concludes] cultural inertia and difficult social and economic circumstances seriously hinder behaviour changes.

"Workplace determinants of health" go well beyond personal lifestyle and the behaviours of employees, and reach into questions of organizational health.

A topic of deep interest to Dr. Len Sperry, Professor of Psychiatry at the Medical College of Wisconsin and a consultant to Fortune 500 corporations on management issues. He is the author of a book called *Psychiatric Consultation in the Workplace*, and believes that corporations can have dysfunctional cultures. Like people, he says, there is such a thing as a 'Type-A' organization.

Dr. Sperry believes **effective management can prevent disability.** Improved health status of employees, as a measurable component of the productive company, is key to this mode of thinking.

In Western culture, one's work is central to identity, and is tied to experiences outside the job. Dr. Sperry compares organizations in a time when they were less troubled, jobs more secure and employment lifelong — to those of today, when some 35% of all middle management jobs in the United States have been eliminated, producing greater insecurity and uncertainty among working people.

Uncertainty in the workplace triggers greater instability at home, greater distress, grief and emotional trauma. The business community has responded by offering crisis counselling services, employee assistance plans and other support measures to manage the emotional effects of today's environment.

Stress, anxiety and depression diminish productivity and cost U.S. corporations $8,000 per person per year, not to mention the dollar and productivity effects of sick leave.

Stress disability claims have increased dramatically and **will lead** all other work disability claims in the 1990's. Pressures on workers — and thus their health — continue to build.

Dr. Sperry calls for comprehensive "population health" studies of American corporations to understand stress-related disorders and other sources of mental and physical distress and the conditions at work that cause them.

He also calls for an integration of primary and mental health services, and he believes an early warning system can be built into corporations that are becoming vulnerable to dysfunction.

Dr. Sperry says organizations have much in common with living organisms. "The health of the company bears heavily on the individual's prospects for sustainable levels of productive and functional health."

He suggests that just as living organisms can become diseased and dysfunctional, so too can organizations. Thus the importance of research into the kind of change that organizations are facing and how early diagnosis can identify dangerous trends that lead to distrust, emotional disorders and reduced productivity of workers in those organizations.

In this light, the kind of environment that will be viewed as healthy in the post-deficit era will recognize the importance of fulfillment at work, flexible work hours, opportunities for personal growth, reduced social and economic distinctions between management and other employees, clear rights to due process, information and free speech inside the workplace, the right to confront those in authority, and the right to be part of the family/team.

These kinds of "interventions to reduce stress and improve employee wellness" represent what the Ontario Institute for Work and Health describes as "workplace determinants" of human health.

People Plans

Companies in the United States that were seen as "a great place to work" were also financially profitable in addition to having a formally integrated "people plan" in parallel to their business plan.

Conversely, negative work environments are characteristically exploitive, arbitrary, abusive, disregarding, bureaucratic, depersonalizing, paternalistic and, worst of all to many employees, inconsistent, "flavour-of-the-month-oriented" and weakly led or drifting.

The healthy organization, research has found, embraces core values that are fundamental to effective working relationships. Values such as mutual trust, confidence and reliability, fairness and justice, recognition of personal effectiveness among employees, dignity and respect for employees, openness, freedom from fear and from "central decrees."

Values like this are practised by management in the expectation that employees will display integrity, commitment, reliability, initiative and cooperativeness in return.

Dr. Sperry notes that there are virtually no comprehensive, well designed epidemiological studies on the impairment of employees. Nonetheless, some estimates say 20 to 25% of all industrial workers in the United States exhibit psychiatric symptoms and, at any one time, about 10% of all employees in the United States experience significant impairment. It is estimated that 25% *of employees* in that country suffer from anxiety or stress-related disorders.

The broad theme of organizational health articulated by Dr. Sperry and others takes us beyond narrowly focused management consulting services offered by non-clinically trained specialists and consultants in the field of disability management. *Needed are new forms of human health management* practiced outside the clinical setting by clinically trained physicians, some with psychiatric certification, and psychologists.

This means linking organizational style with lifestyle, to produce a clear perspective on the resolution and enhancement of conditions that promote the good health of the organization and the people who work in it.

Against this backdrop, we are able to see work and health, and the wellbeing of people, both executives and employees, in a different context than we have seen them up to now. This new perspective begins from a core belief — Dr. Bob Swenson said it earlier — the belief that people want to work, and "grieve" the loss of being able to do so. They want to be productive and useful and more often than not, their place of usefulness is their place of work.

❧ 8 ❧
Sick of Work, Literally

In the analysis of workplace stress commissioned by the Homewood Health Centre, the *Canada Health Monitor* found not only a significant incidence of absenteeism among full- and part-time employed people due to stress-related health conditions, it found that *workplace stress is now more a blue-collar than a white-collar problem*, contrary to common perceptions. Nearly 40% of blue-collar workers experienced stress-related absence over the past year, compared to 25% white-collar workers.

Moreover, blue-collar workers were likely to stay away longer — 60% were absent for more than 13 days, compared to 42% of professional, managerial and administrative workers, and 28% of sales, clerical and services people.

The vast majority of those who were absent from work — nearly nine of 10 — returned to the same job as before, but only two of those same 10 people said anything was done at work to eliminate or change the conditions that caused the problem in the first place.

Discussing his findings, Dr. Earl Berger said it is "painfully obvious that stress and mental and emotional distress take a very heavy toll on the Canadian workforce and the Canadian economy."

The advent of "mental health days" in larger organizations is becoming commoner. Working people seek periodic sanctuary from the rigours of the post-modern work place. Dr. Berger worries that the same refuge will not be available to the growing numbers of part-time, contractual and independent workers working at home. They face the dangers of a new form of workplace isolation.

Dr. Rick Lash, a human resources specialist at the Hay Management Consulting Group in Toronto, says it will be increasingly important for this new and expanding class of "employee" to develop the skills to self-manage. One source of stress they will encounter will be a lack of 'experience of community' that going to work outside the home creates. The vast majority of Canadians say their job is the community they identify with most closely.

Underlining that point, Dr. Sol Sax of Dupont Canada says, "we all know that getting people back to work improves their health." His point intersects with Dr. Bob Swenson's, that doing useful work is a fundamental need of people.

Most of us, at one time or another, have been "sick and tired" of our job. This is literally true more times than we like to think. Stress — or our incapacity to manage it — is one source of the problem. Chronic fatigue syndrome is another. Dr. Sax tells us there are important gender and social issues involved in managing the effects of that "sick and tired of work" experience.

Research indicates, for example, that men react directly to stress on the job, but women do not. Dr. Sax: "Guys get stressed to the max at work, but they go home and veg out and, by and large, can relax. Women bring their work stress home, and men bring their home stress to work."

In an article published by the CMA Journal, he says the quickening pace of technological change will be a constant factor in occupational health. "Technology is booming right now, and it is driving change. It will only accelerate."

Calling for early physician intervention to head off long-term disability of working people who face the pressure of an environment like this, Dr. Sax says, "employees who are taking increasing amounts of time off work in order to cope with their problems are prime candidates for a physician's attention."

The impact of new information technology on the resilience of working people is one thing. Its effect on technical people is another.

Information system (IS) personnel inside companies are under increasing and sustained pressure. Many organizations, if not most, are in some form of transition from one system to another. The demands for service and complaints about service are voluminous, and often both ill-informed and unreasonable.

The Shelf Life of Knowledge
A 1997 survey of 2,000 IS workers conducted by the Angus Reid Group and the Royal Bank of Canada revealed that 65% had lives that were either very or somewhat stressful — and 2% felt close to

breakdown. The number one reason was the congestion at work between the time available to meet a crush of concurrent demands and the need to balance that pressure with obligations at home.

For people in the information technology departments of larger companies, the root cause of stress appears to be the pace of technological change itself. Relationships become frayed. Staff tensions mount. The shelf life of knowledge in one's own job, in the face of rapid-fire innovation in the information field, is creating a quiet but deeply felt desperation.

The flood waters of service requests keep rising and the stress tide rises along with it. Technology companies and departments are learning what businesses generally are re-learning — **that managing the human implications of expansive, relentless change requires sound management, best practices and good leadership.**

Stress is on the rise. Statistics Canada tells us that absenteeism for personal and family reasons — which includes stress — increased nearly three times in the decade ending in 1993. Mercantile and General Reinsurance reports that while absenteeism due to illness and injury fell by nearly a day a week, "long-term disability claims for mental and nervous conditions, many stemming from stress, increased by more than 30% between 1992 and 1994." Total disability claims in the same period increased by just 1.6%. This gives a signal that Harvard's "generally unheralded crisis in mental health" is infiltrating the workplace.

Psychological job strain produced by the combination of little control over one's daily fate and high demands on job performers, represents a looming and divisive presence among *working* people *working* harder than ever. To assess this issue, we turn again to the Institute of Work and Health.

There have been few controlled studies on the health impact of job and organizational change. Still, a correlation exists. High amounts of stress on the body's immune and endocrine systems is one such factor linking health and the environment in which workers earn their livelihood — and believe "the system" is working either for or against them.

Recent studies examined by the Institute have shown a consistent association between the risk of coronary heart disease and mental strain, the latitude to make one's own decisions in the workplace, degrees of social isolation that employees experience, and their ability to relax at the end of the day. For example, according to the Institute:
daytime blood pressure levels appear to be less important than

whether one's blood pressure comes down at the end of the day, which (in turn) depends on whether one is stressed by, or can relax after, work.

Personal outlook on the job counts heavily. The Institute says: Perceptions we have about work may be more important (as a factor in ill health) than what the reality of the workplace is. More qualitative research is needed to explore how we interpret our work experiences.
Nonetheless, studies do indicate that:
the most adverse reactions of psychological strain — fatigue, anxiety, depression, and physical illness — occur when the psychological demands of the job are high and the worker's decision latitude is low.

In this way, the pace and volume of work, the repetitiveness of tasks, and the range of skills used (by the employee) are all related to health outcomes.

A recent review of 36 studies of the relationship between job strain and cardiovascular disease or symptoms — strongly suggests a *cause-and-effect association between job strain and cardiovascular disease.*
The Institute also noted that work-related musculo-skeletal disorders (such as low back pain and upper limb strains) seem to be more prevalent in work environments that are fraught with tension among people, high demands by the job, and high — often ambiguous — expectations of people. Disorders of this nature make up about half of all Workers' Compensation claims in Canada, according to Statistics Canada 1994 figures.
The indirect costs of such disorders plus lost earnings associated with them in the U.S. are estimated to be in the neighbourhood of $65 billion.

The Corrosion of Low Back Pain
With all this in mind, let's take a brief look at one of the most befuddling, emotionally corrosive and painful impediments to worker health: low back pain.
About 15% to 20% of those who suffer low back pain experience the distress for at least a year and 10% of those who take time off work due to low back pain will be absent at least six months, according to a literature review by the Ontario Institute of Work and Health commissioned by Liberty Mutual's Canadian affiliate, Liberty Canada.

(Liberty Mutual is the world's largest workers' compensation insurer.)

The Institute's report was part of *Unfolding Change*, a five-volume analysis of the Canadian workers' compensation system, led by one of the authors of this commentary. The Institute found "limited but growing empirical evidence linking psychosocial risk factors of low back pain." Still, "after decades of international research, very little is known about who does and does not get better quickly and why recovery time varies so greatly."

There are distinct faces of back pain. The outlook for recovery diminishes as one stage succeeds to the next. Three months after the pain first appears, most authorities believe chronic pain syndrome has set in, which complicates treatment further.

The disorder takes a huge emotional toll. The Institute tells us there is "a substantial body of scientific evidence that both physical and psycho-social factors contribute to the genesis of low back pain." The result is a "slow epidemic" of soft-tissue strains including low back pain.

A Netherlands study links these disorders to a frantic pace of work and lack of 'intellectual' (personal) discretion on the job — over and above physical work stressors.

Psychosocial factors and soft-tissue problems are linked in other studies as well. One found that for video display terminal operators, the work load, latitude for making decisions that influence the work at hand, and support from the company and fellow workers, all bear upon the onset and severity of soft-tissue disorders.

The Institute zeroes in on the implications of these disorders on the way we organize work. Part of the process of recovering from these disabilities is returning to work under guarded or modified conditions. This is neither exploitive nor a matter of privilege. It is a wise accommodation. It can head off the employee's slow drift into a dark and lonely emotional corner, increasingly isolated as time goes by and the early good intentions of friends and co-workers to stay in touch fade with time.

Mental isolation is dangerous and destructive, but all too common. Dr. Robert Swenson tells us:

> One patient of mine, a financial analyst and world traveller, became severely ill, made a good recovery, and went back to work, but not at full speed. He was given one project over two years, nothing else to do and barely anyone to talk to.

People are most vulnerable in an atmosphere that combines loneliness, illness and isolation. Chronic pain triggers hostility and frustration. This deepens the self-prophecy of greater isolation socially or at work, and relationships bear the brunt of the behaviour that goes along with the emotional outbursts tied to chronic pain.

Dr. Earl Berger reminds us that for most Canadians, the most important community they have is the job they go to. It is also, ironically, the place that makes them sick and tired most often.

❧ 9 ❧
Epilogue

THE PASSAGE FROM INDUSTRIAL TO INFORMATION ECONOMY IS BOTH DIS-
*tressing and promising. Human health and economic advancement are be-
ing forged by a convergence of global forces. The advent of human capital
as a new currency rivaling financial capital is one manifestation of that
convergence.*

*In the information age, Peter Drucker tells us, machines will be em-
powered by a skillforce known as knowledge workers.*

*As the 90s wind down, surging prosperity in the high-tech sector has
been accompanied by rising rates of mental illness — or at least of diagnosis and awareness. We have turned on the lights in a room darkened by the
absence of either in previous generations.*

*We are experiencing a more hurried and worried society — our self-
propelled rush to deadlines relentless. Work is being redefined, but remains
essential to the wellbeing of us all.*

*In a roundtable discussion among physicians, psychiatric nurses and
administrative staff at the Homewood Health Centre as input for this report, the role of work, the appearance and disappearance of mental symptoms was explored in detail.*

*For example, when a person is working, anxiety symptoms often disap-
pear. When he or she is laid off, they return, and the longer it takes to find
work, the worse symptoms get.*

*The source of the anxiety is not entirely worry about money. It is also a
question of self-image, self-esteem — and their loss.*

The Homewood roundtable continues.

*The burden of being an informal caregiver is a stressor in modern soci-
ety. 'Sandwich generation' defines the early mid-life of millions. Society is
more violent verbally, aesthetically and, for some, physically.*

Evidence from Homewood's core program of psychiatric care indicates that the emotionally troubled are coping with the residue of the inward-turning 'me generation' which is isolating and excluding "others than me." Marital tension and divorce are common.

Domestic violence and substance abuse are, by and large, poorly managed in the primary healthcare system. The drug of choice in today's society has become "more" — more of everything. People and families are never able to get enough. 'Speed' addictions are self-inflicted. And excitement is an "abused substance" of sorts.

Those who suffer affective disorders often experience difficulties sown when they were very young. Uncertainty about jobs and key relationships contributes to levels of anxiety and impairs people's behaviour.

Many people today are both over- and under-employed. Job duties expand as co-workers are downsized. Downsizing, blending of families, aging parents, perfectionism, bankruptcy, reduced healthcare services — in combination, these issues place a greater burden on the capacity of society and its formal systems to meet the needs of people suffering emotional disorders, whether mild or severe.

The Homewood Roundtable focused on economic dislocation triggered by the "sudden" loss of full-time work. Why would a company, they asked, want to invest in health when they can purchase the work they need done from contract employees? Part-time work means part-time obligation.

Even psychologically resilient workers feel they are doing more for less. But there are still large numbers of people who are underfunctioning in the workforce. There are many who have subclinical degrees of depression, anxiety and addictions and are reeling from family stress and loss. Their disorders are underdiagnosed, and may be untreated, mistreated or ignored as the staple of a pressure cooker kind of life.

By the time addiction shows up in the workplace it is usually quite advanced. Before addictive and other disorders affect the work of an individual, they have already disrupted home and family life.

In the short term, it may be commercially profitable to overwork people. In the long run, it is unprofitable and unhealthy. More work is not necessarily better work.

What is the incentive to business people to gain a greater knowledge of mental health, mental illness and the disorders that interrupt one and intensify the other? One may be that psychologically healthy people do more for less, the Homewood roundtable heard.

They will do a better job, and there is a business advantage in understanding how to get and keep people 'up,' as well as preserve conditions that will enhance their health. (An awakening of a corporation's legitimate economic self-interest in a healthy population.)

Everything the Employee Is

"Functionality" is a word gaining in popularity in health circles. Daily occupational functioning is a reflection of one's entire life and relates to everything the employee is.

In trying to measure function, there is literature examining physical capacity vs physical demand. Factors other than demand are in play, however, such as motivation, resiliency, ability to cope, flexibility and adaptability. But these have escaped the eye of investigative knowledge.

Most jobs are "social events" and when people don't return to work, it's because they are unable to cope socially. They are often well enough to return to work, but are unable to function in a specific job or area within the company. If they do, the same problems recur. In all of this, there is a strong incentive to redefine the disability marketplace.

One of the basic platforms of "affective health" is a capacity to deal with whatever happens. The social and economic goal is to combine realism and altruism to create a culture at home and at work that induces healing and preserves health. One of the challenges in designing psychiatric programs of care is to look beyond the narrow reasons why people experience mental disorders. The question that prevails is, what are the broader originating concerns? Often they are of a social, economic or family nature.

At Homewood, clinical staff are encouraged to think not just about the psychiatric issues that are presented as evidence of admission to hospital, but the physical, social and spiritual aspects of the disorder.

Homewood encourages a holistic approach, philosophically and conceptually, an integrated approach to care born 115 years ago with the founding of Homewood itself and the leadership of its first medical superintendent, Dr. Stephen Lett.

Powerlessness

One of the forces touching increasing numbers of people is powerlessness. One of the basic instincts of the human animal is to run from danger. We have modified this instinct and evolved it to a higher state.

The question now is whether we are beginning to lose the capacity to manage the assaults on our sensibilities, forcing us to "run" or retreat simply because we lack the cognitive tools to manage what we face.

Reprogramming one's reaction to pressing events, perhaps through the development of emotional intelligence, is part of the challenge ahead.

This "new" skill has useful possibilities for members of a society that is galloping just to keep up. The tempo of the times we live in is reflected in the fact there is more absenteeism from work today, according to one study commissioned by Homewood, because of stress-related anxiety than as a result of physical injury.

The world seems a more melancholy place than the economic success we are experiencing would seem to merit: prosperity without a smile.

The place of usefulness, for many, needs to be redefined and rediscovered. This is not a medical challenge, but it centrally involves questions of health and behaviour.

And it suggests rather forcefully that the "medical" and the "non-medical" need to be unified around economic and social strategies in which human health is the principal currency of exchange.

❦

Part II

A Universe Unfolding

❧ 10 ❧

Healthcare: a Pooling of Perspectives

BUSINESS AND MEDICINE ARE CROSSING PATHS. THE IMPLICATIONS OF THIS dance are notable for the health and productivity of millions of working people and their families.

In their respective arenas of endeavour, executives and physicians — probably the two most decision-oriented groups among professionals of all stripes — must interpret the practical implications of a social and economic mosaic reflecting:

- Widening income disparity on the wing of one of the most bullish financial markets since World War II
- The lengthening of shadows and deepening of costs from psychiatric disease, most prominently depression
- Transformation from an industrial economic base to an information one, and the advent of human capital as a key resource in this new economy
- Reform of the healthcare system now under way, and displacement of the hospital as the centre of the healthcare universe
- The prominence of non-medical determinants of health — and the role of behaviour in both triggering and preventing disease.

Physicist Dr. David Bohm says in his book, *Science, Order and Creativity*, that the challenge now facing humanity is unique. To meet it, we need a "creative surge."

Part of that creative surge could come from a new partnership of business executives and physicians in pooling their experience and knowledge to grapple with the medical and non-medical dimensions of health, injury and disease as part of a holistic strategy.

This pragmatic unity is not a new idea. More than 20 years ago,

Health Minister Marc Lalonde drew the connection indirectly in his seminal meditation, A *New Perspective on the Health of Canadians.* "Good health," he said back then, "is the bedrock on which societal progress is built. A population of healthy people can do things that make life worthwhile." And he added this:

> The healthcare system is only one of many ways of maintaining and improving health. Of greater importance are the raising of the general standard of living and advances in medical science.

Mr. Lalonde's report still attracts comment internationally. Its topicality is undiminished by the passing of time.

Then, as now, the "underlying causes" of much of the burden of disease are attributable to behavioural factors. In the U.S., studies show that 70% of all early deaths are preventable.

Traffic accidents are projected by Harvard to be among the five leading causes of workdays lost through disability and premature death, while smoking, if present trends hold, will, in 20 years, kill more people on this planet than any other single cause.

The "behavioural issue," though, is not defined exclusively by personal lifestyles. *Dysfunctional organizational cultures and working environments produce illness and disease,* as do social and economic conditions such as unemployment, poverty and hopelessness. These are "behaviours" of a kind rooted in our economic, social and institutional life. They are beyond the reach of the healthcare practitioner or the healthcare system even. As we observed earlier in this report, they would be beyond even a limitlessly funded one.

Mr. Lalonde once again:

> In most minds, the health field and personal medical care system are synonymous. This is one consequence of the traditional view that most direct expenditures on health are physician-centred, including medical care, hospital care and prescription drugs.

The *Globe and Mail* adds this, however:

> No matter how many resources — money, doctors, hospitals, drugs, home care workers, CAT scanners — we pour into the healthcare system, there will always be unsatisfied demand for healthcare — the reality is that Medicare inescapably involves choices about what services will be covered, when and how.

The National Forum on Health has said that the roughly 7% of the Gross Domestic Product that the public sector now spends on healthcare is enough. The Forum has also said, as we reported earlier, that spending more on healthcare does not necessarily translate into better health for Canadians.

Studies have shown that Canadians, particularly as they grow older, do not want to make choices about when, how or if to obtain healthcare services based on their individual cost. *They want the services they need when they need them* — and, at the time and point of purchase, they are looking for value, for results, for the security of knowing they have purchased *quality*.

Quality and Price

The quality movement of the 1980s taught us that value and affordable prices are not anathema to each other. The term "quality" definitively emerged from a recent survey of health organizations by the *Hospital News* in Ontario. The survey sought perspective on the top healthcare issues in 1998. A brief review of their findings merits our attention here.

The Canadian Cancer Society points to the incidence of cancer, the associated rise in lung cancer deaths and the age at which young women take up smoking. The Canadian College of Health Service Executives points to healthcare reform, the shift in resources to community care and the preservation of competence and dedication in the healthcare system. The Canadian Nurses Association advocates comprehensive human resources planning.

The Canadian Home Care Association emphasizes the importance of a comprehensive strategy embracing service integration, primary care reform and pharmacare. The Ontario Hospital Association pushed for "fact finding" to support health policy discussions.

Another Ontario hospital survey produced concerns about burnout among healthcare managers in most Canadian regions; a finding that was documented separately in an unrelated but remarkable survey by high school students in Toronto.

Dilnaz and Dilnoor Panjwani — whose father is a prominent Toronto psychiatrist — set out to investigate "the phenomenon of burn-out" in the healthcare system and its links to depression and alcohol dependence.

"Burn-Out"

Their work drew a survey response from 26% of more than 600 doctors, nurses and teachers. The work included an extensive literature search and professional biostatistical support.

The students — who have received awards for their efforts — found that "the burn-out syndrome is correlated with the biological, psychological, social and spiritual aspects of a professional … and could affect their lifestyle and performance." Sleep was disturbed. Burn-out apparently increased with the excessive consumption of alcohol.

The young researchers call for "policy and planning decisions" to reduce occupational stress in these professions and the promotion of "professional health through early detection." The students' study received co-operation and support from academics, physicians and genetic researchers.

Mr. Lalonde again — 23 years ago:

> One of the most important but least understood environmental problems is the effect of rapid social change on the mental and physical health of Canadians — some is due to technological innovation — but significant disorientation and alienation arise as well from the crumbling of previous social values and their replacement by others whose long-term effect is still unknown."

Do We Need Health or Health Care?

Fast forward two decades. Michael Decter, in his book *Healing Medicine,* describes a revolution:

> a revolution in how we assess the real determinants of our health. Is it the form of a healthcare delivery system or the broader way we live and organize our society that allows us to live longer, healthier lives?
>
> Do more doctors and hospitals make us healthier or just treat us more extensively when we are ill?

The answer to those questions constitute one revolution. Decter anticipates another:

> A debate rages about the appropriateness of care, about what works and how well it works. Re-engineering the supply side of health services is underway. Managing the demand for health services is the next key challenge.

A former deputy health minister, scholar and consultant, Decter says two revolutions constitute the challenge of the late 90s: investing in health, and re-engineering the delivery system. Affordability and quality at the same time require significant change in the system. He adds: "Let there be no doubt about the urgency of the re-engineering challenge. Without improvements, it will drift rapidly into unaffordable crisis."

Minister Lalonde in 1975 and Michael Decter in 1994 arrived at similar conclusions. We need a consumer-centred view, a shift to a continuum of care and less of a public fixation on hospital beds. Mr. Decter: "What was always done by a physician in a hospital might be accomplished by a nurse in a home."

Re-engineering of the healthcare system is not limited to running or replacing hospitals. The new universe will embrace other forms of care inside and outside institutions. It will emphasize public health, and new regimes governing how drugs are prescribed, dispensed and managed.

In 1975, the rate of escalation of health costs outpaced economic growth by 12% to 16%. Mr. Lalonde on this:

> The past twenty years (1955-75) have seen an emphasis on the construction of hospitals and not enough on the other needed health facilities, producing an excess of expensive acute-care beds, coupled with a shortage of alternative treatment, convalescent and custodial care, and increasing pressure on hospital emergency services.

The implication of that trend is at the centre of the restructuring of the hospital system today. Still we struggle, a generation of governments and national experience later, with the fundamental issue of healthcare supply and demand. The effort to quench demand by limiting supply seems timid, almost desperate. Isn't the challenge really to redefine demand, and thus rescript what constitutes supply?

Healthcare and the Information Age

As in every other aspect of life, microprocessing has impacted healthcare, and the future holds no limits. We can anticipate the use of the Internet for enrolling consumers in private health plans. We can anticipate, eventually, the creation of a single health information mega-base, access to which will become one powerful health management tool — and a major privacy protection issue.

More than 5,400 healthcare sites on the Internet's World-Wide Web were linked with 500 health- related chat groups in 1994, as the number of U.S. households able to access such sites grew from 18 million to 25 million. The U.S. healthcare industry now spends over $350 billion annually generating new information. *Business and Medicine Report* calls healthcare the largest information business in the world.

Health management is part of the post-Industrial Age map now being drawn "with a wire" across the face of the earth. Yet it was 20 years ago when Marc Lalonde set the health agenda of the late 90s with his call for "improved ambulatory health centres with round-the-clock, comprehensive out-patient care" — necessary, he said, so that the access to needed care will not be wholly dependent on the individual availability of physicians." Since then, there has been a dramatic movement (mostly in the early 90s) to more day and outpatient surgery.

Michael Decter applauds this trend. It is a step towards making healthcare more affordable while improving outcomes and quality. He says:

Many commentators have fallen into the trap of believing that affordable cost and quality are mutually exclusive objectives.

Quality is quite wrongly seen by some as something added at extra cost. [The fact is that] quality flows from how well the system is organized, from how both consumers and providers are educated and how individual decisions about care are implemented.

Notably, the United States spends considerably more of its GNP on healthcare than Canada, yet this additional spending does not bring better medical care or improved health outcomes.

The quality movement of the 1980's brought to North America verifiable proof that cost need not lead to reduction of quality. Conversely, additional spending does not always improve quality. This realization, coupled with the surge of electronic-age information hardware and software has set the stage for an overhaul of institutional and economic behaviour in the last decade of the 20ᵗʰ century.

On this precipice, healthcare stands — ready to fly with courage or fall with certainty.

Side Trip Into Middle History

Canadian medicare has more than one parent. Tommy Douglas introduced it in Saskatchewan. Woodrow Lloyd, his Health Minister, carried it through a bitter doctors' strike. John Diefenbaker decided it should be studied nationally. Lester Pearson introduced it. Judy LaMarsh, Walter Gordon and other 1960's Liberals advanced it through Cabinet. In later years, Marc Lalonde, David Crombie and Monique Bégin, health ministers all, contributed to its entrenchment and refinement as a Canadian reality. Canadians feel more strongly about public healthcare than any other public issue.

Dennis Gruending, in his 1985 biography of Mr. Justice Emmet Hall, whose Royal Commission led to a national public health insurance system, calls Mr. Justice Hall the patriarch of the healthcare system. For it was Mr. Justice Hall who struck the tone of conscience in pronouncing the need for a comprehensive Canadian plan: "The indigent would be included."

Mr. Justice Hall encountered fundamental questions when he began his Royal Commission in 1962. His hearings became a forum for debate. Author Gruending:

Hall was interested in all health needs, not just physicians' services. And he found plenty to attract his interest — the shocking lack of services for the mentally ill. High drug prices. The need for homecare services. And the tragic state of health among Indian and Inuit peoples.

He was struck particularly by the obvious gaps in the health system, the inequitable access to services and the generally poor health of many Canadians. In 1961, 30% of Canadians had no form of medical insurance. And many of those who did have private plans (because public insurance was not available to most Canadians then) had only a percentage of their medical costs paid in any event.

Originally, Hall advocated a compulsory, tax-financed insurance program not only for hospital and medical care, but for prescription drugs, child dental care and a whole range of services that never made their way into the plan Canada ultimately adopted.

He differentiated his proposals from "state medicine." Only "the payer" changed. Doctors would continue to be self-governing and patients would still choose their own doctors, and vice versa.

In this context, 30 years ago, Hall struck a theme that resonates today. Author Dennis Gruending describes it this way:

Hall took the view that a commitment to improved health services went beyond humanitarian concerns. It was an investment in human capital (the term actually appears in the 1985 biography of Mr. Justice Hall) essential for economic progress in any advanced industrial society.

He argued that in an economy with less than full employment, extra spending on healthcare would actually enhance economic growth.

Eventually, Hall's grand vision of a comprehensive insurance plan gave way to a lesser version of what since has become known as our national medicare system. In fact, public hospital insurance already existed at the time, and insurance for physicians' services was simply added to it to create our universal, national, inclusive, right-of-birth health benefit.

A decade or more later, when doctors began to agitate for billing patients beyond what the public insurance plan covered, Mr. Justice Emmet

Hall was asked to take another look at the system. His re-examination led to the outright government ban on extra-billing, a position that endures today.

The Vision Was Incomplete
Re-enter Michael Decter:

"But there was a flaw in Medicare. The design, with government as the sole insurer, did not solve the leadership question. Nor did it ensure the dynamism to change and evolve."

Tommy Douglas, the father of Medicare, as some see it, commented in 1982:

When we began to plan Medicare, we pointed out that it would be in two phases. The first phase would be to remove the financial barrier between those giving the service and those receiving it.

The second phase [he said] would be to reorganize and revamp the system — and, of course, that's the big item. It's the big thing we haven't done yet.

In fact, the phase Mr. Douglas pined for is the phase we entered just a couple of years ago — pivoting almost entirely on hospital restructuring and aimed at reducing public expenditure. Hospital consolidations may or may not eventually fulfil a broad strategic purpose.

This will only be known as Ontario, Alberta, and British Columbia among other Canadian provinces, strive to institute new forms and structures of service delivery in the aftermath of blunt hospital service curtailments and outright hospital closings.

As we consider the effects of change now sweeping healthcare in Canada and elsewhere like a wind that rises and blows in great gusts, it is important to underline — in indelible ink — two facts that often get lost in the sound and fury of partisan and special-interest debate over healthcare in this country.

The two facts are these. First, Canada's healthcare origins were private, not public. Second, Canada continues to have a mixed public-private healthcare system.

The size of that mixed health economy is **$72 billion a year.** Two thirds of those dollars are for hospital and physician services, which are covered by public insurance; and one third, about $26 billion, for a variety of services, including prescription drugs, home nursing care, dental care, hospital room upgrades that are covered through private insurance or paid for personally by families and individuals.

Public/Private Spending
Spending by the private sector on health services, in fact, increased by nearly 20% between 1990 and 1995. In the same general time period, public spending on a *per capita* basis on health care dropped by one percentage point.

When one of the co-authors of this report (Wilkerson) was President of Liberty Health, a private health benefits company, he forecast a shift in the percentage split between public and private spending on healthcare, with the latter portion expanding.

This shift will not occur because of the private sector's entry into the category of "essential medical services" provided under Medicare, but more likely because the kinds of services covered mainly by private insurance will be consumed on a greater scale.

Foremost among them are prescription drugs, which in the majority of cases, fall outside Medicare.

The fear of "privatization" of Canada's healthcare system is, by and large, groundless — unless there is a national will to put hospital and physician services into the hands of publicly regulated insurance companies, which is not likely. There is no sure bet that the private sector would want the new territory, and it *is* a sure bet Canadians have no intention of giving it to them, a view the authors of this report share.

Frequently, another version of privatizing physicians' services on a limited basis materializes. That is allowing individuals who can afford it to pay for specialized physician services, or medical tests, on a private basis — out of their own pocket — while continuing to support most Medicare services with tax revenues.

The difficulty of this concept is that there is no doubt private insurers would market a "product" to this high-end segment of the population and in time, we would create a two-tier "essential service" health insurance marketplace. The profitable, high-premium specialist market, and the rest of us or residual markets supported by government insurance. The implications of that are at best unclear. It seems likely that employers would begin to use the selective, high-end insurance and executive benefits would then officially sanction the present boot-legged process of queue-jumping.

A Voice of Business — Pro-Medicine
Confusion about the public-private nature of Canada's healthcare

system regularly invades a rational discussion of healthcare, particularly when business interests are involved. A grand example of this was the 1996 "Health Summit," which was conceived by one of the authors of this report when he was President of Liberty Health and sponsored by the Canadian Medical Association, Liberty and two other corporations.

A considerable amount of the press coverage of the event dwelt on the suspicions of various groups that the Summit's purpose was to undermine the concept of public health insurance in Canada despite the statements by the Summit Chairman, Red Wilson, then CEO of Bell Canada Enterprises, that "Canada's healthcare system represents a real source of comparative advantage particularly *vis-à-vis* our U.S. competitors." And this: "There is a very compelling business case for preserving and strengthening our system."

In fact, the Summit, attended by business leaders and a wide range of health, community and labour spokespersons, endorsed the fundamental principles governing Canadian Medicare. Mr. Wilson again:

> Our healthcare system is one of Canada's greatest successes — our system was built on strong traditions of community service and voluntarism, compared with what might be called the 'enterprise' system.

And, he said:

> Our beliefs about healthcare help define us as Canadians. Where Americans are fond of saying they are all equal before the law, Canadians take pride in being equal before the healthcare system.

A former Assistant Deputy Minister of Finance in Ontario and Chair of Executive and Professional Programs at the School of Policy Studies at Queen's University, Dr. Bryne Purchase discusses the question of healthcare as a comparative business advantage. He says:

> the manner in which Canada's public health insurance policy is implemented compared to that in the United States, relieves Canadian firms of an added business risk, reduces management costs and avoids protracted contracting disputes with labour."

Further, Dr. Purchase finds that:

> to the extent that healthcare adds years to life and enhances the quality of life, far from reducing savings and investment (due to its cost), it may actually increase them.

But we don't know. The country has not yet developed a clear measure of its business or economic returns inside and outside the healthcare system itself. But researchers at Queen's and the University of Ottawa took a fair whack at the question.

The Inflation of Health

The study by Queen's and University of Ottawa was influential because the government of Ontario Premier Mike Harris paid a lot of attention to it and it set the stage for much of the confidence exhibited by the Ontario Government in the belief that major cuts could occur in healthcare without diminishing service. Entitled *Sustainable Healthcare for Canada*, the analysis concluded that "significant cost savings are feasible with no reduction in health status by shifting to less costly modes of delivery." The researchers said they found approximately $7 billion in potential cost reductions, which represent about 15%* of public health expenditures in Canada.

The savings were concentrated by this study in two main areas: more appropriate use of facilities; and the introduction of "better practice" benchmarks. At the same time, the researchers **emphasized the importance of incremental change,** interestingly enough a point the government in Ontario has seemed to distance itself from.

The Queen's and University of Ottawa study sets out four main stressors that affect the delivery of healthcare services in Canada. These are:

- fiscal constraints on governments,
- the lack of public knowledge about links between healthcare and health status,
- the complexity born of ethical issues that influence the allocation of scarce dollars, and
- the need for a new regulatory framework that embraces incentives for efficiency.

The study notes that by 1995, runaway healthcare costs had been slowed by the ebbing of general inflation. In turn, cost pressures on the system were relieved somewhat by the determination of the provinces to clamp down on physicians' costs and hospital compensation.

This useful study says that a huge gap still exists in our understanding of how to get value for money from the delivery of healthcare services. System improvements cannot be won without it.

Sustainable Health notes that healthcare is not just one factor affecting health — it is **the one** that absorbs the most money. Interestingly, the Queen's/Ottawa study calculated a price index for hospital care and found that the prices charged by hospitals and other

* The percentage figure is subject to discussion.

healthcare providers have risen faster than prices for food and housing, outpacing the consumer price index itself.

The researchers found that the forces driving healthcare costs higher were both economy-wide — and thus outside the control of the healthcare system — and specific to the healthcare system itself. The study shows that 38% of healthcare costs relate primarily to wage and price inflation among hospitals; secondarily to service intensity; and finally, and least of all, to increased number of patient treatments.

At the same time, 46% of hospital expenditure growth has occurred as a result of economy-wide inflation, while 20% has been due to population growth and the aging of the population itself. Interestingly, the "aging boom" represents just 3% of the total.

Crucially, the study isolated the impact of prescription drugs. Growing use of prescribed drugs represents 61% of total hospital expenditure growth. This, in turn, is about evenly split between wages and prices, and intensity of service. Additional drug therapies are a very tiny factor in this context. The cost impacts of population growth and aging represent about 15% of the total expenditure growth for prescription drugs. Aging itself has less impact than has been generally assumed up to now.

Cost Savings and Health Status

In summary, the Queen's/University of Ottawa study found that expenditure growth for health services overall has been driven by both system-specific and economy-wide inflation, split about 40-60 between the two.

The researchers conclude that significant cost savings are feasible without intruding on people's health status. That is, by shifting to less costly modes of delivery. They say $7 billion, or about 10% of the taxpayer's portion of the total health bill in this country, could be found in better use of facilities and a shift toward "better practice benchmarks."

The authors say their estimate of savings along these lines is conservative. Specifically, *Sustainable Health* sees a need for reductions in acute-care beds and length of stay (20% in each case), a substitution of continuing care for acute care, reductions in rate variation, and a greater emphasis on facility substitution and deinstitutionalization. The outcome of all this should be lower costs and, importantly, more appropriate care settings. Events have unfolded pretty well along those lines.

The point made by *Sustainable Health* is an important one. Across the board cost reductions, which are generally characteristic of the present restructuring process in Ontario, is like giving a patient surgery without a recovery room. The system needs time and alternatives to ensure that people are located in appropriate care settings. This will not happen as an automatic outcome of deficit-driven cost reductions.

In other words, *major changes in the current system should not be implemented until the new model is ready to pick up the slack.* The study notes that transition costs associated with structural change were not accounted for in calculating potential savings.

Sustainable Health calls for alternatives to employee layoffs within the health system in order to ensure that alternative services in the community are up and running before any facility is closed, though it recognizes that systemic change will be an *ongoing process and not a one-time event.* The involvement of health employees in the decision-making process was therefore seen by this study as a must, not an expendable option.

National Perspective

Sustainable Health points out the need for Canada to tackle health issues on a national basis without necessarily changing the mix of responsibilities between the federal and provincial governments. *That means sharing experiences and learning from each other.* It points out the pros and cons of efforts made in a number of provinces to come to terms with health spending and to police cost reduction in a broader strategic context.

For example, it notes that British Columbia has held its total *per capita* healthcare expenditures below the national average by concentrating and controlling admission rates to hospitals and by placing patients in less costly facilities where services were delivered more efficiently.

The downside of B.C.'s approach — from a narrow cost management perspective — is that wage rates for healthcare providers and workers are well above the Canadian average. Perhaps in the long term, however, this latter fact works to the advantage of British Columbia in ensuring that the skilled work force is duly motivated to help implement necessary changes.

Ontario has held *per capita* expenditures for both hospital and residential care facilities close to the national average, but has experienced higher *per capita* costs overall because more physician services were offered in Ontario than in other parts of Canada — and fees for those services were, by and large, higher than the national rate.

Quebec tackled the wage issue by paying lower salaries and lowering admission rates to hospitals and residential care facilities. The success of those policies as a device to manage cost was only partial, because patients stayed longer and used more costly types of facilities. Again we see one province's experience differing from another. By sharing experience, the provinces could learn valuable lessons.

The Hospital of Tomorrow

Hospitals of the future will be different. *They will become healthcare centres for defined communities of people, providing a continuum of services and a new mixed economy of public medical services on the one hand, and private supplementary and specialized services on the other.* This means fewer hospitals and less hospital-based care, a trend well established in the United States and already taking hold in Ontario.

For example, in 1982, for every 1,000 people, Americans logged 1,132 nights in a hospital bed. Ten years later that was down to 607. By 1995, this was down to 160. And over the next decade, most health markets will log only 70 or 80 nights in a hospital per year for every 1,000 citizens, according to U.S. data.

In Ontario, between 1989 and 1995, prior to the current restructuring process, government eliminated over 8,000 hospital beds, but no hospitals. That is obviously changing.

Globally and locally, the blueprint for change in healthcare contains medical advances in healthcare and telecommunications as well. This is part of the wired world in which we live. Electronically and digitally, Canada is among the most wired countries of all.

Michael Decter on a variety of these points: "Changing the setting for delivering healthcare services has been the major shift in the hospital sector over the past five years." In 1989, he noted, Ontario hospitals had 50,000 beds. By 1994, the number was 8,000 less. The reason was a shift to outpatient and day surgery.

In 1993, the Saskatchewan Health Services Utilization and Research Commission said hospitals in that province could save $16 million a year by increasing day surgeries and reducing pre-surgical admissions. Not only would the steps cut costs, the Saskatchewan authority believed, it would enhance quality.

Getting What Money Can Buy

Decter said such measures require effective homecare services that are communicated clearly and completely. As for benchmarking, he describes it as "a powerful technique for comparing your performance to the performance of peer organizations in comparable circumstances." He describes the *Practice Atlas* distributed to Ontario hospitals as a superb source of comparative data for benchmark purposes. The calculation devised by the Harvard School of Public Health, Disability-Adjusted Life Years (DALYs) is a significant new tool for benchmarking on an international scale.

Benchmarking is an established business technique. In 1992, Arthur Andersen and Co. completed a review of best practices in 120 ambulatory surgery facilities in the United States. The survey demonstrated differences that occurred in average arrival and discharge times. The firm identified 43 best practices and benchmarks in 11 areas, such as patient registration, physician relations and diagnostic testing.

But the stubborn dilemma remains. Neither physicians nor health service managers have enough information on medical costs and outcomes to understand the cost-effectiveness of different interventions.

Government cannot realistically regulate how often people visit the doctor each year or the number of pills they take, but it can change incentives to encourage cost-effective use of healthcare. The Queen's/ University of Ottawa researchers: "That is why solid information on resource use, cost and outcome is essential to support sustainable healthcare in Canada."

Structural Reform
Healthcare service changes are a big part of the blood and thrust of frontline cost-cutting and system change. Structural reform issues are not far behind. Integrated delivery systems are on the horizon. They raise, bluntly, the issue of physician compensation.

The Ontario Medical Association, in fact, has itself proposed a system of physician rostering which — unlike what Mr. Justice Hall conceived — will restrict unlimited patient choice in order to achieve what was described as a "better balance" between supply and demand.

This *concept of balance is key to an integrated system of healthcare* as well. It contains a series of "building blocks" around healthcare and population health that impose greater discipline and achieve stronger management of healthcare resources. In this we find a new emphasis on disease prevention.

The new model puts a premium on performance standards and

on measuring which medical practices and treatments work. It says health is a strategic matter. Diagnosis and treatment are supportive tactics.

There is an inherent complexity in this model, whether from "loosely" coordinated efforts to "tightly" vertically integrated structures. In turn, the new model foresees rostered populations in specific geographic areas and accountability for their health shared by healthcare providers. The Ontario Health Services Restructuring Commission notably separated out mental, women's and children's health as discrete "services".

Within the integrated care model, "capitation funding" is the principal financing tool. Population rosters would be geographically based in large municipalities, ranging in size from 100,000 to 500,000. In a delivery system of this nature, Canadians would receive one-stop-shopping medical care.

"What we're talking about is bringing together primary care together with home care, hospitals and long-term care into integrated systems," Tom Closson, former Chief Executive Officer of the Sunnybrook Health Science Centre, told a Toronto news conference. "Right now, we have thousands of family physicians in Ontario, most of whom are working in offices of one or two."

"We also have 44 hospitals and a number of long-term care facilities, such as nursing homes and homes for the aged. Many have their own governance structures, their own boards. What we're talking about here is trying to collapse those hundreds of thousands of entities into a lot fewer entities."

Competitive systems of integrated healthcare would be set up in heavily populated areas. Patients would sign up with one and, if they were unhappy with the service, move to another. Up to 10 such organizations would be established in Metropolitan Toronto alone. In less populated areas, all medical services within a geographic boundary would be pulled together.

Integrated systems would be publicly governed, while delivery of healthcare services could be provided by either profit or not-for-profit organizations. "We're not talking about two-tier medicine," Closson adds quickly. "We already have the private sector involved in lab services [and]... in nursing home services."

The American Bogeyman
We made this point earlier, but it's worth underlining: **Canada already has a mixed private-public healthcare system.** Medicare pays

for physician and hospital services, the "medically necessary" component. As prevention becomes a strategy of the future, this component of the system will be relied upon less.

Nonetheless, proposals calling for an integrated healthcare system inevitably trigger concerns that this line of thinking would push us toward the American version of managed care and U.S.-styled "HMOs" (health maintenance organizations).

The foreboding centres on two things:

- the fear of a cost-driven healthcare system that may sacrifice quality, and
- the creation of a two-tier system along a rich-and-poor divide.

Lorne Zon, the Executive Director of the Toronto District Health Council, on the other hand, says equating an integrated system in Canada with "all that is wrong with healthcare in the U.S. is, itself, simply wrong."

While the U.S. has a public insurance component — Medicare and Medicaid, aimed to assist the poor and elderly respectively — millions in that country don't have access to health insurance of any kind. This raises the spectre of backbreaking medical bills and simple lack of access to care.

Managed care is not the law of the United States, nor is it uniquely American. It is not a philosophy. It is an approach to planning and coordinating patient-care services, monitoring results, and, theory has it, controlling costs as a natural outcome of the right care at the right time. Thus its comparison to the concept of integrated care that is being advocated in Canada.

The comparison fades — and the theory is pierced — by a crucial point in the U.S., where cost-consciousness became cost-zealotry. In effect, what's best for the patients was sacrificed by administrators over-ruling physicians, clouding the first principle of quality and necessary care: the needs of human beings.

There are surface similarities between the U.S. HMOs and integrated healthcare in Canada. But there are more powerful differences rooted in the distinction of **who pays.**

In the U.S., "who pays" for essential medical services is employers, employees and consumers — but employers mostly. In the U.S., taxes pay for healthcare services for the needy and aged.

The Canadian system differs fundamentally. The taxpayer finances **all** essential physician and hospital services, and in some cases, underwrites the cost of prescription drugs.

At the same time, Canadian employers, employees and families pay for supplementary health services including upgraded hospital rooms, prescription drugs, dental care, home oxygen, various disability-management services, and other forms of care and therapy.

In this mix, there is a parallel between healthcare reforms unfolding in Canada and those in the U.S., the two biggest spenders in healthcare. Both are now seeking to tackle healthcare needs strategically. Both are looking to reduce costs without torpedoing quality — but the jury on those reforms consistently returns verdicts of public apprehension, doubt and outright anger.

In the quest for cost and quality as the harmonies of an orchestrated healthcare service system, Canada and the United States approach the matter from opposite funding poles.

But both confront an issue that transcends the funding question, and which represents the most pressing service issue facing either system in either country: prescription drugs.

The wonder of 20th-Century science and technology has become the central figure in a war against cost and abuse.

❦ 11 ❧
The Other Drug War

THE DRUGS OF CHOICE FOR THE BABY-BOOM GENERATION ARE LEGAL. WE are experiencing a surge in tranquilizers, anti-depressants and sleeping pills. Canadians use codeine more than any nation in the world. It seems we are a people super-sensitive to pain.

Chemical dependence is an issue of the times. With an aging population, it will intensify. In fact, Canadians today spend more money every year on prescription drugs than we do on physician services. *Drug interactions are a leading cost-driver of emergency hospital services.*

A University of Toronto study released in April 1998 estimates that more than 100,000 people a year die in American hospitals from adverse reactions to medications. This makes drug reactions one of the leading causes of death in that country. The study said that physicians were not to blame. The deaths occurred because virtually all medications can have side effects. Combinations can be deadly.

Prescription drugs represent about 15% of all annual health spending in Canada. It has been estimated that anywhere from 8% to 12% of Canadians do not have health insurance, and among those who have, many feel their coverage is inadequate. In addition, drug benefits are expensive. In Saskatchewan, the birthplace of Medicare, public drug insurance carries an $850 deductible and even then, the government pays only 70%.

The nature of prescription drug insurance coverage varies widely among private and government plans. The critical public health and policy question is better framed by how we use and abuse prescription drugs, how they get prescribed and how formularies — lists of drugs approved for consumption — are scripted and used.

*The cost of drugs is growing **faster** than just about any other compo-*

nent of the healthcare system, approximately 14% a year. Researchers warn us about worldwide patterns of consumption centered on wrong or ineffective drugs being prescribed and expensive prescription drugs being used when cheaper over-the-counter alternatives would work just as well.

Recent U.S. studies tell us that Americans saved an estimated $2 billion in 1996 by using over-the-counter medicines for treating common ailments.

Prescription drugs are big news today.

Ninety per cent of the strains of one of the most common disease-producing organisms in the human system now resist penicillin and other antibiotics. According to the National Centers for Disease Control and Prevention in Atlanta, Georgia, the capacity of disease-producing bacteria to resist antibiotics — the kind of bacteria most commonly found in hospitals — increased 20 times between January, 1989 and March, 1993.

According to the American Society for Microbiology, there is no national or global surveillance system for monitoring antibiotic resistence in animals or humans. As a result, the resistance crisis is a threat not only to human health but to economic health. A threat to food production is one facet of that.

Scientists have also discovered new strains of tuberculosis resistant to proven drugs. The National Center for Disease Control and Prevention ties the bacterial resistence wave to the misuse of antibiotics by physicians, consumers, and industries that use them in mass inoculation of livestock. A 1998 study by the University of Toronto found that the use of expensive antibiotics went up when the patient had complete insurance protection, and down when physicians themselves were reminded of the cost involved.

Two earlier studies by Dr. Robert Coambs of the University of Toronto tell us that physicians writing unnecessary or wrong prescriptions, combined with their patients not complying with them anyway, could be costing the health system more than $42 billion a year. This is over and above the base cost of the prescription in the first place.

Only Half Comply

The Coambs study indicated that only 50% of patients correctly take medicines prescribed for them. A proportion of these don't take them at all. Researchers estimate that the cost of inappropriate prescriptions by physicians alone exceeds $2.5 billion a year. According to

Dr. Coambs, "we are now in an era when our own behaviour has a tremendous influence as to whether or not we take our medication or whether the physician writes the right prescription. Those behaviours have a tremendous influence on healthcare expenses."

Dr. Coambs says the failure to deal with the problems of misuse of medication will lead to greater costs and greater loss of life as the population ages. He says some of the worst problems occur with well established medications such as tranquillizers and anti-infective agents such as penicillin.

He stresses the importance of continuing medical education for doctors as a key to both cutting costs and saving lives. He cites the need to arrest the misuse of medicines for high blood pressure and hypertension that are taken by about six million Canadians a day.

He estimates that more than 60% of hypertensives are not taken properly. As many as 20% of patients don't even get their prescriptions filled, and more than half stop taking them after a few months. He estimates that in turn, at least 12,000 deaths a year are the result of prescription drug non-compliance, and says this is a conservative estimate.

Medical studies show that for any particular medical visit, *patients forget 30% to 70% of what the doctor tells them by the time they leave the office.* **This points to the need for education.** And need for **listening and communication skills** on the part of physicians and patients alike. A process in which the physician orally communicates little, the patient accepts everything the doctor says, and there is little, if any back and forth of what the patient heard or understands, is fundamentally flawed.

Medical patients are becoming consumers in the classic sense of the term. According to surveys, Canadians want more information about healthcare choices and treatment options. In 1995, *Maclean's* found that 80% of Canadian consumers want more information about prescription drugs. And were frustrated by the lack of it. Dr. David Kessler of the U.S. Food and Drug Administration says, "there is still more information on a box of Wheaties than what comes with most prescriptions."

The Executive Director of the Clinical Research Centre at Montreal General Hospital, Philip Gold, says the development of new and more effective medicines is essential to the quality of life as well as life expectancy. Optimistically, Dr. Gold predicts life expectancies of 100 years inside a generation. His optimism extends to the advancement of prescribed medications.

In 1988, total expenditures for drug research and development was $902 million in Canada. By 1995, that figure had grown to $1.7 billion.

At the same time, a very important shift in the source of research spending has also taken place. *The pharmaceutical industry represented 18% of those expenditures 10 years ago. Today, it makes more than **one third** of all drug research expenditures.* Spending by universities has declined from one quarter of all dollars spent to 16%. Federal spending dropped as well, down from 28% to 21%, and the provincial governments from 10% to 8%. Non-profit and foreign-funded spending for pharmaceutical R & D declined proportionally.

Last year the Canadian Medical Association and the Canadian Pharmaceutical Association set out on a co-operative effort to improve the management of prescription drugs in this country. They defined in detail the respective responsibilities of physicians and pharmacists to further the quality of drug therapy.

Meanwhile, Johns Hopkins University finds the task of enhancing drug therapy hampered by continuing gaps in available data from hospitals and research institutions. The Ontario Hospital Association recently worried aloud about the obsolescence of data collection and record-keeping in hospitals.

According to the Queens/University of Ottawa study, increased use of prescription drugs represents 61% of the growth in total hospital expenditures.

As the disease burden of psychiatric illness grows worldwide, costs associated with prescription drugs will inevitably keep pace. Drug therapies are a significant and strategic modern tool for treating mental disorders. In this context, the "**other war**" on drugs will require new unity among the physician, education and business communities to advance the knowledge of practitioners in family and psychiatric medicine. *A cohort strategy — perhaps one of the most important in the entire expanse of healthcare reform — is called for, one that will take into account this reminder: in the Canadian healthcare system, prescription drugs are mostly not an essential medical service as defined by the* Canada Health Act (1984). *Employees and employers, as a result, pay for the bulk of the increasing drug costs through private insurance.*

❦

☙12☚
The Cohorts
of Health Reform

EARLIER, WE DISCUSSED THE IMPLICATION OF CO-MORBID DISORDERS, SPE-
cifically mental illness co-existing with physical disease, and their
combined effect. We return to this point.

It has been estimated that **1.5 billion people worldwide** suffer
mental disorders, including alcohol and drug addictions. Only **1%** of
that number receive adequate treatment. In a study by Paul Revere
Life Insurance Company in the United States, fully **one third** of the
7,000 employees surveyed reported *experiencing stress and anxiety trying to balance work and family responsibilities.* In established market
economies, fully **one fourth** *of all years lost to disability and injury result
from neuropsychiatric conditions.*

Research tells us that about 25% of medical outpatients and 30%
to 60% of medical inpatients suffer from significant co-existing psychiatric disorders. This places an enormous burden on the diagnosis
and treatment of physical health alone.

Further, the mentally distressed account for 40% of all in-hospital days. As numerous studies tell us, the impact that mental disorders have on general medical patients is both common and poorly
recognized, while at the same time responsible for excessive "utilization costs" associated with general medical services, including prescription drugs.

The cross-over effect of mental disorders on physical symptoms
takes a number of forms. Panic disorders are often masked by symptoms resembling cardiac or neurological distress. Eating disorders look
like high blood pressure, diabetes or pancreatitis. Mental disorders
have an insidious effect on the efficacy of healthcare generally.

Chronic Disease and Mental Disorders

Studies tell us that *arthritis, cancer, lung disease, neurological disorders and heart disease are strongly associated with mental disorders*. Startlingly, *42% of those with a chronic disease may have a mental condition*. Mental disorders among medical inpatients lengthen the stay in hospital, and increase emergency room visits and re-hospitalizations.

The shadow of this data lengthens further. A study at Johns Hopkins University tells us that anywhere from 12% to 30% of hospital or medical patients screened positive for alcoholism, and fully one fourth to one half of the cases went unrecognized during treatment of the medical condition. Further, physicians were less likely to identify alcoholism among patients with higher incomes and higher education levels, and among women.

The dollar impact of these facts widens on a family level. A four-year analysis of U.S. insurance claims found that families with alcoholics generated twice the healthcare costs as families without. The Center for Health Studies in Seattle, Washington found that the healthcare costs for treating primary care patients suffering mental disorders was nearly twice that for treating those without. Primary care treatment alone cannot and will not reduce the use and cost of healthcare services by the mentally ill.

Dr. Robert Swenson of the Ottawa General Hospital specializes in treating heart patients who suffer from depression. He tells us that severe depression impairs those it afflicts as much or more than coronary artery disease, indeed as much or more than "eight other major, chronic medical conditions" including disorders such as diabetes and respiratory illness.

If coronary artery disease and depression co-exist in the same person, the functional impairment suffered by the individual is "roughly twice" that caused by either ailment alone. (Flash back to Dr. Garfinkel's observation that the co-morbidity of heart disease and depression ups the odds of sudden death five times.)

Depression amplifies the symptoms and disability of chronic illness. It confuses not only the outcome of medical treatments but often the physician doing that treatment.

Depression saps the motivation of the patient to do what he or she needs to do to recover from a chronic medical condition. And *depression can have adverse physiological effects on the course of chronic disease.*

Mental illness and physical illness are two sides of the same coin.

Dr. Swenson: "We cannot separate the mind and body — they are connected intimately," he says. Mental disorders in some people "can be totally caused by biological functions. Depression associated with hypothyroidism is one example. More often, however, mental disorders arise from a combination of biological, psychological and social factors."

Things Mental and Physical

The connections between "things mental and physical" are significant and numerous.

The brain connects with the nervous and hormonal systems. The psychological stress a person experiences creates nervous impulses in the brain. These impulses are dispatched in a variety of directions. The source of the stress, in turn, may be social or economic, or result from a sense of drift or prolonged uncertainty that a person may experience for clear or vague reasons.

Dr. Swenson tells this story. Ray (not his real name) had been treated for depression for two or three years. He hated his job, but toughed it out — day after day as weeks became months, and his life, in his eyes, became directionless and angst-filled.

Ray tried to work out his own personal finances in order to take early retirement. But it was tight. No elbow-room financially. Nearly 55 and without enough savings to get out of the prison that the relationship with his boss had become, his "day pass" home at the end of each work day produced longer evenings and nights of deepening depression.

Then freedom. The company amended its early retirement plan. This produced a "buy-out" package aimed at the middle-aged Rays in the company. Dr. Swenson saw a big improvement in Ray's condition from that point forward.

"In time, he was off his pills, and he never looked back. And it taught me a big lesson — you can never take for granted the cause of severe depression," he said. "The brain is often not disordered first — there is a triggering mechanism; in Ray's case, a job he hated, which translated to a neuro-chemical experience."

Neuro-chemical experiences of this kind produce a range of distress impulses. If the chemical changes that result from the process persist long enough, chemical abnormalities occur in the brain and the emotional makeup of the person can be radically altered for the worse.

Dr. Swenson notes, for example, that there is a higher rate of depression among epileptics. The brain is chemically disordered, and the emotional balance of the epileptic person is upset. Mental illness in this case is caused by a physical state. Most people have a high threshold of resistence to mental illness. But anyone can get it, like the flu. With the right kind of stressors, individual predisposition, or genetic makeup "anyone has the potential to develop depression or ultimately, a total breakdown," Dr. Swenson says.

The body-mind connection is evident in the activity of the thyroid. When it fails, hormonal changes take place in the body and brain. The implications are both mental and physical. Slowing of the heart rate is one. Difficulty concentrating is another. "The brain chemistry changes," Dr. Swenson notes. If the condition persists, it can produce irreversible dementia.

The body manufactures chemicals to combat the effects of stress. Produced by the body to combat stress, cortisol levels can increase dangerously and suppress the immune system.

In this dynamic, we see a dangerous intersection of "causes and effects" implicating both the immune and nervous system, activated by a variety of circumstances. For example, the immune systems of medical students facing final exams was shown in one study to be suppressed by the stress of the experience.

"Mental illness must be approached from three perspectives: biological, social and psychological," Dr. Swenson says. "These factors are common to all types of mental illness."

After centuries of myth and shame, science has proven what the heart knew all along: *mental illness is an inherent dimension of being human, equitably distributed among all of us in its potential to strike indiscriminately.*

Dr. Harvey Skinner, Chairman of the Department of Public Health Sciences at the University of Toronto, reminds us that dualism — the theory of separation between mind and body — is held by a minority of civilizations, most of them culturally and geographically in the West.

We are now surrounded by evidence disputing the myth.

The Mind and Body — A Single Authority
North Americans tend to worship athletic achievement. Inherently and obviously, *successful athletes must unify the mind and body as a single authority.* Mental preparation is a big part of any athlete's competitive itinerary. Baseball slumps, whether in the little leagues or the big leagues, are mostly a question of mind over matter, combined with

usually small adjustments in the player's batting stance or throwing motion. The physics of hitting home runs are three parts batter's swing, wind and ball motion/speed — and two parts courage and intelligence.

In basketball, medium-skilled players use emotional intelligence and game smarts, to make the varsity team and then get into the game.

A nervous speechmaker, standing in front of a critical audience, may have a great text and a strong voice, but when the emotions surge, his or her mightiest weapon is an ability to breathe, a physical act to facilitate emotional calming.

Back to sports. Mega-star Michael Jordan once apologized to his teammates for not passing the ball over a period of several minutes in the late stages of a big game. He described himself as "being in the flow" — a state of exclusive concentration in which he unleashed his paranormal basketball skills, to fly as only Michael Jordan flies. A mindset unleashing unstoppable and disciplined physical skill.

Glen Sather is President and General Manager of the Edmonton Oilers of the National Hockey League, and one of the smartest strategists in hockey. In an interview specifically for this report, he talked about the connections between "mind and body" at the highest levels of athletic performance. "Superstars perform at a level that other players can't reach because of their intelligence. It has less to do with their physical skills."

He said of hockey's greatest player, Wayne Gretzky: "His awareness and attitude are so superb. In all the years I've known him, he's never been down." He attributes Gretsky's greatness in the most physically demanding of all major league sports as "pure intellectual capacity."

"Athletes are motivated to get physically better when injured, and their motivation comes from a pursuit of excellence — trying to be as good as their teammates want them to be."

"Professional athletes have mental attitudes that help their bodies get better. They almost seem to self-heal sometimes. And this attitude is something they learn, something they acquire in the environment in which they work and associate."

Depression and Heart Disease

From one generation to the next — in cases of fame and anonymity — we have seen mental and physical forces combining to influence each other. Sometimes helpfully. Sometimes not. *Outlook, mindset, behaviour, and physical "doing" are linked.*

The biological dimension of mental illness is apparent when depression and heart disease mingle. Among heart patients, depression "should not be regarded as secondary to their medical condition." The converse may also occur.

Dr. Robert Swenson, in a 1997 article in the *Journal of Psychiatry and Neuroscience*, writes that depression "might predispose patients with damaged hearts to arrhythmia and sudden death." Psychological stress among heart patients can set off a series of events that increase the risk of a fatal heart attack.

A study from the Rand Corporation states how important it is for physicians to identify depression as a means of managing the "physical" disease. The publication *Family Practice*, which bills itself as "the Canadian Newspaper of Primary Health Care," says flatly that "family physicians are preventing cardiovascular disease when they treat depression."

U.S. epidemiologists cite an impressive number of studies showing that depression is a predictor of cardiovascular disease, independent of cardiac function. It is believed depression can increase the odds of a heart attack. Medical scientists are also looking, in the same light, at the effects of prolonged and chronic negative emotions — hostility, extreme competitiveness, attempts to dominate other people, pessimism, hopelessness and a depressed mood — on recovery from heart disease.

Certain types of hostility appear to promote heart disease. A study in empirical hostility found that "those who are cynical about other people, suspicious and not trusting, had more ischemia during the study than other groups." Outwardly, these people tend to show a different face, and "come across as very charming. They make good politicians."

The Montreal Heart Institute, in research described by Columbia University as "most convincing" in tying depression to higher cardiac mortality rates, found in a study of 222 post-heart attack patients over an 18-month follow-up after hospitalization that the risk of death from cardiac causes for those in the depressed group was 14% higher than for the non-depressed group.

The Institute's Dr. François Lespérance concluded that "our research shows that depression increased the risk of mortality after [a heart attack]." He estimated "the risk increased three- to fourfold over one year." According to *Family Practice*, experts estimate that as many as 20% of heart-disease patients suffer from depression.

Can depression be objectively measured in terms of the limitations it imposes on the capacity to function of those it afflicts?

The Rand Corporation and the UCLA Neuropsychiatric Institute found depressed patients had health problems beyond the symptoms of the depression, and their physical and social function was more limited than those who suffered only chronic physical ailments, including coronary artery disease. In fact, the study found, functional limitations were "significantly worse" for those with both depression and an advanced heart condition.

Functioning Is Worse

"The functioning of depressed patients is comparable to, or worse than that of patients with major chronic medical conditions."

The presence of depression is often masked by physical symptoms. The Rand Study also reversed earlier thinking and concluded that depression mimics chronic medical conditions.

Over 20 years ago, in May of 1977, the American Psychiatric Association reported:

increasing evidence that patients with medical illnesses such as cardiac disease, cancer and stroke are at a greater risk for major clinical depression. For instance, one of three who suffered an acute [heart attack] also suffered from major depression.

Depression is also a predictor of death and serious complications among sufferers of heart disease. Dr. Wayne Katon, Chief of Psychiatric Services at the University of Washington School of Medicine in Seattle says this:

Depression has a profound impact on patients with chronic medical illness, and those suffering one or more chronic medical disorders have a 41% greater risk of having had a recent psychiatric disorder compared to patients without chronic conditions.

Is it coincidence, according to the Harvard *Global Burden of Disease* study, that depression and ischemic heart disease are expected to become 1. and 2. on a list of diseases that shorten life or cause disabilities in the entire world population?

In a paper published in the *American Journal of Psychiatry* in 1998 by the College of Physicians and Surgeons at Columbia University, depression was linked to death and disability associated with ischemic heart disease, and with cardiovascular conditions generally.

The authors, Drs. Alexander Glassman and Peter Shapiro, said "it is amply clear that depression is strongly associated with more frequent and more malignant cardiovascular disease."

"In fact," they said, "it is likely that depression's effect is not limited to cardiovascular disease but involves all vascular disease including stroke."

Researchers at the U.S. National Centre for Health Statistics report this year that a high level of depression increases the risk of first-time stroke for men by 56% and for women by 85%.

The Yale Cardiovascular Centre in New Haven, Connecticut says there is evidence "to support the idea that depression may cause a stroke or other cardiovascular events. By treating depression, physicians may be able to lower the incidence of stroke."

The Columbia study continues:

Evidence (from medical outcomes studies) is that depression is as much a cause of disability as any major medical illness except heart disease — and our review of the evidence suggests that depression is actually a major contributor to the course and severity of heart disease and that the two conditions later in life may well be synergistic.

The Columbia study and other research tells us that while depression carries a psychological cost, it also has what Drs. Glassman and Shapiro describe as "very real and dangerous physical concomitants."

When depression and medical illnesses co-exist, Dr. Wayne Katon found, the patient is hospitalized longer and "is twice as likely to be re-admitted compared with non-depressed patients."

Centuries Old and New as Well

Shakespeare wrote 400 years ago "my life... sinks down to death, oppress'd with melancholy."

For centuries, the mind and body have been connected in literature and folk idiom. The conviction that mood and the heart have a relationship has been time-tested, but until recently, not scientifically tested.

"Nevertheless," Drs. Glassman and Shapiro of Columbia University say in their paper, "Depression and the Course of Coronary Artery Disease," "it is now abundantly clear that depression is associated with ischemic heart disease."

Inquiry into this heart-depression convergence goes back 60 years, but fell dormant for several decades.

By the 1980s, studies found an "excess of deaths" from cardiovascular disease among depressed patients. The studies continued into the 90s. Canada led the way. through Dr. François Lespérance, Dr. Nancy Frasure-Smith and the Montreal Heart Institute are stars in this galaxy.

By the late 1980s, it also became apparent that links between depression and smoking threatened to raise the mortality risks facing heart patients with depression even higher.

Six Scandinavian studies presented to the 1998 annual conference of the American Psychiatric Association, and reported on June 19th by the *Toronto Star*, demonstrate that depression is a factor beyond the destructive behaviours it induces.

Star science reporter Joseph Hall: "The studies followed depressed people who did not smoke, overeat or have high blood cholesterol, and showed the illness played a large role in bringing on heart ailments." These studies also showed the singular impact of depression: "When they controlled for all known cardiovascular risk factors — weight, smoking, cholesterol levels, family history — depression still turns out to be a very important risk factor for developing heart disease over the course of a lifetime."

According to Dr. Wayne Katon of the University of Washington, "for heart patients, the impact of depression on the risk of dying is at least as significant" as the cardiac dysfunction or patient's history of heart attack. In fact, in the post-heart attack period, depressed heart patients have a three to four times greater risk of death over the ensuing six months.

In a study, researchers at the West Virginia Medical Institute chronicled a 71% increase in the risk of a heart attack among those with depressive disorders compared to those without.

Scientists have also found that the prospects for survival and quality of life for *heart patients suffering depression* are improved by drugs that control the depression. Dr. Charles Nemeroff, Chairman of the Department of Psychiatry and Behavioural Sciences at Emory University School of Medicine in Atlanta, said it is now known that depression is associated with "platelet activation, reactivity and cardiac events" — which in layman's terms, means that depression can trigger physical illness.

In this light, a question lingers unanswered: is depression an illness of the mind, as we commonly perceive it, or an illness of the body and brain, often set off by external forces such as stress?

A burgeoning data base [Dr. Nemeroff says], first from epidemiological studies, and more recently from clinical studies, provides strong evidence that depression is a major risk factor for cardiovascular and cerebrovascular morbidity and mortality. In short, *depression heightens the risk of disability and death for heart and stroke patients alike.*

In one study, researchers in Finland found that men with no prior history of heart attacks, but with elevated levels of depression, were more likely to have a first heart attack even after biological and behavioural risks were accounted for.

Another study found that about one in five patients with coronary artery disease met the formal criteria for major depression.

The Columbia review said "this depressed group turned out to be about two and a half times more likely to develop a serious cardiac complication over the next 12 months.

Meanwhile, Dr. Steven Roose, Professor of Clinical Psychiatry at Columbia University in New York, describes as "critical" the need to find effective treatments for depression in people suffering ischemic heart disease. One concern is the effect anti-depressants can have on the cardiovascular system, including heart rates. They can be insidious and detrimental and therefore, research is needed to harmonize the treatment of depression with cardiac considerations, where the two diseases co-exist.

The *Journal of the American Medical Association* reports: "Patients with chronic conditions account for the majority of U.S. healthcare expenditures — this in a country that spends absolutely the most dollars on healthcare." (Canada is second.) Dr. Jerrold F. Rosenbaum, Director of the Outpatient Psychiatry Division at Massachusetts General Hospital in Boston, notes that depression is "associated with many physical symptoms such as pain complaints, chest pain, fatigue, bowel dysfunction and a less vigilant immune system."

"In ill and frail populations, depression is a significant risk factor for death," Dr. Rosenbaum notes. "Researchers are still studying whether treating associated depression can actually alter the course of medical illness such as cancer."

In a *Toronto Star* news report, Dr. Roose says doctors also believe that depression, caused by chemical alterations in the brain, can actually increase blood clotting.

Runs in The Family
Biology plays a role not only in the effects of depression, but in its onset.

According to the Canadian Mental Health Association, the disease can run in the family. The identical twin of a depressed person, for example, is four to five times more likely to experience mood disorders, given the genetic similarity.

Experts in the United States tell us that about 2% of children and 5% of adolescents have a serious depressive disorder.

"Depression is a family affair in more ways than one," writes Dr. Jane E. Brody in the *New York Times*.

Not only does depression in one family member affect everyone else, depression in one or both parents greatly increases the risk that their children will also become depressed or develop other emotional disorders.

This "familial vulnerability" may stem from the actions of a depressed parent or from an inherited brain abnormality.

Dr. Brody, of the National Alliance for Mentally Ill Children and Adolescents, says that regardless of the cause, depression can persist across generational lines.

The College of Physicians and Surgeons at Columbia University in New York, in a groundbreaking study in 1996, found what Dr. Brody described as a "frighteningly higher risk of depression and other problems in the children of depressed patients."

Under these circumstances, children are at "high risk" for depression, anxiety disorders and substance abuse. The risk factors range anywhere from three to five times the experience of children whose parents are not depressed.

Depression in children is similar to that in adults — appetite and weight loss, excessive sleeping, difficulty getting up in the morning, chronic fatigue, agitated behaviour, feelings of worthlessness, inappropriate guilt, indecision. Dr. Brody:

In addition, previously normal youngsters might develop antisocial behaviour, loss of self-control, outbursts of violence; they may skip school, lose interest in hobbies or friends or experience stomachaches or headaches.

Dr. Weissman at Columbia: "If such symptoms are not just a passing thing, if they go on for several weeks, it's time to pay attention to them."

The Spiral of Social Setback

The biology of mental illness — as exhibited by depression — materializes by way of chemical imbalances in the brain. According to the

Montreal Heart Institute, depression is an "independent factor" in the risk of death six months after a heart attack. As noted earlier, additional research is needed to determine whether treatment of depression can influence the chances of surviving a heart attack.

The impact of depression is not restricted to post-heart attack patients. Preliminary results of another study conducted at the Montreal Heart Institute have documented a negative impact of depression on cardiac prognosis (recovery outlook) among patients admitted for unstable angina. Admissions for angina are now more common than those for myocardial infarction (heart attack). The study found that depression following hospitalization for unstable angina *quadruples* the risk of cardiac-related death or a non-fatal heart attack within a year.

"There is also evidence that psycho-social factors including life stress, low educational level and social isolation influence the outlook for recovery following a heart attack." The Institute noticed that the "poorly educated" are at risk of job loss and a "downward spiral toward poverty can follow [a heart attack]."

"And for those who live alone, the future may be even more bleak," thus calling into question the will to live.

The Institute found that "depression is associated with the lack of close friends." This underscores the importance of a support network to help fuel the recovery process. In a later study, the Institute called for more research into the interaction among relationships, job issues and social factors — and depression as an influence on the outcome of treating cardiac disorders.

Researchers also see the need for research to nail down treatment options. If depression increases the odds that heart patients will die during the aftermath of a cardiac crisis, what factors produce a fatal event? What are the "biological mechanisms" that swing into action?

One is behavioural, Dr. Swenson's point earlier. The patient's failure to do the things necessary to contain the risk of further cardiac trauma, such as diet, conforming with medication rules, smoking, drinking and facing off with killer stress:

It is reasonable to argue [Dr. Swenson says] that depressed patients who have lost interest in their usual activities, who are unable to concentrate, who are thinking about suicide, are less able or willing to take medications, exercise, stop smoking and change eating habits.

Another possible mechanism of cardiac death triggered by depression among recovering heart patients pertains to the way in which the heart beats to do its work. Depressed cardiac patients experience what the experts called "decreased heart rate variability" over a 24 hour period. Translated, the heart's rhythm is abnormal. Blood clotting may also be increased by depression. This can lead to "fatal arrhythmias."

It also places depressed cardiac patients at a greater risk, since clotting in the arteries that supply the heart muscle with blood and oxygen is one cause of heart attack.

Still, the exact mechanisms ignited by depression that threaten heart patients remain unclear. But medical interventions targeted at the 15% to 20% of heart attack victims who show signs of depression during hospitalization would help reduce deaths.

Nearly Always Sudden Death

The Columbia review of evidence meanwhile, cited the study by Drs. Lespérance and Frasure-Smith that found that higher mortality rates among heart attack victims almost always took the form of sudden death which, in turn, is almost always tied to ventricular arrhythmia, a condition characterized by irregular, chaotic impulses in the heart system.

There is also considerable evidence that certain fluctuations in the function of the nervous system cause problems in the workings of the ventricular system of the heart, producing sudden death. In turn, fluctuations or changes in the nervous system are considered an integral part of serious depression and, according to Columbia University "the direction of those changes is such that one would anticipate an increase in sudden death."

"This could easily explain a good part of the increased mortality associated with depression following [a heart attack]," the Columbia research team concluded.

Other studies suggest alterations in the metabolism of depressed patients may increase the risk of vascular disease.

Further, it is conceivable that atherosclerosis — the degeneration and hardening of the arteries and valves of the heart — could be a cause both for depression and heart disease and, in fact, there is evidence that late-onset depression may be one outcome of arteriosclerotic disease in the brain.

Bottom line so far though, is that science doesn't know conclusively why cardiac patients with depression are more likely to die.

Montreal Heart Institute researchers produced a second study suggesting that symptoms of depression among heart victims may predate heart attacks by "many years." Studies from the Netherlands indicate that a condition known as "vital exhaustion" — involving a combination of fatigue, irritability and poor morale — frequently exists for several months before the heart attack.

The Montreal Heart Institute concludes, therefore, it is possible that, in addition to increasing the risk of becoming depressed after a heart attack, a prior episode of depression may impact the cardiac recovery process.

A 1996 study found that among 35 patients who met the diagnostic criteria of depression in hospital, seven died inside one year; 15 experienced sustained depression or relapses during the year; and *only nine of those 35 both survived the cardiac threat and eventually threw off the depression.* "This is in sharp contrast to the 72.2% survival rate of heart patients who were not depressed in the hospital."

Business Awareness of Chronic Disease Depression

Dr. Swenson believes that knowledge of the "heart-depression link not only helps turn up the heat on making sure depression gets treated but will, in time, through awareness, research and treatment, reduce depression as a cardiac risk." *At present, four out of five cases of depression never get diagnosed or treated at all.*

Greater awareness in business circles of the impact that negative stress has on employees, and the extent to which it affects health, will also encourage efforts to control conditions that produce stress which, in turn, contributes to both depression and cardiac illness. Occupational mental health is beginning to get the attention it deserves, which is long overdue, says Dr. Swenson.

The case for defeating depression as a way of reducing the rates of death and disability becomes quite obvious in these studies. Even though the implications of treating depression itself — in this context — must still be clarified through research.

Impairment of human functions stemming from depression has also been a singular subject of study. Researchers from the Rand Corporation, UCLA and the New England Medical Centre conclude that "depressed patients in the general medical sector tend, by far, to have the worst mental functioning and wellbeing — a comparison that held true after two years.

Notably, patients suffering from depression but being treated by mental health specialists fared better than those in a general medical facility. Last October, the Canadian Psychiatric Association announced a plan to improve communications between family doctors and psychiatrists — the objective being to improve the care given patients suffering the mingled effects of mental and physical illness. The initiative reflects a reality for the medical profession, caregivers and society generally — that mind and body are interdependent.

Dr. Pierre Beauséjour is Chairman of the 3,500-member Canadian Psychiatric Association, an associate professor of psychiatry at the University of Ottawa and Director of General Psychiatry at the Royal Ottawa Hospital. He announced the joint plan along with the College of Family Physicians of Canada. It flowed from a report published earlier by the two organizations.

National Strategy on Mental Illness

Dr. Beauséjour says the objective is to build "closer working relationships" between general physicians and psychiatrists. Working together, the two groups will seek to reduce referral waiting lists and influence the reform of healthcare through a model of "shared care."

Last year, the Canadian Psychiatric Association called for a "national strategy" to confront mental illness and promote prevention, treatment and rehabilitation across the country.

Dr. Beauséjour said Canada's mental health system will face increased demand from "an aging population, a highly stressed youth population, and employment issues." He also cited the psychiatric residue of health problems, including AIDS.

The Canadian Mental Health Association embarked upon a national campaign of its own. "A Framework of Support" brought families, now the largest group of caregivers in the community, "into the loop" of consultation to promote community mental health services.

The CMHA promotes consumerism in mental health and underscores "knowledge and information" as a principal weapon in containing the impact of emotional disorders.

The biology of mental illness — or, in this case, its biochemistry — is evident in the hallucinations of schizophrenia. The may see things and hear voices that aren't there. But the visual and auditory regions of his brain are active. Where those ghosts come from, science is unsure.

Brain imaging — one of the breakthrough technologies in 20th Century medicine — shows a "biopic" of one contemporary disorder which had a credibility problem for some time — post-traumatic stress disorder (PTSD), a specialty of the Homewood Health Centre.

When syndrome victims begin to relive their traumatic experience, such as in the case of war veterans, the brain swings into motion. Researchers found that PTSD sufferers, in fact, have a predisposition to the disorder due to differences in brain structure. Similarly, anorexics display unique brain characteristics relating to structure and metabolism.

Dr. David Wright is a psychiatrist at Homewood. He specializes in the treatment of trauma and Homewood has Canada's first and largest inpatient program for disorders of this nature.

Patients come from all over Canada for six weeks. The program draws on a multitude of disciplines from psychiatry and occupational therapy to recreation, creative arts and pastoral care.

Dr. Wright and his colleagues, leaders in an emerging field of psychiatric medicine, discuss their work regularly at international gatherings of physicians and disability managers.

Those suffering PTSD have what he describes as a "social wound." They are often victims of abuse. They relive "the event."

"The (Homewood) therapeutic community offers an environment where social wounds get the necessary social healing."

PTSD often appears with other problems — such as addictions or mood disorders.

The outlook for those suffering this disorder, first profiled in the aftermath of the Vietnam War, is fairly optimistic. Dr. Wright says "positive change can occur in our patients' lives."

In an address to the American Psychiatric Association, he said Homewood has treated native Canadians and trained native community workers to use the Homewood model.

"The number of traumatized people in the Arctic is very high and the level of community violence much higher than in southern Canada," he said. Extending successful treatment to entire communities would indeed be an example of stopping the cycle of violence."

Affection and the Heart
William Harvey erased the line between the mind and body nearly 400 years ago when he wrote, "...every affection of the mind that is attended with either pain or pleasure, hope or fear, is the cause of an agitation whose influence extends to the heart."

Less poetically, Dr. Robert Swenson discusses these connections with us:

Authors: *Can medical problems trigger mental disorders?*

Dr. Swenson: It is possible for serious medical illness to represent for the sufferer intolerable psychological loss — the loss of autonomy, capacity to work or to interact with friends or family. This may lead to overwhelming anxiety or profound depression.

Authors: Can that happen to anyone?

Dr. Swenson: It can, but some of us are more vulnerable than others — such as those with a previous episode of depression or anxiety, with drug or alcohol abuse problems, the inability to keep a job, a family history of psychiatric illness, unstable personal relationships, repeated major losses in their life or disabilities requiring ongoing medication.

Authors: You mentioned earlier that the attention being given mental illness will increase the pressure on business people to do more to help detect and deal with it in the workplace. What should they be looking for among workers or family members?

Dr. Swenson: For one thing, depression may take the form of a sad or withdrawn appearance, poor motivation, a difficulty in remembering things or concentrating. Anxiety symptoms may include shortness of breath, shakiness, dizziness, weakness or chronic chest pain.

Authors: Can anyone detect these symptoms?

Dr. Swenson: On the surface, yes, but physical complaints associated with depression or anxiety need careful professional evaluation.

Authors: Is depression connected to other psychiatric disorders?

Dr. Swenson: Sometimes. Sometimes not. For example, a **primary** depressive disorder is the first appearance of psychiatric illness in the patient's lifetime and is not associated with other psychiatric illnesses or, intrinsically, with a physical illness.

A primary depressive disorder may be **unipolar** (major depression only) or **bipolar** (manic and depressive episodes). A secondary depressive disorder may occur in a patient with other psychiatric or medical illness.

Authors: How prevalent is depression among heart patients?

Dr. Swenson: Depressive and anxiety disorders may occur in up to 25% of patients who have cardiovascular disease.

Authors: Among [heart attack] victims, who is most vulnerable to developing a depression?

Dr. Swenson: Those who have memory and concentration problems, marital conflict and interpersonal strife in their lives, are unable to modify the behaviour that poses a cardiovascular risk, or who have marked work stress or a marked reluctance to return to work. These are some of the indications.

Authors: *Is depression like having a chronic physical illness?*

Dr. Swenson: An important study has shown that impairment in daily functioning from depression is comparable to or worse than the impairment uniquely associated with any of the eight chronic medical conditions, including coronary artery disease.

Studies also show us that the effects of depression [in combination with] medical conditions [compound each other]. For example, the combination of advanced cardiac artery disease and depressive symptoms [essentially double] the impairment in social functioning [that is] associated with either condition alone.

Authors: *In short, greater disability?*

Dr. Swenson: In this sense, depression often amplifies the symptoms of the chronic medical illness, adding to the patient's disability and confusing the treating physician.

Depression may also decrease the patient's motivation to care for his own [chronic] illness, and it may also have adverse physiologic effects on the patient's disease.

Authors: *Anyone can feel down when they're sick. Does that mean we are all depressed?*

Dr. Swenson: A normal sadness is a predictable response to life's problems and disappointments. Depression differs from this in the combination of specific symptoms and duration, which have a predictable course and respond to treatment, as in the case of a major depression.

Some depressed patients, often elderly, do not complain of their mood but describe symptoms such as fatigue, insomnia, lightheadedness, or possibly nausea as their major problems. They may also complain of chronic pain and blame their everyday lack of living on their physical problems.

Authors: *How do the complaints appear to those around the person?*

Dr. Swenson: Often family members will say "he just doesn't try anymore." The complaints, though, require thorough medical investigation, especially in someone with prior cardiac disease.

Authors: *What does the successful treatment of depression depend on when there is also a chronic disease involved?*

Dr. Swenson: It is essential to integrate the patient's psychiatric and medical care. [For one thing] many depressed patients are reluctant to be referred for psychiatric care but will accept treatment for major depression if encouraged in that direction by their family physician or cardiac specialist.

The creation of an alliance between patient and physician is critical to help the patient understand the "disease concept" of depression and the fact it is impairing their everyday life.

Authors: How important is the support of family and friends?

Dr. Swenson: Social support plays an important role in [helping depressed patients] adapt to and recover from cardiac disease. It is also important in the primary prevention of [heart attack]. For example, the degree of emotional support was found to be independently related to risk for death in the subsequent six months after [a heart attack] among 195 elderly patients hospitalized for acute myocardial infarction [heart attack].

Authors: Can depression directly influence the process of recovery from a cardiac event?

Dr. Swenson: Yes, and with respect to cardiac rehabilitation, it should be kept in mind that most patients who have a depression disorder also have diminished motivation and interest in daily life along with the overwhelming fatigue that accompanies a major depression. Certainly, the patient's progression with cardiac rehabilitation is often slow or non-existent.

Authors: Are there other mental disorders that have similar implications for the recovery process?

Dr. Swenson: The most common and clinically significant in a cardiac rehabilitation practice are panic disorder and generalized anxiety disorder.

Panic disorders can produce a sudden onset of somatic symptoms (chest pain, for example) and patients experience these attacks as evidence, in their mind, of a serious underlying illness.

Generally speaking, the average age for the onset of a panic disorder is the late teens or early 20s, although some develop it in later years in association with a medical illness.

Authors: What vulnerabilities are associated with panic disorders?

Dr. Swenson: People with panic disorders are at increased risk for major depression, alcohol abuse and suicide, while generalized anxiety disorders are usually characterized by uncontrollable worry, accompanied by a variety of physical symptoms.

Authors: What is the connection between our nervous and cardiovascular systems?

Dr. Swenson: There is developing literature [on the subject] and an increasing awareness of the relationship between stress, the autonomic (involuntary) nervous system and the neural (brain) regulation of the cardiovascular system.

There is an association between emotion and changes in the heart rate and blood pressure, and therefore heart muscle oxygen requirements.

The studies of mental stress in patients with coronary artery disease have documented a reduction in left ventricular function, coronary artery spasms and abnormalities [in the pumping motion of the heart with certain types of mental stress].

The Unity of Physicians

As we ponder the broad cohort effect of mental disease and chronic illness — in terms of healthcare costs and human suffering — we notice the narrow track that healthcare reform in Canada and the United States has followed.

Up to now, reform has translated into a restructuring of health delivery systems and overhauling hospital services. Models of integrated care are the stepchildren of this. However, questions of structure and organization are not the only issues requiring attention. Far from it. Long-term health goals must attract a concentrated effort by institutions and individuals alike.

In many respects, restructuring the healthcare system mirrors the corporate and industrial approach to the pressures of rising costs and diminishing markets.

In deciding how the healthcare system of the future will look organizationally, let us also consider the challenge it will be called upon to meet. The cohort status of chronic and mental disease is part of a shift occurring globally. The impact of disability is only beginning to be clearly understood.

Again, let us remind ourselves of Harvard's position: depression will be the leading cause of work years lost through premature death and disability in the developed world by 2020 if present trends continue. In these terms, psychiatric illness is growing faster than cardiovascular disease.

The exploration of the implications of the mind and body as one complex is being advanced by Dr. Walter Rosser, Chairman of the Department of Family and Community Medicine at the University of Toronto.

Dr. Rosser graduates more family physicians every year than anyone else in the world — more than 100. His department has more than 600 faculty members and exports its knowledge to countries such as Brazil and Saudi Arabia, with graduate student programs having been taken by individuals from 14 countries. He wants general practitioners and psychiatrists to get closer to each other, a theme sounded earlier by Dr. Pierre Beauséjour, Chairman of the Canadian Psychiatric Association.

Dr. Rosser believes that training of future physicians must take into account the intricate interplay among clinical, social and emotional factors affecting human health individually and at the population level. Compressing patient problems into finite and mutually exclusive diagnostic classifications is wrong-headed.

For example, symptoms of anxiety may not match formal diagnostic criteria, but nonetheless affect the wellbeing of their patients. Dr. Rosser has introduced a training program aimed at arming physicians to manage these less intense but intrusive forms of mental distress.

New understandings from drug studies linking human psychology and our immune system demonstrate that a medical model segregating problems of the mind from those of the body is obsolete and insufficient.

The Dividing Fault Line

Dr. Rosser likens this segregationist custom to a geographical fault line with medical specialists on one side, psychiatrists on another and family physicians straddling the two. Yet in reality family physicians focus on undifferentiated problems of both mind and body. The majority of personal health needs met in primary care — combined with the trust that develops between physician and patient over the years — effectively blurs any division between mind and the body. This unity between mind and body is acknowledged by the Institute of Medicine in its definition of primary care.

Individuals suffering symptoms of anxiety are seen in family practice at the rate of three to four per 100 visits, while patients with symptoms meeting the strict criteria for referral to a psychiatrist are seen, on average, less than once in a thousand visits. Nonetheless, these "lesser"symptoms still impair function and quality of life.

Undifferentiated anxiety problems are often resolved by personal reassurance by the physician. Primary care is often focused on problems that may never be resolved by definite diagnosis.

In fact, Dr. Rosser says, 40% of visits to a family physician produce a conscious decision by doctor and patient to do nothing for a week or so and see what happens. This kind of decision, according to Dr. Barbara Starfield, is not an "absence of action," but a conscious decision.

(Dr. John Gates of the Carter Center in the United States, meanwhile, tells us that more than half of all physician visits in the United States do not produce a specific or formal diagnosis.)

Dr. Rosser says that between 40% and 50% of vaguely or poorly defined patient symptoms arise from family, job or life stresses. Often support and reassurance by the physician are the preferred therapy.

Meanwhile, the traditional medical undergraduate curricula cram huge amounts of information into students; the focus tends to be on learning about "disease entities" with little attention paid to prevalence of the disease among the population. Rosser says problems of the mind and body are usually dealt with separately in medical education. Clinical exposure in this critical learning phase occurs by way of blocks of time spent with each specialty, typically using hospitalized patients.

Dr. Rosser is looking for ways to alter the mix of educational experiences that physicians get.

ᴦ13ᴥ
Medicine: on a
Frontier of Change

As of 1990, according to the World Bank, public and private expenditures on health services were estimated to be **$1.7 trillion —
or 8% of the entire world's total production.** An attention-getting
perspective.

Dr. Harvey Skinner, Chairman of Public Health Sciences at the
University of Toronto says that:

> over the past 30 years we have been spending our way toward health.
> Healthcare costs consume about 14% of the Gross Domestic Product in the United States now, and by 2030, it will top 20%.
>
> [Dr. Skinner continues:] Over the past 30 years, health costs
> have risen faster than income in the United States, and projections to the year 2030 indicate that health costs ·could exceed *per
> capita* income if corrective action is not taken.

And he adds, "Many of the Fortune 500 companies are seeing their
net profits overtaken by rising healthcare costs."

In this light, Dr. Skinner draws a tight link between business interests and healthcare — and the connection is strengthened further
when one considers the emergence of human capital as an essential
instrument of economic growth in the 21st Century. The tide is turning to find the most effective ways to keep the human asset of health
as strong as possible.

Dr. Skinner asks the question: "Will we be healthier if spending is
increased on healthcare services?" Conventional wisdom may say yes
but the evidence, as pointed out earlier, says something else. Countries like Japan spend less, and appear to have healthier populations.

Common indicators of the overall health of a population are infant mortality rates and life expectancy. "Interestingly," Dr. Skinner also notes, "countries that spend less *per capita* on medical care, such as Japan and Sweden, have better population health indicators with respect to both measures."

"Data such as this," Dr. Skinner says, "have stimulated a resurgence of interest in population health perspectives."

Meanwhile, the National Forum on Health, a panel appointed by the Canadian federal government to study the healthcare system, called for the expansion of Medicare in this country to include homecare and prescription drugs, saying "we must restructure the system to ensure that Canadians receive the care they need." These items, the Forum says, are medically necessary, but are currently covered mainly by private health insurance.

Over the past three decades, technological and therapeutic enhancements have made it possible to shift an emphasis... towards non-institutional care [the National Forum said], and since the release of the highly-acclaimed Lalonde Report... we have broadened our understanding of the factors that contribute to better health.

Devastation of Child Poverty

Initially, the focus of government population health policies was on lifestyle choices and healthy public policy (*e.g.*, seatbelt legislation)... The focus has now shifted to the social level beyond the immediate control of health professionals.

"The social and economic determinants of health merit particular attention," the National Forum concluded, headlining its comment "The bigger picture of health — what really matters." The Forum underlines the devastation of child poverty.

Evidence suggests that deprivation during childhood can impair development of cognition and speech. The impact on children's mental and physical health can only be partially offset by interventions later in life.

Unemployment has far-reaching and extremely damaging effects on health for many individuals — the stresses and strains that accompany job loss erode the physical and mental health and have significant repercussions on the health of other family members. Research also shows that recovery of health after re-employment is neither immediate nor complete.

On the same theme, the University of Toronto's Dr. Harvey Skinner says acknowledging the reality of "social determinants of health" pushes health reform "upstream towards disease prevention and health promotion."

The National Forum tells us that the health status of the Canadian population is improving, not so much due to what we've done to care for the ill, but due to the fact that we are not as sick as before.

Medical treatments — including such 20th Century landmarks as immunization — play a role in achieving and maintaining good health. But very significantly, so does a higher standard of living and a healthier working environment.

Worrisome signs are appearing," the Forum reports, "such as an increase in stress-related diseases and mental health problems associated with unemployment… and increases in suicide rates among youth.

Pressure points: child poverty, involuntary retirement, labour-force restructurings, and the ever increasing pressures of work on families, which could lead to declines rather than increases in life expectancy.

We offered earlier that the Canadian Minister of Finance probably has more impact on human health than the Minister of Health. The National Forum Working Group on this point: "People who have been unemployed for a significant length of time tend to die prematurely, and have higher rates of suicide and cardiovascular disease." Spouses of unemployed workers experience increased emotional problems. Children, especially teens, whose parents are unemployed, are at higher risk of emotional and behavioural problems.

The Coping Crisis

The Forum Working Group once again:

The main economic variable that can positively affect the health of Canadians is a monetary policy that emphasizes jobs and growth. The more equal a society, the more widely shared are feelings of self-esteem and control, the more empowered are its members and the better its overall health status.

For millions in the post-deficit society, coping is a way of life. Studies reveal that people who cope poorly have a substantial outpouring of hormones, particularly steroids, that suppress the body's basic defence against disease. Our capacity to resist the causes of disease is reduced materially when our hormones are elevated for any considerable time. Abnormally high hormonal levels also affect the functioning of the brain. These dynamics demonstrate further the connection between the mind and body.

Coping skills — the mechanism that contains or unleashes these forces — are usually set in place early in life when the brain is most pliable. "How the cortex of the brain develops is of fundamental importance in understanding how we cope with the challenges of everyday life," the National Forum Working Group says.

Thus the importance of "nurturing in the early period of life." This grounds one's capacity to learn at school, cope with adult life and combat the risk of disease.

Early childhood development has a strong relationship with the eventuality of suffering chronic diseases in adult life. The period from birth to six years is critical because this is when the cortex of the brain is undergoing its most rapid development — this affects competence and coping skills in later life.

The Lives of Women

We also must come to understand what the National Forum describes as "the unexplained — gender differences," which influence how health factors affect the lives of Canadian women differently than men.

"Although women may seem to be healthier than men because they live longer, other health and socio-economic indicators suggest that this may not be the case." The Forum notes that "biological factors explain only part of the phenomenon" and "our limited understanding of these factors in women's lives demands more research on the non-medical determinants of women's health."

One of the great ironies — and gross deficiencies of healthcare in its various forms — has been the very fact of allowing such "limited understanding to persist after decades of male-centred research such as in cardiology, which then claimed to speak for women and men alike.

Heart disease kills as many women as men; women are more likely to die from their first heart attack. Cardiovascular disease is the biggest killer of women. Yet cardiac research has virtually excluded women over the years.

Dr. Susan Abbey and Dr. Donna Stewart of Toronto Hospital are seeking to correct this imbalance.

In a study to document reasons for the gender differences in symptoms between men and women suffering ischemic heart disease and depression or anxiety, the researchers say there is some evidence already that either women are undertreated or men overtreated in the management of heart disease.

But there is little literature overall dealing with gender difference. Recent research tells us that untreated depression and anxiety have negative implications for men suffering heart disease. But the research has not been done "in a meaningful-sized sample of women" to appreciate the gender implications.

Symptoms of heart disease or depression can resemble each other — chest pain, smothering sensations or difficulty breathing. Misread, they can lead to incorrect diagnoses and wrong treatments, producing significant risks either way.

Studies indicating an increased risk of cardiac death among patients with depression have been conducted exclusively or mostly among men — "despite the fact that depression is twice as prevalent in women as men in the general population, and cardiovascular disease is the leading cause of death among women," Dr. Stewart told the XVIth Congress of the World Association of Social Psychiatry in Vancouver in 1998.

Very little is known about the prevalence or impact of depressive symptoms in women after a heart attack, but it is known that depression accompanies a cardiac event in one of three men.

Women and Anxiety

The topic of depression and heart disease is discussed elsewhere in this report — and is the theme of Canada's first World Mental Health Day at Markham, Ontario in 1998.

Anxiety, meanwhile, may be another independent factor in the management of cardiac disease.

Once again, however, no studies have been done on its prevalence or impact in women suffering ischemic heart disease, despite the fact unveiled earlier that depression is twice as common in women as men. Nor, in fact, has there been research into the impact of psychological symptoms on the way men and women "present" heart symptoms.

In the face of growing evidence of the links between depression and anxiety, and the suspected rate of death and disability among heart patients suffering them, Abbey and Stewart conclude it is essential that the gender differential be assessed in the ischemic heart disease population.

Meanwhile, "there is preliminary evidence that women may have more psychological difficulties following a heart attack, including more depressive symptoms, more anxiety and more sleep disturbance."

"Women are also less likely to be enrolled in cardiac rehabilitation," and when they were, they entered with significantly more symptoms and functional impairment and exited with a deepened depression.

In the month preceding a heart attack, women have been found more likely than men to report chest pain radiating into the neck and jaw, feeling tired — like a "battery losing power" — and to have sensations of fainting, indigestion and vomiting.

Women were less likely than men to consult a cardiologist in the face of their symptoms in the month before they were admitted to hospital — reflecting, perhaps, adherence to their own myth that women rarely have heart problems.

In addition, Drs. Abbey and Stewart said women were "significantly more likely" to report that their heart symptoms began during a period of emotional stress.

The Toronto Hospital study is breaking with the past in seeking out scientifically based gender variations between men and women in the presentation of chronic and mental disorders. Their study is not alone in this quest.

"Yielding to the influence of a women's health movement that dramatically gained momentum two decades ago, the North American medical establishment has started to alter ingrained habits," reports *Maclean's Magazine* in its cover story on women's health in January 1998.

Women's hospitals and clinics, in many parts of the country, as well as regulatory agencies, are pushing for clinical trials of new drugs to include women as well as men. And for good reasons. *Maclean's:*

> There is abundant evidence, for example, that physicians prescribe tranquilizing drugs and sleeping pills for Canadian women and for older men at a far higher rate than for men in general.

Research funds for women's health are up, and five regional Centres of Excellence for Women's Health, created in 1996, are studying issues once considered outside the scope of medicine — issues such as poverty, male violence and the media's influence on women's health.

The focus on women's health has also produced attention on "socially constructed" illnesses.

York University's Professor Georgina Feldberg says women occupy a disproportionate number of "front-line jobs" such as school teachers, bank tellers and nurses, and as a result are disproportionately exposed to the stress-filled fallout of government cutbacks and corporate downsizing as well as the stresses inherent in these jobs.

Women, Work and Health
In an article for the *Canadian Journal of Community Mental Health*, Dr. Susan McDaniel of the University of Alberta makes this point: "The relationship between work and health is not well understood generally, although knowledge is accumulating (particularly with respect to) women and health."

Yet few mental health promotion programs for women in the workplace have been attempted except as part of general help packages such as employee assistance programs."

At the same time, Dr. McDaniel says data:

suggests women who are employed generally experience better overall health than women who work at home. It is also the case that women in the paid labour force experience considerable stress as a consequence of lower pay and lesser job security, less mobility, greater pressures associated with combining work and home responsibilities, the strain of sexual harassment and generally less than satisfactory self-images.

Women, research shows, are more vulnerable to stress. Studies show an estimated 75% of all women have been prescribed tranquilizers at one time or another — and aside from a bevy of potential issues associated with frequent intake of these drugs, Dr. McDaniel points out that this prescribing trend suggests to the woman, her family, employers and fellow workers that *she is the problem* and, as such, women more than men are encouraged to learn to cope with their situations. Women are working for longer periods in their lives, with:

the increased recognition that many work absences and loss of productivity are due to non-physical problems. The workplace is an important site for the promotion of mental health among women.

In saying this, Dr. McDaniel reaches out to the concept of organizational health. The creation of a work setting that cultivates the essential undergrowth of human health — trust, satisfaction, truth, clear purposes and a sense of place among those doing the work — employees — and in most cases, not just for money alone. If research tells us anything, it tells us that the workplace fulfils human needs that go beyond the elementary goal of earning a livelihood.

Dr. McDaniel referred to women, but could have included men, when she said the benefits of mental health promotion in the workplace would produce "substantial benefits to management and to society".

It is clear that such programs, in order to be successful, must attend to structural problems that employees face rather than simply encouraging mental wellbeing and responsibility for mental health at the individual level.

The work and health concerns of women were underscored in a Statistics Canada report in May of 1998, which showed that female Canadian workers miss 50% more time from work than males. Women were sick for 7.5 days last year compared with 5.3 days for men — and they spent an average of 1.5 days off for family reasons compared to slightly less than a day for men.

Fatigue and stress are factors related to women's burden of taking on a greater share of responsibility for the care of others. In turn, worrying about an elderly relative or having other home-related problems may have an effect on the immune system or contribute to disorders such as migraine headaches.

Among companies with largely female staffs in the United States, depression was the main cause of exploding mental health costs. Companies that brought those costs down did so by expanding access to insurance coverage and support services, such as counselling. In one case, mental health costs were cut in half.

The hotel giant, Marriott International, meanwhile, offered mothers-to-be $100 to take advantage of the company's prenatal services. The results: fewer delivery complications and reduced hospital stays.

Biology is implicitly and explicitly a substantive issue in defining women's health. In some cases greater knowledge of biological dynamics shifts the perceptions of "what is and what is not" an emotional disorder.

A study by the National Institute of Mental Health questions the view that premenstrual syndrome is an emotional disorder. It suggests that the symptoms stem from an aberrant neurological effect of blood level changes in the hormonal system.

Author Dr. Peter Schmidt said "women with severe PMS respond differently to normal hormone levels. We're beginning to appreciate the complexity and relevance of hormones in human behaviour."

In a special section on women's health called "Not Created Equal," *New York Times* writer Dorian Sagon observes that:

it turns out that steroids, a class of compounds that includes sex hormones, may play an important role in the mood swings of menstruation.

These hormones directly affect brain cells. The neuroactive steroid allopregnano, made from progesterone, dampens the sensitivity of brain cells. It works like... Valium... When the progesterone level is high, a woman is calmer, when it is low, she may feel more anxious and irritable. Moreover, women with PMS become insensitive to the calming effects of Valium-like drugs.

In keeping with increasing recognition that some powerful mind-altering substances are internally produced by hormones, it is no wonder that adolescence is often a time of emotional turbulence.

Why Women Aren't Men

In the same *New York Times* article, we learn that science is demonstrating that women can do some things better than men as a result of a variety of "biological and cognitive advantages."

Science and medicine are finally realizing that differences that exist between men and women necessitate developing distinct therapeutic treatments addressing the specifics of physiology.

Women's College Hospital in Toronto is an example of that theory in action. Notably, however, this unique institution was founded 100 years ago, which suggests the penny drops sooner for some than for others.

Women's health research is a fledgling in the adult world of medical science. Something like 5% of all medical research dollars are currently spent on health problems exclusively affecting women, despite the fact that women constitute 52% of the population and represent 70% of patient visits to a doctor.

In November 1997, the women's health program at Toronto Hospital received the Commonwealth Award for Excellence. Its leader, Dr. Donna Stewart, who holds the Lillian Love Chair in Women's Health, cites seven priority areas for research at this world-recognized teaching hospital, ranging from basic biological sciences to clinical projects in cardiovascular disease, the neurosciences, mental health and eating disorders, organ transplants, arthritis and auto-immune diseases, cancer and reproductive health.

Dr. Stewart says catch-up is needed in many areas of research in women's health. Women were at times deliberately excluded from research trials because of the complications presented to researchers by female hormones and the supposed risks of exposing women's reproductive systems to investigative therapies.

"However well intentioned such restraints," Dr. Stewart said in a *Globe and Mail* supplement earlier this year, "the result has been that the healthcare of women has often been guided by the findings of research conducted primarily on men."

Women have unique health needs. Their social circumstances often differ from men's — the impact of poverty, violence, discrimination and lack of access to the care they specifically need are notable differentiators — along with anatomical variations which, among other things, make for smaller blood vessels around a woman's heart. This creates "trickier" interventions in the case of cardiovascular disease, which women get as often as men, contrary to official myth.

The Centre for Research in Women's Health was created by the University of Toronto and Women's College Hospital, and is the first facility dedicated to researching all facets of women's health. It is part of a growing international network of universities and hospitals dedicated to women's health needs.

The Centre is also notable for its corporate support. Pace-setting grants in the millions of dollars have been received from corporations such as General Motors and the Canadian Imperial Bank of Commerce.

Meanwhile, a handbook released this year called *Behavioural Medicine and Women* notes that most of the research into the consequences of chronic environmental stress on human disease have been conducted with men.

Cruel Irony

That must change. Women are a growing part of the workplace, of course, at all levels — but, by and large, they are continuing their child-rearing roles.

On top of that, it is mostly women, not men, who get sandwiched by conflicting responsibilities between home and work, an issue compounded by the dramatic increase in the demands on working women to care for an elderly parent.

Dr. Diane Whitney, a psychiatrist at the Homewood Health Centre in Guelph until this fall, when she joined Women's College Hospital and the Faculty of Psychiatry at the University of Toronto, says it is "a cruel irony" that women are finally progressing in the world of work, where they were limited or shut out for a long time, only to face "role overload."

Dr. Whitney believes there is a correlation between the growth in women's multiple roles as income earner, breadwinner and informal caregiver, and higher rates of depressive symptoms among women.

Dr. Whitney points out that most women are at higher risk of encountering depression during their childbearing years — a time of genetic vulnerability.

Studies have found that among women working in large corporations, the single most important predictor of blood pressure problems was "the climate in the company they worked for." This ranked higher, according to the *Behavioural Medicine and Women's Health Handbook*, than more typical risk factors including obesity, age and family history of hypertension.

In a Swedish study, female managers felt greater conflict between the demands of their work and their home life than male counterparts or female clerical workers. Their blood pressure remained high when they returned home, in marked contrast to male managers working in the same plant, and it tended to remain elevated if they had small children to go home to.

For women, like men, coronary heart disease is the leading cause of death. Research has found that women suffering cardiac disorders and who have few sources of support, including a spouse, friends, church or social groups, have a three times greater risk of death than those who enjoy support of this nature.

The effects of social support can be demonstrated in laboratory studies which have shown that cardiovascular reactivity to a stressful task can be reduced by the presence of a friend. This applies to both sexes.

the *Handbook* says, in a chapter authored by Thomas G. Pickering.

The Safe Place

The Homewood Health Centre conducts a core program of recovery for women in depression. Many in this program have experienced what Homewood describes as "a loss of voice in their melancholy," not seeming to be heard.

"I should be happy but I'm not. I don't speak up. I should, but don't because I might be wrong. I don't want to risk conflict." The fear of rejection, of becoming overtly angry. "I'm stupid... I can't live without him."

In *Silencing the Self* by Dana Crowley Jack, depression among women centres on relationships and "visions of self".

Depression resembles grief because, in both, feelings of loss and sadness dominate the emotions. Depression, however, is distinguished by a fall in self-esteem and a syndrome of specific symptoms that affect thought, sleep, appetite, energy level and behaviour.

Women, prone to depression at a rate twice that of men, become depressed "most often over disruption or conflict in close relationships, whereas men are lowered into a depression by the loss of an ideal, achievement-related goal or performance issues," Dr. Jack says.

The "relationship focus" for women is rooted deeply in the culture of a society which has taught girls throughout childhood to "anticipate and react to male needs."

In Jack's book, a mother recalls time spent alone with her daughter. "A lot of time when [her husband]'s gone, we are all relaxed and happy, harmonious... he'll then drive up in the driveway and I see Jane start looking around the house thinking, 'Now what can we do to make sure that Daddy is not set off? Is the room picked up? What are we going to have for dinner tonight?'"

The mother is concerned by the mannerisms and instincts she observes in her daughter. Passed on from mother to daughter, the cultural cycle perpetuates itself.

The so-called post-modern age we are now entering is characterized, among other things, by the "superwoman" image.

In one survey chronicled by *Silencing the Self*, 11 women listed standards such as wife/partner, weight/appearance, mother/homemaker, employment/finances, self-esteem/self-assertion. Failure to live up to these benchmarks produced comments such as "I don't *feel* pretty enough."

"...can't earn an acceptable income."

"...gained weight, eat whatever."

The cultural weave in the fabric of thinking between women and men shows up not only in their perceptions of failure — relationships versus performance, for example — but in their perception of success.

Dr. Susan Schenkel in her book *Giving Away Success* says "men tend to attribute their success to ability, women tend to attribute their success to luck rather than skill," thus, automatically denying their ability and transforming themselves from active to passive participants.

From this, the sense of control and competence is lost. "Giving away success" in this way "embodies some of the basic canons of traditional femininity: putting others first, self-sacrifice and modesty."

The Overlooked

U.S. studies claim that women attribute their success to hard work, and men to ability. For women, ability didn't enter into it. One businesswoman summed up this way: "I get myself coming and going. I blame myself for my failures and don't give myself credit for my successes." Such patterns are self-defeating. And they represent what women have been taught to do.

"Research has demonstrated that people evaluate each other on the basis of sex-role stereotypes," Dr. Schenkel says. This conditioning tends to ascribe women's success to luck, not ability.

Case in point: Rosalie is an employee who noticed something intriguing about the sentence structure of her performance evaluation. On a negative note, the supervisor uses an active tense. "Rosalie is often late." On the positive, he uses the passive tense. "Functions organized by Rosalie always run smoothly." Instead of saying she was a good organizer, her boss drifted into an oddly ambiguous representation of her performance.

Historically, society has tended to devalue the feminine. Perhaps, then, it becomes nearly inevitable that rates of depression among women have been historically higher than men.

In a woman's experience, depression is both an individual and social experience, in the sense that relationships — a key determinant — place the woman in a social context where "mind and self come into being through communication with others," says Dr. Jack.

"One cannot heal the self in isolation," Dr. Jack notes. In this light, the core program at Homewood emphasizes group therapy as a principal vehicle of recovery. The program embraces a model merging the biological, psychological, social and spiritual aspects of the disease and the process of recovery from it.

Group work can be a powerful antidote to the immobilizing consequences of sex role socialization (stereotyping), according to Homewood.

Providing a "safe place" for rediscovery of one's inherent human strengths, the challenge of recovery, in this light, allows one to question the status quo and develop new standards for measuring oneself.

The differences between men and women in the origins and incidence of depression are well documented, — but according to research conducted at Homewood, the coping mechanisms employed by the sexes may not be as different as previously thought.

The Homewood study, presented to the Canadian Psychiatric Association and McMaster University, contradicted earlier literature on the subject, which portrayed coping styles along predictable gender lines of crying, eating, withdrawal and confronting feelings on the one hand, and aggressive behaviour on the other. Men sought isolation and escape to cope with depressive symptoms, women turned to blaming themselves and acting out their feelings.

Where Men and Women Don't Differ

A team of Homewood clinicians sought coping patterns among their patients to determine if, in fact, there were gender differences. The hypothesis said there were. Their findings did not.

The Homewood research team found no statistically significant differences in the way men and women coped with their depressions. Both withdrew, pushed away others and tried to find out what was bothering them by themselves.

In neither case was there a reported propensity to turn to drugs or alcohol or, contrary to earlier research about the male response to depression, to become aggressive.

But something else emerged from the Homewood research — something both troubling and instructive.

Fully three quarters of the 186 patients Homewood surveyed had previously experienced some form of abuse — physical, sexual or emotional. More than half had witnessed violence or abuse earlier in life and one quarter "identified themselves as committing some form of abuse."

Further, there were no "statistically significant gender differences in experiencing, witnessing or committing some form of abuse."

A number of factors may have contributed to the Homewood findings — including the relatively small sample and the "self-reporting" nature of surveys among patients early in the admission stage. Homewood will expand the inquiry to validate these preliminary but noteworthy findings.

In all of this, what is not in question is that treatment of severe depression must include securing a safe place for those afflicted by it — emotionally and, sometimes, physically — in which to probe the issues that have helped trigger the biological and experiential factors behind its onset.

The heart of the Homewood program is to relieve "unresolved pain in the context of external relationships." That is most likely to happen in a safe place where a sense of the self is re-established through new connections to the principles of equality and mutual respect. ❧

Part III

A Quest for Empathy

🐦14🐦
The Friend Within

FOR THE FIRST TIME IN HUMAN HISTORY, A LIGHT IS BEING CAST UPON A deep mystery, the human brain, and how it operates when we think, feel and imagine. One of the reasons why this knowledge has been late in coming, author and *New York Times* columnist Daniel Goleman says, is that "the place of feeling in mental life" has been generally overlooked by research and left unexplored.

Neurological data now allows us to see how the emotional habits of children, for example, can be shaped for the better. At a time when polling and demographic surveys, including Michael Adams' book *Sex in the Snow*, indicate that people are increasingly looking for instant gratification, the ability to rein in impulsive behaviour takes on considerable importance.

Emotional intelligence is a capacity to understand and read other people. It grounds the concept of empathy as a leadership tool. It becomes the search for skillsets which cultivate healthy relationships, shared values, co-operation, as benchmarks of the productive workplace in the information economy.

Dr. Goleman says intelligent management of human emotions is relevant to some of the most basic bread-and-butter questions facing us today, among them, civility, safe streets, effective jobs and systems of mutual support during a period of sweeping social and economic distress.

Science now tells us that feeling, not reason, is the principal shaper of decisions and actions, and has as much influence as clear thinking in arriving at solutions or decisions.

While society has placed a large value on a purely rational basis of behaviour, we are now learning that IQ is a less reliable measure of success and future behaviour than emotional intelligence. The pace of change in modern society is producing new realities that we must now learn to live with. Dr. Goleman tells us the inborn instincts of human beings to deal with speed and rapid change are less developed than those we have historically relied upon to think and react with. There is danger in this. Our response to change is often like that of a hunter confronted with a threatening beast. We are both aggressive and fearful at once. At the same time, the development of the capacity to undo these instincts, to rein them in, is teachable and learnable. This supposition flows from new knowledge that the brain itself is malleable and changeable through experience.

The Biology of Emotional Health

Without learning these emotional skills, Dr. Goleman tells us, people will tend to confront dilemmas of the post-deficit society with an emotional repertoire more suited to the kinds of threats our food-foraging distant cousins faced in pre-history. In other words, the repertoire is obsolete.

Dr. Goleman cites a three-way connection among biology, emotion and health. Every person has two minds, one to think and one to feel. Science now knows that the brain mechanisms influencing feelings are triggered quicker than those influencing rational thought. The emotional centre takes its cue from the most "primitive root" in the brain itself, the brain stem.

The question that presents itself is whether emotions can be intelligently managed. Goleman says they can. *Emotional intelligence is a new frontier* with implications for the prevention of emotional conflict and for how we build relationships. *It is a business and leadership tool of considerable potential.*

Emotional intelligence is a new platform to help laypeople, including those in leadership positions, to comprehend the connections between mental health and biology. Severe stress can change the way the brain functions biologically. When people are isolated, the brain reacts differently than when they have social association and support.

Emotional disorders can be inherited. Genetics determine the size of one's brain. The environment in which a child lives can heighten or reduce the odds of depression later in life. Imaging technology reveals differences in brain-cell function between persons with mental disorders and the mentally healthy.

Until recently, scientists thought the brain was like a computer inside the human head. They now know differently. Scanning technologies allow us to watch the brain think — images of words being spoken appearing on a monitor through the brain scanning powers of Magnetic Resonance Imaging (MRIs) and Positron Emission Thermography (PET). On these display screens, parts of the brain light up as the scanner detects changes in the metabolism of the brain triggered by the mental stimulus. These shed new light on the nature of mental illness.

Unlike a computer, the brain is continually changing in response to experience. Science is undergoing what has been described as a "free-for-all" of discovering new pathways to knowledge of human behaviour.

For example, anorexia, obsessive-compulsive disorders and depression all display unique structural or metabolic characteristics. The phantom limb, and phantom pain syndromes, are now better understood through new knowledge of the brain. Scientists studying the latter conditions say the brain is "not static, it is dynamic, a chemical soup."

That the brain is malleable — a characteristic called "neural plasticity" — is, according to some observers, the single most important neuroscientific discovery of the past decade.

Perhaps there is no more significant application of this new knowledge about the mechanics of the brain than to the development of a child.

As scientists now know, the brain is not a computer. They know it begins working long before its development is finished. They also know that the same processes that wire the brain before birth also drive the explorations and learning that occur immediately after birth.

These discoveries have massive social implications. For example, in this light, parenting logically becomes a focus for behavioural health-planning on a family level.

Deprived of a stimulating environment, a child's brain suffers. At Baylor College of Medicine in Texas, researchers found that children who don't play much, or are rarely touched, cuddled or talked to by their parents, develop brains 20% to 30% smaller than normal for their age.

At a time when parents must struggle for more time with their children, the implications of failing to achieve that are becoming more apparent, and more distressing.

At the same time, there is a bright side. Scientists find that the brain during the first years of life is so malleable that even young children who suffer strokes can still mature functionally. Research is proving that a strong partnership exists between nature and nurture.

Targeting the Physics of Mental Disorders
Like all great concepts, the brain's construct is simple and elegant. Neurologists, psychiatrists and biologists are keying in on the physical causes of mental disorders.

In doing so, they confront a deeper mystery. What is the mind, where is it located, how does it work, and does it arise from purely physical processes and chemicals, or does it have less tangible origins? Is the mind a bridge to the human soul?

These questions have been debated for centuries by philosophers. They are now on the scientific agenda. In fact, in the 400 years since the scientific revolution began, since our knowledge of the universe grew, since the exploration of the origins of life began, since mankind discovered the four-dimensional space-time continuum, the brain has remained almost a perfect mystery. But things are changing. As one writer put it, "new discoveries are piling up."

Mysteries concerning the mechanics of the brain are less impenetrable. As a result, the fight against Alzheimer's disease, depression, drug addiction, schizophrenia and traumatic brain injury is making progress. Specific institutes have been created to explore brain functioning. Canada's own Dr. Philip Seeman at the University of Toronto is a leader in the field. Toronto Hospital has established a $21 million fund for brain research.

Based on technologies that were pure science fiction three decades ago, imaging systems are discovering differences between the brains of men and women, the smart and less smart, the mentally healthy and mentally ill. A picture of the brain is now emerging that is different than one we saw before.

One of the most breathtaking parts of that picture, according to some, has been the discovery that the electrical activity of brain cells changes the structure of the brain. In the case of child development, it becomes apparent that the environment in which the child lives will profoundly influence his or her wellbeing and growth. Child abuse, therefore, is not only a crime against the child at the time it happens but a blow to society that can be felt years later.

Children who are physically abused early in life develop brains that are exquisitely tuned to danger, reports *Time* magazine.

Emotional deprivation alters the brainwave patterns of change. In addition, children born to mothers suffering depression have different patterns of brain activity in the left side, where the brain has its centre for joy and other light-hearted emotions. In short, the kid gets depressed too. Even more telling, the patterns of brain activity displayed by these children closely track the ups and downs of their mother's depression.

At the age of three, children whose mothers were more severely depressed or whose depression lasted longer continued to show abnormally low readings. Strikingly, not all children born to depressed mothers developed these patterns, however. What accounts for the difference appears to be the emotional tone of the exchange between mother and child, a remarkable insight, followed by this one: mothers who are depressed, but who can pull out of the depression in order to give their child care and nurturing and sounds and sights that are constructive and positive, will help save that child from exhibiting the kinds of mood swings that their own disease is imposing on them.

Scientists tell us that if a mother snaps out of her depression before her child is a year old, the brain activity in the left frontal lobe of the child quickly picks up. However, the ability to rebound declines markedly as a child grows older. Knowledge of this kind is useful in parent training and in the treatment of depression among women who are of child-bearing age or who are in fact raising a family.

What we have always known is that children go through a formative period of life when they are young. The brain's greatest growth spurt, scientists have now confirmed, ends around the age of 10. After that, the brain destroys its weakest synapses, preserving only those that have been transformed by experience.

This magic — the magic of this transformation — and the survival of **only** those synapses shaped by the experience of the child seems to be encoded in the genetic makeup of the child herself [the *Time* report says].

By age eighteen, the brain has declined in plasticity but increased in power. The product, at that point, of the child's upbringing is pretty well cast in stone. Talents and latent tendencies nurtured through infancy, childhood and adolescence are now ready to blossom, for good or ill.

The Integrity of Intuition

Emotional intelligence can be a useful business management tool. It describes the concept of applied integrity.

Integrity in business, in these terms, is not just being honest and doing the right thing. According to the authors of the book *Executive EQ*:

> It is accepting full responsibility, communicating clearly and openly, it is keeping promises, it is avoiding hidden agendas and not practising them, it is the courage to lead, it is the courage to be honourable, it is the courage to be consistently honest both intellectually and emotionally.

Emotion and passion are intuitive judgments of the most important kind. From them, integrity is born and upheld. According to Steven Carter, a professor at Yale, business integrity is discerning what is right and what is wrong, acting on that discernment even at personal cost, and saying openly that you have done so based on your understanding of right from wrong.

Executive EQ refers to one large corporation where an objective was set to expand the *trust radius* of the company's executives. This had early payoff. Profits grew. New people were hired, as more people trusted each other.

The CEO of Visa International set out a doctrine for hiring and promotions. People should be hired first on the basis of integrity, second on the basis of motivation, third on the basis of capacity, fourth on understanding, fifth, knowledge and last, experience. In this *Executive EQ* case reference, he explained his thinking this way:

> Without integrity, emotion is dangerous. Without motivation, capacity is impotent. Without capacity, understanding is limited. Without understanding, knowledge is meaningless. Without knowledge, experience is blind.

At its best, emotional intelligence is not about influence and manipulating people or exerting authority over them. It's about proceeding, learning, relating, innovating, making priorities, and acting in ways that take into account emotional valence, rather than relying solely on logic or intellect or technical analysis alone. **This whole concept applies to the practical management of the post-deficit pressures.**

The Last Frontier of Ignorance
Dr. Philip Seeman holds the Anne and Max Tannenbaum Chair in Neuroscience at the University of Toronto. Dr. Seeman granted the authors an interview for this report — as did Dr. Mary Seeman, herself a leading figure in the clinical treatment of schizophrenia at the

Clarke Institute of Psychiatry. She holds the Tapscott Chair in studies on this tormenting disease.

The Seemans are a powerful team, she for her distinguished work in the most serious quarter of mental illness, and he for his world standing and contribution to that field. Dr. Seeman and his research colleagues at the U. of T. isolated the receptor in the brain most responsible for hallucinations and delusions, opening the way to a new generation of drug therapies — and for his standing in the world as a neuroscientist.

Near his "real office" — his lab in the Medical Sciences Building at the University — Dr. Philip Seeman begins his assessment of the status of the human brain with vivid understatement:

> It is [he said] very different from anything below the neck. It is dominant and complex. For one thing, the brain has more different types of cells than the rest of the body, 50% of the body's genes and about 10 billion nerve cells — each one of which connects with at least 2,000 other neurons producing ten trillion connections in all.

Nor does the brain stand still to be investigated and understood. "The brain is not hard-wired. It is always changing." The human neurosystem is built for change and evolution. It is built for survival. It has enormous reserve.

In fact, about 90% of the brain's nerve cells play backup to a crucial 10% we need to function, to walk and move around. Every day we lose 10,000 of those cells. Not a problem, though. There are plenty more.

Dr. Seeman acknowledges that technology has broken through some of the mysteries associated with the brain. Revolutions in imaging technology and DNA have helped convert to science our perception and management of disorders associated with the brain.

"A third major revolution" has occurred in medications. Five to 10 million North Americans are on Prozac alone. Another two to three million on anti-psychotic drugs.

"The brain is the last frontier of ignorance." Brain research, Dr. Seeman said, has "barely scratched the surface." Nonetheless, that frontier has been crossed in one area. New knowledge about the brain tells us that mental illness — once seen as a curse or character flaw — has a biology. "Medications tell us that if drugs work, then it was a bio-chemical problem. The drugs controlled the effect, much like putting oil in the car."

Brain abnormalities are beginning to be understood through brain imaging, though not enough for diagnostic purposes yet. Dr. Philip Seeman: "There's no blood test to prove the Unabomber is mentally incompetent." Dr. Mary Seeman on the same point in reference to the clinical diagnosis of schizophrenia: "There is no x-ray, no biopsy, with which we can determine the presence of this disease on clinical grounds."

Dr. Philip Seeman once again: "The psycho-motor aspects of mental illness can be picked up through imaging technology, they are observable." Brain imaging allows neuroscientists to see emotions, thought patterns, as well as patterns of feeling, voice and motor movements (arms and legs). But they cannot tell what a person is thinking. "There is no physical trace of a memory."

The evidence that a memory exists is found in the circuitry of the brain that revolves around the experience being recalled. Parts of the brain will light up when we think something, when we see, when we hear.

The brain is highly regionalized. When a person is depressed, "only part of the machine is broken."

The brain has a region that specializes in loyalty and friendship." Other regions mirror other features of the personality — and enough separation exists for us to be both subjective and objective at the same time, for example, remaining friends with someone we consider a pain in the neck.

The massive complexity of the brain is not just in the state of the equipment neurologically in place — but, even more, in the changing nature of the brain's wiring. This fluidity creates the resilience of the human brain. Dr. Seeman tells us, "every neuron has an influence on every other neuron — as a result, the number of possible influences on the possibilities of human behaviour and functioning is virtually infinite."

The brain can change, Dr. Seeman reiterates, but only "within limits." Genes control its gross structure, giving us distinct character and attributes. "Perfect pitch" is one example.

External influences can fine-tune the wiring of the brain. Culture, attitudes, religion, upbringing — these can influence the way a brain comes to function. Prejudice and rebellion are aspects of a personality.

The immune and nervous systems are linked. Stress affects our antibodies and thus our immunity to certain diseases, and these forces interact with the brain.

Dr. Seeman cautions that the search to unravel the mysteries of the brain has barely begun and will take "hundreds of years" to complete, if ever — meanwhile, the search for the mind is an ill-defined enterprise that may not have begun at all.

One definition of the mind offered by Dr. Seeman is that the mind is the output of the structure in which it resides, the brain.

If the brain is the structure, and the mind the output, is there a third entity involved in the essence of being human? The soul, perhaps? Dr. Seeman: "Now, that's the big question." He pauses, then offers:

There are times when an individual is brain-dead, and the body is going. In that moment, in that second before physical death occurs, there is a loss of glisten in the eyes and then a final expiratory breath. Who knows, perhaps that is the moment when the soul leaves the body and proceeds elsewhere.

Perhaps — the notion adds a felt-like cover to the topic of human consciousness. A topic we will now explore with one of the world's leading cognitive scientists.

How the Mind Works

Dr. Steven Tinker is a professor at the Massachusetts Institute of Technology and Director of MIT's Centre for Cognitive Neuroscience. He was educated at McGill University in Montreal, and taught at Harvard and Stanford universities in the United States. Dr. Tinker authored a bestseller called *How the Mind Works*. A brief and virtual conversation with him, by way of the pages of his book, gives us dimension on that elusive element of the human system, the human mind.

Q: Does science know what the mind is, where it is?
Dr. Tinker: Well, first, we don't understand how the mind works — not nearly as well as we understand how the body works and certainly not well enough to design Utopia or cure unhappiness.
Q: What have you learned in the process of writing your book on such an intriguing topic?
Dr. Tinker: I have selected from many disciplines, theories that offer special insight into our feelings and thoughts. My goal was to weave the ideas into a cohesive picture using two even bigger ideas that are not mine, the computational theory of mind and theory of the natural selection of replicators.

Q: Can you define the mind?

Dr. Tinker: The mind is a system of organs of computation, designed by natural selection to solve the kinds of problems our ancestors faced in their foraging way of life, in particular, understanding and outmanoeuvering objects, animals, plants and other people. The mind is what the brain does; specifically, the brain processes information and thinking is a kind of computation. The mind is organized into modules or mental organs, each with a specialized design that makes it an expert in one arena of interaction with the world.

Q: Where does genetics come in?

Dr. Tinker: The modules' basic logic is specified by our [individual] genetic program. Their operation was shaped by natural selection to solve the problem of hunting and gathering life by our ancestors in most of our evolutionary history.

Q: Is your book about the brain, as well as the mind?

Dr. Tinker: [Of course], the book is about the brain — and that is because the mind is not the brain but what the brain does, and not even everything it does, like metabolizing fat and giving off heat. The brain's special status comes from a special thing the brain does that makes us see, think, feel, choose and act. This "special thing" is the processing or computing of information.

Q: And computation is at the heart of the mind-body theory, is it not?

Dr. Tinker: Computation theory is, in fact, one of the great ideas of intellectual history for it solves one of the puzzles of the "mind-body" problem — how to connect the ethereal world of meaning and intention, the stuff of our mental lives, with a physical hunk of matter like the brain. Why did Bill get on the bus? Because he wanted to visit his grandmother and knew the bus would take him there.

For millennia, this has been a paradox. Entities like "wanting to visit one's grandmother" and "knowing the bus goes to Grandma's house" are colourless, odourless, and tasteless. But they are also causes of physical events, as potent as any billiard ball clacking into another...

The computational theory of mind resolves the paradox. It says that beliefs and desires are information incarnated as configurations of symbols. The symbols are physical bits of matter like chips in a computer or neurons in the brain. They symbolize things in the world because they are triggered by those things via our sense organs and because of what they do once triggered.

Q: Consciousness and intelligence are greater mysteries than our conventional use of the terms implies, would you agree with that?

Dr. Tinker: The two deepest questions about the mind are "What makes intelligence possible? and "What makes consciousness possible?" With the advent of cognitive science, intelligence has become intelligible. But consciousness or sentience, the raw sensation of toothaches and redness and saltiness is still a riddle wrapped in a mystery inside an enigma. Parts of the mystery have been pried off and turned into ordinary scientific problems.

Q: *How would you define intelligence?*
Dr. Tinker: Intelligence is the ability to attain goals in the face of obstacles by means of decisions based on rational rules. Intelligence consists of specifying a goal, assessing current conditions to see how the situation differs from the goal and then applying a set of operations to reduce that difference. By this definition, human beings are intelligent — we have desires and we pursue them using beliefs.

Q: *Are the physical properties of the brain commensurate or synonymous with intelligence?*
Dr. Tinker: The tissue in the human brain is necessary to our intelligence but the physical properties are not enough, just as the physical properties of bricks are not enough to explain architecture. Something in the patterning of neural tissue is crucial.

Intelligence has often been attributed to some kind of energy flow or force field. No, intelligence does not come from a special kind of spirit or matter or energy but from a different commodity, information — which is a correlation, a mathematical and logical concept, between things. Information itself is nothing special; it is found wherever causes leave effects. What is special is information *processing...*

Q: *Which brings us back to how the processing of information works. Is the computational theory of the mind reliable — in other words, why should we buy into it?*
Dr. Tinker: Simply because it has solved millennia-old problems in philosophy, kicked off the computer revolution, posed the significant questions of neuroscience, and provided psychology with a magnificently fruitful research agenda.

[Having said that,] generations of thinkers have banged their heads against the problem of how mind can interact with matter. [Quoting a source]. "Self-pity can make one weep but so can onions." How can our intangible beliefs, desires, images, plans and goals reflect the world around us and pull the levers by which we, in turn, shape the world?

Q: *How far has the influence of the computational theory of mind spread?*
Dr. Tinker: For one thing, it has quietly entrenched itself in neuroscience, the study of the physiology of the brain and nervous system.

No corner of the field is untouched by the idea that information pro-cessing is the fundamental activity of the brain. [This] is why neuro-scientists are interested in neurons.

Information-processing even defines the legitimate questions of the field. The retinal image is upside down, so how do we manage to see the world right side up? If the visual cortex is in the back of the brain, why doesn't it feel like we are seeing in the back of our head? How is it possible that an amputee can feel a phantom limb in the space where his limb used to be? How can our experience of a green cube arise from neurons that are neither coloured green nor in the shape of a cube. These are "pseudo-questions," because they are about properties of the brain that make no difference to the transmission and processing of information.

[Dr. Tinker adds:] Plato said that we are trapped inside a cave and know the world only through the shadows it casts on the wall. The skull is our cave and mental representation are the shadows. Research in cognitive psychology has tried to triangulate the mind's internal representations by measuring people's reports, reaction times, and errors as they remember, as they solve problems, recognize ob-jects and generalize from experience. The way people generalize is perhaps the most tell-tale sign that the mind uses mental representa-tions, and lots of them.

Q: *Finally, let us return to the question of consciousness. Where does it fit in the current effort to understand how the mind works?*

Dr. Tinker: In the study of the mind, sentience (consciousness) floats in its own plane high above the causal chains of psychology and neu-roscience. If we could ever trace all the neurocomputational steps from perception through reasoning and emotion to behaviour, the only thing missing by the lack of a theory of sentience would be an understanding of sentience itself. The concept of sentience underlies our certainty that torture is wrong and that disabling a robot is the destruction of property but disabling a person is murder. It is the rea-son that the death of a loved one does not impact us with just self-pity at our loss but with the uncomprehending pain of knowing that the person's thoughts and pleasures have vanished forever.

Q: *A final word?*

Dr. Tinker: (Just this, perhaps.) Mental states are invisible and weight-less. Thinkers define them as "a relation between a person and a propo-sition." The relation is an attitude like "believes-that, desires-that, hopes-that, pretends-that." The proposition is the context of the be-lief. It lives in a different realm from the facts of the world itself. ❧

❧15❧
The Visibility of the Mind

In Tinker's words, the mind is colourless, tasteless, beyond touch. It is what the brain does. It computes information. Here rests the great paradox of mental health: the wellbeing of the human mind, invisible in its own right, is a process, not a thing. There are things on all sides. Brain matter. The physical world. The cave known as our skull. And behaviour. The mind is connected to visible, touchable things and as a concept, is a computing, actionable force. *Mental health, therefore, can be seen and touched.* Just as mental illness, its nemesis, assumes discernible and, in many respects, physical form.

That being said, its discernible form is often mistaken for something else. Often the symptoms of mental illness are treated only for their physical effect on patients — by family physicians.

Earlier in this report, Dr. Walter Rosser of the University of Toronto reminded us of the need for family physicians to be trained to handle the emotional root causes of physical disorders and complaints.

U.S. experts agree. Behavioural (mental) health specialists and primary care (family) physicians there frequently share clinic space. In Canada, psychiatric departments are common in general-care hospitals. The question of collaboration, however, is not so clear in either case. The need for close ties is abundantly evident in the combustion created by the commingling of mental illness and chronic disease — particularly among physical conditions such as coronary arterial disorders, diabetes and irritable-bowel syndrome.

At one Seattle-based health management organization that has family and mental health physicians in neighbouring offices, "we make no distinction between patients seeking primary care and those seeking mental-health care."

In short, they erase the line between mental and physical illness. This can reduce healthcare costs by cutting back the demand on the medical care system while improving the health of medical patients. This reflects the pervasive effect of mental disorders on physical health.

Writer Joseph Burns observes, "When physicians in traditional settings miss 50% of the depression cases [that come their way], underlying health problems will not be addressed and patients will not get better."

Unifying Detection Strategies

Erasing the line between physical and mental health is not a matter of blurring the distinctions between conditions of one nature versus another. The opposite is the case. It aims to unify detection strategies and sharpen the distinctions between mental and physical disorders by diagnosing each for what it is while separating symptoms that often mask each other. This, to isolate, understand and correct them, much like a hockey referee separates hockey players in a brawl in order to sanction the principal offenders and preserve the integrity of the game.

Data in the United States paints a fairly dramatic picture. One HMO in Minneapolis, for example, Health Partners, says that over the past 12 years, by treating patients under the integrated model, they experienced a 27% reduction in hospital admissions, the same in bed days, a 10% reduction in physician office visits and a 34% increase in referrals to hospice programs.

U.S. and Canadian observers, without advocating the HMO concept for Canada, agree on a fundamental point that emerges like a shaft of light from this data. That is, **that harmonizing the diagnosis of treatment — and prevention — is an important strategic goal.** The Homewood Health Group has established "erasing the line" as just that.

Erasing the arbitrary fault line between health services is a vision that articulates what health management (proactive and strategic), in contrast to disease management (reactive and tactical) is all about.

It is a companion to "life course" planning, which engages the belief that health is a continuing process, that must be vitalized and protected from disease triggered by medical and non-medical events alike.

As one psychiatrist grittily put it, "Shit happens and we can't prevent everything bad that comes our way," but we can be mindful of "the goodness of here and now" and at the same time, better understand what we need to do long-term to enjoy a better quality of life. *Longevity is an empty promise if we are simply surviving poorer health longer.* One healthcare provider captures the point thus:

> We have to move from disease management to health management. Up to now, we've set up shop at the bottom of the cliff and we're waiting for sick people to fall off so we can treat them. Instead, we have to go to the top of the cliff and keep them healthy so they don't fall off in the first place.

Erasing the line between mental and physical health is not strictly a medical matter. It is a cultural one. Healthcare providers in both the U.S. and Canada recognize a number of attitudinal patterns that reflect human experience and upbringing.

For one thing, patients often believe physical symptoms are the key to getting in to see a doctor. Even then, individuals and their family physician may resist the evidence of a mental disorder. The risk of discrimination in employment and insurance coverage is too strong. This is less true in Canada as administrative insurance practices neutralize some of the discriminatory features of obsolete but still active policies. This very point is discussed later in this report.

Family physicians may feel ill equipped to deal with emotional problems and their schedules may be weighted against investing the time needed for the diagnosis and treatment of mental illness and emotional distress. In this, there is evidence of stigma and fear, an ancient, even inbred perversion of the public's acceptance and understanding of mental illness.

The point remains: mental illness is a human tragedy and, prospectively, the foremost disability of the 21st Century, crippling the productive capacity of more people than cancer, AIDS and violence.

In that glare, let us look at mental illness through the curtains of history once drawn around the medical discipline created to investigate and confront it, psychiatry.

Eternal Fear and Perennial Hope

We walk into this world through the eyes and writings of several authors in the field. Dr. Franz G. Alexander, a force in psychiatry who died in the late 1960's, and his co-author, Dr. Sheldon Selesnick, served at Cedars-Sinai Medical Centre when the two wrote an influential book, *The History of Psychiatry*, 30 years ago.

In the forward to *The History of Psychiatry*, Dr. Jules Masserman says: "It is a history of man's eternal fears, perennial hopes and the physical, social and philosophic devices that evolved in various guises into modern psychiatry."

It was once written that humankind has three principal sources of anxiety: physical well-being, social security and our place in the scheme of things, which, in turn, assigns us a sense of usefulness and identity.

Our wellbeing has been culturally defined as physical. Yet, as Drs. Alexander and Selesnick write, "the mentally ill have always been with us — to be feared, marvelled at, laughed at, pitied or tortured, but all too seldom cured. Their existence shakes us to the core of our being, for they make us painfully aware that sanity is a fragile thing."

Psychiatry was born, the authors said, because "man has always known that sanity is a fragile thing, and to cope with his ills, man has always needed a science that could penetrate where the natural sciences cannot probe — the universe of man's mind."

In the universe, we constantly contemplate our place *in* time, and our time *and* place. Drs. Alexander and Selesnick speak to us through the pages of a three-decades-old report in which they scan the evolution of mental prehistory to our present times. Let's listen in for a bit:

> Mental illness has been embraced since primeval times by philosophers, physicians, artists, clergymen, scientists, and eventually "medical men" specially trained for the purpose — psychiatrists.
>
> Mental illness strikes at the very essence of man's nature, because we are all intimately involved in the problem of mental health — the struggle to understand and to deal with mental illness has encompassed broad areas of our civilization.
>
> Yet for the past 300 years, most of the best scientific minds have dedicated their efforts to the exploration of the physical universe. In this period, man has brought about revolutionary changes in his physical, cultural and social environment. Emphasis on the physical sciences strongly affected medicine. Medical science became essentially an applied natural science.
>
> Medical science dramatically affected humankind's existence. Life expectancy increased. Diseases were wiped out. Survival rates of infants improved. Considering this, it is not surprising that the predominant view of the nature of man was long governed by the concepts of the natural sciences.
>
> Man's physical being, based as it is upon cellular structures, was viewed as part of a larger universe based on atomic and molecular struc-

tures. [This] made [human beings] a rational mechanism, a combination of intellectual and moral free will, operating in a context of biological determinants.

Given this viewpoint, it was to be expected that medicine would come under the sway of natural sciences.

In our century, [however,] a scientific revolution has taken place; psychiatry has come of age. On the strength of substantial achievements, it has ceased being medicine's neglected stepchild and has become one of the more prominent fields in medicine.

The close relationship between emotional problems and physical illness has been dramatically illuminated.

And as the momentum of awareness and involvement gathers, it becomes increasingly evident not only that psychiatry has come of age but also that our civilization may have entered an age of psychiatry — this evolution has meant more than the betterment of psychiatry; it has meant the advancement of all medicine.

Psychiatry and The Biochemist

This point resonates in the emergence of what the authors describe as "the organic approach" to psychiatry. This is the first inkling of a unity between the psychiatrist and biochemist, the first signs of multidisciplinary thinking and teams and erasing the line between mental and physical health. Drs. Alexander and Selesnick, once again:

Neuropsychiatry continued to make significant contributions to the understanding of mental illness during the 20th Century. Specialists began to apply, wherever possible, newer medical theories of disease to the problems of mental illness.

Microbiology became extremely important through the medical world during the first three decades of the present century. Increased knowledge of microbes as major assailants of tissues was extended to mental disorders.

Syphilis of the brain and its care by induction of malaria became a model of organic mental illness and treatment.

Work in the field of diseases resulting from nutritional deficiencies produced a model for organic therapy of psychotic conditions when it was discovered that a deficiency of vitamin B led to serious disorders of brain metabolism that cause psychotic symptoms.

Research in heredity and genetics has led to the discovery that chromosomal aberrations are responsible for the errors in metabolism [which cause] mental deficiencies. Moving with great momentum [have been investigations] of chemical changes within tissues… and [as long ago as 1929], scientific studies showed that variations in the electrical activity of the brain could be recorded… an invaluable tool in diagnosing brain abnormality.

Increasing knowledge about biochemical relationships was applied to the study of the endocrine system… [this] offered hope that with increasing knowledge of the complicated interplay of the endocrine glands, the physiological basis of mental illness could be understood and made accessible to effective therapy.

Areas inaccessible before, such as the heart and the brain, are now searchingly penetrated. Progress in [North America] in neurosurgical procedures has been outstanding. Dr. Wilder Penfield of the Montreal Neurological Institute initially opened the cranial cavity to treat a localized form of epilepsy.

The physiological mechanism by which psychological repression occurs and by which experiences formerly repressed came into the framework of the conscious mind are problems [of the future].

A multidisciplinary approach has become as necessary in dealing with neurophysiological problems as with other medical specialities.

However divergent the psychological and organic orientations may seem, their integration is well on its way. The current model of etiology holds that not one but many causative factors produce diseases. One modern model suggests that psychological and organic, or human constitutional vulnerabilities, together with emotional stress, lead to a given mental disorder.

The authors of A History of Psychiatry reached conclusions in 1960 that resonate today.

Human motivations — love, hate, hope, despair, revenge, the actual content of a person's life, all his most significant and real experiences — can be meaningfully explained only psychologically. The basic position of the present-day body constitutes an indivisible whole, and that medicine must approach personality problems and their bodily effects with a combination of psychological and somatic [physical] methods of treatment.

Psychology and biology deal with the same complex organism but represent two different aspects of it.

Molecules and Mental Health

Fast forward 30 years to April, 1998 and Dr. Eric Kandel, in the *Ameri-*

can Journal of Psychiatry:

> When historians of science turn their attention to the emergence
> of molecular medicine in the last half of the 20th Century, they will
> undoubtedly note the peculiar position occupied in this period by
> psychiatry.
>
> In the years following World War II, medicine was transformed
> from a practicing art into a scientific discipline based on molecular
> biology.
>
> During the same period, psychiatry was transformed from a
> medical discipline into a practicing therapeutic art.
>
> [He continues:] The decade of the 1960s marked a turning
> point in psychiatry. To begin with, new and effective treatments, in
> the form of drugs began to be available. By the mid-70s, the thera-
> peutic scene had changed so dramatically that psychiatry was forced
> to confront neural science if only to understand how specific (drug)
> treatments were working.

The advent of drugs, Dr. Kandel says, brought psychiatry "back
into the mainstream of academic medicine."

This progress flowed along several lines. Psychiatry now had effective treatments for the major mental illnesses and something ap-
proaching practical containment for two of the three most devastating — depression and manic-depressive illness.

The profession now had the means to validate and objectively
measure clinical diagnosis, and a renewed interest in the biology of
mental illness, specifically the genetics of schizophrenia and depression. At the same time:

> the years since 1980 have witnessed major developments in the
> brain sciences, in particular, the analysis of how different aspects
> of mental functioning are represented by different regions of the
> brain.

Psychiatry has had the opportunity, therefore, to contribute to a
broader understanding of the working of the brain, and to do so by
defining the mental functions necessary to comprehend the biology
of the human mind.

Dr. Kandel calls for a "rapprochement" between neural science
and psychiatry — perhaps like that embodied so uniquely by Drs.
Phillip and Mary Seeman, discussed earlier.

He says all mental processes derive from the workings of the brain.
The mind is a range of functions carried out by the brain. The brain
undertakes not only simple motor behaviours such as walking and

eating but complex cognitive actions — thinking, creating works of art. Behavioural disorders are disturbances of brain function even when the cause is environmental in origin.

Genes — particularly combinations of genes — contribute to behaviour, including social behaviours. Genes do not explain all mental illnesses. Social factors also contribute to behaviours and, in turn feed back on the brain, changing how genes are expressed or animated in our system. This, in turn, alters the function of nerve cells. The way genes are expressed is influenced by all forms of learning. This gives rise to changes in the patterns of connections within our brain. These changes not only contribute "to the biological basis of individuality but imitate and maintain behavioural abnormalities."

A psychiatric patient's learning experience from psychotherapy or counselling can yield long-term results.

In his essay, Dr. Kandel rejects the notion that biological processes are strictly determined by genes, thus ruling out social forces. Dr. Kandel on this point:

- A gene serves as a stable template that can be replicated reliably. This occurs in each cell of the body. Each succeeding generation receives copies of each gene.
- Genes determine the structure, function, and other biological characteristics of the cell in which they "live." This is called the transcriptional function of the gene. This means each gene oversees the manufacture of specific proteins in any cell.
- Whereas the "gene template" cannot be influenced by social experience, the "transcriptional function" governing the biology of the person can be.

Stated simply [Dr. Kandel said], the regulation of gene expression by social factors makes all bodily functions, including those of the brain, susceptible to social influences.

These social influences will be biologically incorporated into the altered expressions of specific genes in specific nerve cells in specific regions of the brain. These socially influenced alterations are transmitted culturally. They are not incorporated in the sperm and egg and therefore are not transmitted genetically.

[He continues:] In humans, the modifiability of gene expression through learning is particularly effective and has led to a new kind of evolution: cultural evolution. ...the capability of learning is so highly developed in humans, that we change more by cultural evolution than by biological evolution.

And further:

Measurements of skulls found in the fossil record suggest that the size of the human brain has not changed since *Homo sapiens* first appeared approximately 50,000 years ago; yet, clearly human culture has evolved dramatically since that time.

A theme akin to that sounded by Dr. Daniel Goleman in his bestseller, *Emotional Intelligence*. Dr. Goleman:

The hippocampus and the amygdala were the two key parts of the primitive brain that, in evolution, gave rise to the cortex and then the neocortex. To this day, these limbic structures do much or most of the brain's learning and remembering. The amygdala is the specialist for emotional matters.

"All passion depends on the amygdala," Dr. Goleman says. "Most intriguing for understanding the power of emotions in mental life are those moments of impassioned action we later regret, once the dust has settled: the question is how do we so easily become so irrational."

Dr. Goleman says that, through evolution, humankind obtained a "feeling mind" before a "thinking mind" and emotions, not rational thought, have the upper hand in matters of behaviour. In fact, he says, "the brain has two memory systems, one for ordinary facts and one for emotionally charged ones."

A special system for emotional memories makes excellent sense in evolution, of course, ensuring that animals would have particularly vivid memories of what threatens or pleases them. But emotional memories can be faulty guides to the present.

As recently as 1970, psychiatric illnesses were traditionally classified into two major categories: 'organic' and 'functional' — *organic* meaning conditions associated with impairments to the nervous system that show up as psychiatric symptoms, such as dementias and Alzheimer's as well as "toxic psychoses" such as drug and alcohol addictions. Meanwhile, *functional* mental illnesses include depressive disorders and schizophrenias.

These distinctions originated from autopsy observations of architectural distortions of the brain in the 19th century. In effect, diseases that produced brain lesions (anatomical evidence) were called organic; the rest, functional. Apparently this distinction no longer holds. Dr. Kandel:

There can be no changes in behaviour that are not reflected in the nervous system and no persistent changes in the nervous system that are not reflected in structural changes on some level (in the brain).

He says everyday sensory experience — what we see, hear or smell, what we are deprived of and what we learn can probably lead either to a weakening of synaptic (brain) connections or a strengthening of them. "We no longer think that only certain diseases, the organic diseases, affect mentation through biological changes in the brain and that others, the functional diseases, do not," Dr. Kandel said in his *American Journal of Psychiatry* article, concluding that: "The basis of the new intellectual framework for psychiatry is that all mental processes are biological and therefore any alteration in those processes is necessarily organic."

Mental Processes are Biological

We now need to ask [Kandel continues,] how biological processes of the brain give rise to mental events and how in turn do social factors modulate the biological structure of the brain? And to what degree is this biological process determined by genetic and developmental factors, by environmental and social influences, or toxic and infectious agents?

Even the mental disturbances that are considered to be most heavily determined by social factors must have a biological component, since it is the activity of the brain that is being modified.

The implications of Dr. Kandel's thesis run on at least two levels. He himself calls it intriguing to suggest that insofar as psychotherapy is successful in bringing about substantive changes in behaviours, it does so by producing alterations in "gene expression" that produce new structural changes in the brain. The same applies to drug therapies.

The psychiatrist of the future will need to have expert knowledge of the brain. Dr. Kandel also foresees "an era of new co-operation between neurology and psychiatry" and this will have greatest benefits in the treatment of disease such as autism, mental retardation and the cognitive disorders of Alzheimer's and Parkinson's diseases.

Dr. Kandel offers this note of caution in considering his biological framework for psychiatry. "We are only beginning to understand the simplest mental functions in biological terms." He says that most biologists sense that "we are in the midst of a remarkable scientific revolution that is transforming our understanding of life's processes — the nature of disease and of medical therapeutics.

Most biologists believe that this scientific revolution will have a profound impact on our understanding of the mind.

The connection — perceived and proven — between body and mind is not a new medical or philosophical construct.

The originality of the concept goes back to the father of medicine, Hippocrates, who insisted that medical students give full weight to emotions both as a contributing cause of disease and a factor of recovery. Aristotle talked at length about the role of emotions in health and illness.

The University of California at Los Angeles (UCLA), more than a decade ago, created a department to evaluate the interaction of the mind, body and society. Norman Cousens — in his book, *Head-First, The Biology of Hope* — says illness is not just what went into a person's stomach, but also what went into their minds, their family relationships, their ambitions and hopes.

"Medical science might not always be able to conquer or ameliorate all these forces..." he says in his remarkable treatise.

Only recently, relatively speaking, has scientific knowledge accumulated on the immune system, which is affected by "practically everything" including emotions and behaviour.

The pathways along which the human mind makes its registrations on physiology are being probed more deeply than ever before. A biology of emotions is coming into view [Dr. Cousens writes].

[Out of research has come] a much clearer picture of the way ideas, emotions, experiences and attitudes can create biological change."

Some cancer patients become nauseous from the anticipation of chemotherapy. Shouts of "Fire!" in an auditorium can produce a constriction of blood vessels and blood pressure changes and even a rupturing of the muscle fibers of the heart.

Chronic stress can increase one's vulnerability to latent viruses, while the enhancement of positive emotions can stimulate the antibodies that attach them. Dr. Cousens:

What the world's greatest literature tells us about medicine is that few things are more important than the psychological management of the patient. A person's outlook on life can be a vital factor in the onset and course of a disease — the science and art of medicine converge at the point where physicians become basically concerned — as traditionally poets have been — with the whole of the human condition.

Anesthesiologist Dr. Henry Beecher of Harvard Medical School, a pioneer in his field, says the usefulness of *any* given drug is a combination of its chemical ingredients and "the confidence of the patient that it *will* work."

Studies at UCLA showed that depression can produce profound physiological change, Dr. Cousens reports, affecting the biochemical balance of the body.

Those same clinical studies also matched a decline in the depression among a trial number of cancer patients and produced an increase in certain immune cells.

Treating our Humanity

The American Psychiatric Association editorially tackled some of the issues concerning the role of psychiatry in the age of biology. "What is psychiatry?" was answered: "the care of patients with brain disorders, such as Alzheimer's Disease."

"Psychiatrists also study and care for patients with other brain diseases of known etiology such as HIV infection of the central nervous system," the *Journal* said. "Our science is busy searching for the brain and the biological mechanisms of these mental illnesses just as Alzheimer did 100 years ago."

The issues facing psychiatry touch the basics of life, the boundaries between normality and disease, the role of traumatic grief in creating a vulnerability to mental illness, the effects of normal aging on memory or the challenges of coping with life that confront the terminally ill.

Simply, psychiatry is the medical specialty that studies and treats a variety of disorders that affect the mind. Our minds create our humanity, our sense of self, and in that light, psychiatry can be seen to be that branch of medicine that reaches into the core of a person's existence.

All mental illnesses revolve around one common theme. They are expressed in signs and symptoms that reflect the activity of the mind — memory, mood and emotion, fear and anxiety, sensory perception, attention, impulse control, pleasure, appetite drives, willed actions, executive functions, the ability to think in representative ways, language, creativity, imagination, consciousness, introspection and a host of other mental activities.

Mental health is the essence of being human. In most healthcare systems, it is also a narrow band of service where research is massively underfunded.

The *American Journal of Psychiatry*:

> When disruption occurs — in the multiple systems of the mind, psychiatrists observe disorders that we diagnose as dementias, schizophrenias, mood disorders, anxiety disorders and other mental illness.
>
> The speciality of psychiatry is defined by the patients these doctors treat, not by the treatments they apply. If psychiatry deals with diseases of the mind, does it also deal with diseases of the brain? Unequivocally, yes, and what we call the mind is, in fact, the expression of the activity of the brain.

Or what Dr. Philip Seeman described earlier in this report as the "output dimension of the brain."

Mind is an abstract term that refers to mental functions as a collective noun — functions such as memory or mood. The brain, meanwhile, is the neural assembly of molecules, cells and circuits that produce those functions.

The two are as inseparable as the "dancer and the dance," to quote W.B. Yeats; and in this light, psychiatrists are physicians to both the mind and brain; they use psychotherapies that address mind mechanisms such as memory or consciousness, and what works at the neural level by producing changes in the brain.

Psychiatrists also use medications that work directly on the brain while their effects are shown in the mind as a lifting of depression or a diminution of hallucinations.

At present, mental illnesses include some with known brain mechanisms such as Alzheimer's Disease and others suspected to have such neural connections (like schizophrenia) and others that are stirred by the brain and personal experience as in the case of post-traumatic stress disorder.

Troubled Ruminations

Dr. Samuel Guze is Vice-Chancellor of Medical Affairs at the Washington University School of Medicine, a professor of psychiatry, and formerly the head of that department at Washington University.

In a book published in 1992, he tells his readers that, yes, psychiatry is a branch of medicine and "deals with the most characteristically human problems in all of medicine — disturbances in our sense of self, our relations with the rest of the world, our perceptions and memories, our capacity for love, our ruminations and ability to communicate."

He examines a horizon of change upon which disorders such as epilepsy, mania and other psychoses have shifted from "a magical or theological orientation to a medical one." And that medical orientation, in turn, is increasingly focused on getting people back on their feet, and functioning quicker.

"Mental illnesses can be every bit as painful, disabling and frightening as many other medical conditions, often involving increased mortality," Dr. Guze notes. Yet, *public sentiment is often prejudicial because of the absence of black-and-white physical or anatomical evidence of its existence and origin, if not cause.*

In these terms, the "integrity" of mental illness as a "legitimate disease" is challenged. But if that challenge has merit, it should also question the "disease status" of conditions such as high blood pressure, which can exist for years without triggering any consistent physical or biochemical changes in the body. On top of that, there are ambiguities in the scientific basis of blood pressure. Yet no one doubts high blood pressure ought to be considered a disease, and a dangerous one at that.

In fact, certain cardiac disorders present a face similar to that of mental illness. Dysrhythmia, for example, occurs without recognizable abnormalities in the body or its chemistry. Yet, such disorders often complicate existing conditions of gross heart disease, may be connected in "cause and effect" to depression, and, as Dr. Guze says, "even when no satisfactory explanation for the abnormal heart rhythm is available, it may be associated with great fear and disability — and may be life-threatening."

In the great majority of cases of epilepsy, "consistent neuropathological changes cannot be detected... and epilepsy was as difficult to define and classify as many psychiatric disorders are today before the electrical activity of the brain could be measured by the electroencephalograph (EEG)"

"But who," he asks, "would argue that it became a disease only after the EEG was developed?" Nobody, presumably. Dr. Guze:

> It may be said there is no such thing as disease; there are only diseases. The concept of disease may be a myth, but, if so, it is a myth when applied to all medical conditions and not just when applied to psychiatric disorders.

The Non-Existent Body

Harvard's global mental health report points out the "costs to the healthcare system that rise as resources are expended on searching for the causes or treatment of 'non-existent physical conditions.'" (Non-existent in the sense that the real, underlying ailment is a mental disorder masked as a physical condition.) Harvard says:

Despite the prevalence of depression, only a minority of depressed patients receive appropriate treatment. Primary healthcare workers often fail to recognize and diagnose depression.

Depression patients suffer as much disability and distress as patients with chronic medical disorders such as high blood pressure, diabetes, coronary artery disease and arthritis.

Depression runs in families, reflecting an inherited vulnerability. There is equally strong evidence that childhood experiences, such as loss of a parent, also produce vulnerability to depression and that losses experienced in adulthood can precipitate depressive episodes.

[Harvard continues:] *Depression is thus both biological and social in origin. (Interestingly), researchers have reported sizable increases in rates of depression in Taiwan over a 30-year period during the island's rapid modernization.*

We do not know the specific causal pathways that transform social experience into [mental illness], nor do we know the specific links between changing socioeconomic development and changing rates of depression, although the correlation of job loss and recession, and increased rates of suicide and hospitalization for psychiatric disorder indicates a link between the two. Similarly, there is a documented tie between depression, social uprooting and refugee status.

[Harvard again:] *Current research provides strong evidence that all mental disorders are biosocial and that wherever physiological processes are involved, the quality of a person's social environment influences both vulnerability to mental illness and the course of that illness.*

Mental disorders are not simply symptoms of broader social conditions; nevertheless, poverty, lack of security, violence, the lack of healthy family relationships during childhood and the trauma of significant loss are crucial factors for mental illness. Indeed, although mental illnesses can be categorized and diagnosed, they most often are found in constellations that bind together biological forces, social conditions, cultures and particular forms of illness.

❧16❧
The Solution of Addiction

At several points during this commentary, the masking and un-masking of mental illness found addictions in the foreground of the misery millions experience in all walks of life — and as a secondary expression of deeper disorders.

Dr. Graeme Cunningham now guides us through various thickets that make up the addictive experience. He is the Director of Addiction Medicine at the Homewood Health Centre in Guelph, Ontario and President of the newly founded Addiction Institute of Canada, a physician education venture led by Dr. Cunningham and Dr. Russell Joffe, Dean of Health Sciences at McMaster University in Hamilton, Ontario.

The addict, Dr. Cunningham observes, is "more lost than any-thing," trapped in a destructive "reward system" which produces "so-lutions" for his or her cravings. The alcoholic, for example, drinks to "get normal" as he or she defines normalcy. The addict may also seek gratification further afield, for instance, by working 100 hours a week. Addictions are intimately tied to "reward systems" (and symptoms), mirroring — in both cause and effect — broader imbalances we find in daily life. Between men and women, for example.

Dr. Cunningham — whose leadership in his field has wide recognition across the country — says that in 80% of the cases where the husband is alcoholic, his wife stands by him. When the opposite is the case, and the wife is addicted, the husband leaves home — with-draws his support — 7 times out of 10.

When the recovering alcoholic is male, society may encourage and even cheer him on. When *she's* not a *he*, the reaction by family, friends, co-workers is more along the lines of "it's about time she got back to her family responsibilities." On top of that, addicted women get sicker sooner and receive treatment later. They are also younger — about 32, on average, compared to addicted men, who are typically 42 years of age.

The Disease Soliloquy

Dr. Cunningham says we must remind ourselves that addictions are a disease. In most cases, he says, "the issue is not the alcohol or the heroin — it is the addict saying, 'this is my solution.'"

Homewood provides a non-religious spiritual framework for its world-famous addictions clinical programs. (*The storied Betty Ford Clinic sometimes calls to compare notes.*) And through his clinical experience, Dr. Cunningham sees the progression of addiction corralling the addict's closest relationships. The inner circle suffers first and most, including the kids. When the problem shows up at work, he's "well into it."

By then, unpredictability becomes the measure of the man or woman. Doesn't return phone calls. Absent a lot. Irritable. Eruptions, even.

When signs mount, Dr. Cunningham advises co-workers or employers to seek out health-related reasons first for the employee's or executive's inexplicable behaviour before seizing upon the job performance issues that spring up at times like this. Particularly when the destructive or 'different' pattern of behaviour consistently defies precedent or abruptly signals an irrational change in the conduct or outlook of the individual.

The crisis facing the addict is not "stopping" — it is an inability to stop *starting*. When the alcoholic stops drinking, the destructive emotions and feelings continue. There is still danger — and managing this danger has nothing to do with being weak or strong. It is a question of genetic predisposition, environment, uninvited cravings. We return to this point shortly.

The Aura of Age

The tragedy of addiction is not the visitation of a corrosive affliction on younger people alone. Dr. Cunningham fears for those vulnerable through the passing of the years.

Abuse of prescription drugs by the elderly is often inadvertently facilitated by physicians who renew medication without even seeing their frail patient. Often, the objective is to "calm" them in the face of complaints about being unable to sleep.

For the elderly, addictions carry a great burden of shame. Dr. Cunningham says men and women of this generation have particular difficulty seeing alcohol or drug abuse as a disease. They usually suffer alone, isolated and fearful. And suffer they do.

Often, the addiction crisis in the life of an elderly person living alone is discovered only when he or she falls and is treated for an injury such as a broken hip.

When governments are looking for new strategies in homecare, Dr. Cunningham advocates services that will help spot the emergence (or presence) of addictions among the isolated elderly before a secondary crisis — like a serious fall — happens.

In fact, Dr. Cunningham says, injuries from falls often occur because of the side effects of casually prescribed sleeping pills. In addition, dementia can be deepened by the invasive properties of drug and alcohol abuse.

More generally, though addictions darken the horizon for millions of Canadians, Dr. Cunningham sees a light beyond. For those treated at Homewood, the goal line for recovery is usually five years out. That is, he says, after five years, the addiction is usually in remission; at least for 60% to 80% of the patients treated by the Homewood clinical staff. This "remission" (the author's words) is defined as a state of recovery in which the buffeting of daily life does not trigger a relapse.

As Dr. Cunningham described it, an addiction is a latent state that the sufferer is unaware of until it is set off. "The alcoholic doesn't know he's one until he drinks. It is a neuroscientific fact that it is totally impossible to crave alcohol until you drink it." And for recovering alcoholics, the longer the abstinence, the less likely a relapse.

Two other points from Dr. Cunningham:

- The stigma of addictions seems to run even deeper than that of mental illness, reflected, he says, in the fact that disability insurance is denied to anyone with a history of drug and alcohol abuse.
- In 1935, alcoholism could not be treated in hospitals generally. We've come a long way on that front, but are just starting out on another. Gambling and sex addictions are in the same boat now. But both are growing in Homewood's famous portfolio of addiction treatments.

The Pathways of History

Dr. Graeme Cunningham has a Scotsman's directness — but he also skillfully navigates the subtleties of human emotion. And he has a wide compassionate streak. Professionally, in his position at Homewood, he is the descendant of others bearing like arms in the fight against addiction.

Homewood, history books tell us, was the first "asylum" in Canada to treat the disease of drug abuse "to any great extent." It also housed the country's first addiction specialist, Dr. Stephen Lett, the first superintendent of Homewood. (The hospital named a lecture series in 1998 to commemorate Lett's "before his time" innovative style.)

Lett's treatment of addictions at Homewood, according to archives, reflected his embrace of the "medical model" of addiction treatment — a theme being reawakened in the 1990s as a more effective conduit between psychiatry and its patient constituency of the dawning 21st Century.

Lett was an early proponent of the disease concept of drug abuse — more than a century ago — and, even in those early years, decried those who saw addiction as "a vice that the patient can at once abandon if he only wishes to do so."

Dr. Cunningham would easily travel arm-in-arm with Dr. Lett down that path were it not for the generations of patient suffering and care that separate them. Having said that, Dr. Lett's concept was more narrowly cast than Cunningham's. Lett saw the nature and treatment of addicts in "strictly physiological terms," his biographer confides to us.

Dr. Cunningham and his modern-day colleagues see the recovery process as reaching beyond pharmaceutical or clinical limits. Spirituality is an expression of that additional dimension.

Ironically, addictions were a "growth business" for Homewood 115 years ago. If you cared to consider the matter in those terms, the same is true today. Except that the marketplace has grown into new "climes of the times" — sex and gambling addictions.

In Lett's time, opium was a treatment standard. The shadow and scent of that drug, in fact, has soiled many pages of history. Hong Kong and its territories came under Western control as a direct result of the 19th Century opium wars waged by Britain to force China to allow its importation. Opium and morphine were at one time believed to be non-addictive ameliorates for addictive and other symptoms.

The Ultimate Hijacking

The long memory and mosaic of addictive behaviour continue to reach deeply into lives, societies and cultures the world over. According to a 1994 report from the Robert Wood Johnson Foundation in the U.S., the annual cost to American society of alcohol abuse is nearly $100 billion. The annual social costs of tobacco use are estimated by some sources at $65 billion — and more than half a billion deaths annually are attributable to alcohol and tobacco use.

"Substance abuse is unquestionably a major societal problem," Science Magazine concludes obviously. "A problem that has so far resisted any single approach to reducing drug use, drug supplies or the multiple adverse consequences of drug use."

A U.S. public television special hosted by social analyst Bill Moyers, once press secretary to U.S. President Lyndon Johnson, says the dilemma facing addicts is simply this: "The addict's brain is hijacked by drugs — and relapse is normal." (Moyer's own son is fighting a drug and alcohol habit.)

Science Magazine, meanwhile, reports that "scientists have identified neural (brain) circuits that subsume the actions of every known drug of abuse and they have specified common pathways that are affected by almost all such drugs."

The author of the article is Dr. Alan Leshner, an associate of the U.S. National Institute on Drug Abuse. Skeptics apparently claim the Institute is on a campaign to promote the "brain disease" theme. Nonetheless, Dr. Leshner goes on to say: "Researchers have also identified and cloned the major receptors for virtually every abusable drug as well as the natural ligands for most of the receptors." They have also ridden the "biological cascades" within the cells of the brain that occur after the drug has triggered the receptor activity.

All of which, to the laity, means we seem to know a lot more about the great "brain drain" that addiction produces and becomes. Dr. Leshner: "There is a wide gap between the scientific facts and public perceptions about drug abuse and addictions." An example — most people, he writes, see drug abuse and addiction as social problems, to be handled only with social solutions, particularly through the criminal justice system.

On the other hand, science has taught that drug abuse and addiction are as much health problems as they are social problems. The result of this gap (in information) is a significant delay in gaining control over the drug abuse problem.

One major barrier to raising public awareness is, of course, stigma. The only thing worse than a drug user is a drug addict.

The Myths of Withdrawal

Dr. Leshner says that too often — contrary to clinical and scientific knowledge — the public focus of attention on addiction problems zeroes in on the wrong aspect and, consequently, "efforts to deal with it are badly misguided."

Questions of addiction often pivot on the nature of dramatic withdrawal symptoms. Are there any? The question invokes this assumption — the more severely evident the withdrawal visuals, the more serious or dangerous the drug must be.

"This thinking is outdated," Dr. Leshner says. "It does not matter what physical withdrawal symptoms, if any, occur — many of the most addicting and dangerous drugs do not produce severe physical symptoms upon withdrawal." Crack cocaine and methamphetamine are clear examples, and produce nothing like the physical symptoms that go with alcohol or heroin withdrawal.

The Essence of Addiction

What does matter tremendously is whether or not a drug causes what we now know to be the essence of addiction: compulsive drug-seeking and use, even in the face of negative health and social consequences.

Dr. Leshner moves to the "reward symptom" that Dr. Cunningham acquainted us with earlier. And he says various drugs travel a common path into the human system. "Virtually all drugs of abuse have common access, either directly or indirectly, on a single pathway deep within the brain."

"Not only does acute drug use modify brain function in critical ways, but prolonged drug use causes pervasive changes in brain function that last long after the use of the drug stops."

The addicted brain is different from the unaddicted brain — and the "common effects of addicting substances suggest common brain mechanisms underlying all addictions." Addiction is tied to changes in brain structure and function and this is what makes it fundamentally a brain disease, according to the Drug Institute writer.

Researchers at the Laboratory of Molecular Psychiatry at Yale University tell us that at its core, addiction involves a biological process — the effects of repeated exposure to a biological agent (drug) on a biological substrate (brain) over time. The brain's neurons are altered. And so are the networks of operation called neural circuits.

"This leads eventually," the Yale team says, "to the complex behaviours such as dependance, tolerance, sensitization and craving." And *that* — craving — is the essence of addiction. Homewood's Graeme Cunningham reminds us that 90% of the population drinks responsibly. Ten per cent don't. It is that one person in 10 who is driving the broadly-stated costs of addiction up.

Accountability

Dr. Sally Satel, an American psychiatrist, writing in the *New York Times*, raises the question of addict accountability in the framing of addictions as a brain disorder. Acknowledging that it's a "logical scientific leap" to say addiction is a chronic and relapsing brain disease, she then disputes both points.

Addiction, she says, is not a brain disease, and relapse is not inevitable. She says there is wide disagreement on what the brain imaging results say about the invasive effect of addictions on the neurosystem. There are voluntary aspects of addictive behaviour, she writes, and "addicts' brains are not always in a state of siege."

"During these periods, it is the individual's responsibility to make himself less vulnerable to drug craving and relapse." The addict can learn how to fight urges and find alternative ways to meet emotional and spiritual needs. Dr. Satel prefers to call addictions a behavioural condition. Fair enough.

Dr. Stephen Lett, 115 years ago, seemed dedicated to the more tightly scripted medical model. Nonetheless, his Homewood legacy has blossomed beyond that into something Satel would appreciate, while recognizing Cunningham's fundamental point.

That is, addiction is not about being strong and weak. It is about being lost. Looking for solutions. Drinking to become normal. In these conflicts — and in the residue of what nature bestows on millions of us — we find the essence of addiction, craving, and the essence of the struggle to escape the grip of its clawed fist.

Constellations of Torment

These times of rapid change and invasive uncertainty are bound together in constellations of torment for growing millions of people in all walks of life, in countries the world over. This is the realm in which psychiatry works. A world of hope and fear, definition and ambiguity, fast rising new discoveries about the unity of mind and body, and the convergence of psychiatry as both art and science.

Nonetheless, the "real world" is a place of physics and systems and things. A world that resists mental illness as a priority in the face of "real diseases" such as cancer, heart disease, and more recently, Alzheimer's and AIDS.

Harvard University confronted the issues surrounding mental illness and psychiatric services in its 1995 assessment of mental conditions worldwide.

"A widespread misconception is that psychiatric conditions are not 'real' illnesses, amenable to the kind of definition, identification, evaluation, treatment and research that is possible for other medical conditions."

The research community itself contributed to this. For many international health researchers, "mental illness" was by and large a vague domain of psychological distress and general human unhappiness.

Years later, dramatic changes appeared in approaches to psychiatric research —including the advent of effective drug therapies — and this provided a basis for rethinking mental illness in a global, multicultural context.

Yet Harvard laments the failure of research, even today, to sufficiently examine "social factors so obviously important to understanding the burden of mental illness."

In the face of profound demographic changes, the rise of neuropsychiatric disease — depression most particularly — will wipe out the productive working years of more people over the next 20 years than any of these "real" diseases. Dr. Guze:

Until very recently, laboratory tests played only a limited role (in the diagnostic process) in psychiatry because our understanding of possible pathophysiologic mechanisms has been limited. In the last few years, however, that's been changing.

He comments on the advent of laboratory testing using a range of laboratory indicators of various brain functions.

"While the results thus far are still modest and inconsistent, there is reason to be optimistic that before too long, laboratory findings may begin to play a role in clinical psychiatry similar to their role in the rest of medicine."

Dr. Mary Seeman, at the Clarke Institute of Psychiatry, patiently notes the obvious. "There is no blood test to detect schizophrenia." Since she is a clinician of great reputation, it would seem easy to take her word for that. But that apparently wasn't the case for one insurance adjuster who argued with Dr. Seeman about the condition of one schizophrenic employee who "seems all right to me" and "I really don't get it why she can't go back to work. Isn't there a test you can give her so we can see something that proves she's sick?"

There isn't much to offer those who can't accept the clinical judgment of an internationally known Canadian physician, when the word of a less acclaimed physician would invariably be good enough in the case of a muscle strain, respiratory disorder or low back pain. While there is no blood test for schizophrenia, thanks to the work of Dr. Mary Seeman and others, the boundaries of clinical knowledge are expanding and the biology of mental illness is forming like a silhouette behind a lighted screen.

Dr. Guze once again:

In some depression, patients show greater resistence to cortisol secretion in their systems under certain circumstances, and less in the onset of rapid eye movement in sleep.

Some patients with schizophrenia have enlarged and smaller brain parts as revealed by CAT scans and MRIs. Such findings are also encountered in patients with other psychiatric conditions. In other words, alterations in anatomy or physiology which may be relevant to the genesis and treatment of these disorders.

Research into characteristics of this nature shared by people suffering depression could produce insights into other variables which contribute to psychiatric disorders, including family and social experience.

Agonizing Variables

At present, however, psychiatric diagnoses are still based mainly on an analysis of the patient's history and mental status. Some people begin to show evidence of disorder in childhood, others later in life, still others in old age itself. Some experience brief episodes, others suffer the disorder chronically all their life. Some have little impairment, others are severely disabled. Some mental illnesses are more common in women than men. Some people experience hallucinations (pictures in the mind) and delusions (strong but wrong beliefs in the face of overwhelming contrary evidence), while others suffer neither.

The same kind of variables exist across a range of phobias, obsessions, memory failure, manias and learning difficulties. The differing experiences of the mentally ill may one day point to how people's experiences and the conditions in which they live and work affect their mental health. Temperament, social and economic background and family interaction all play a role in the development and course of mental illness.

Co-morbidity — discussed at some length earlier in this report — is what Dr. Samuel Guze calls "a new concept in psychiatry that bears directly upon psychiatric diagnosis." The outgoing Secretary General of the World Federation for Mental Health told the authors of this report that it is an appropriate line of inquiry in the search for solutions to mental illness.

Co-morbidity refers to the presence of a multiplicity of syndromes in the same patient. In short, having two or more different problems at once that complicate the treatment of each single disorder, as in the case of depression and heart disease discussed earlier. Dr. Robert Swenson, a psychiatrist at the Ottawa Heart Institute, told us earlier in this report that drug therapies for treating depression in heart patients are currently the subject of extensive research. This is critical.

A co-morbid condition might see the sufferer seeking help for one but not both conditions. Side effects can be created in the treatment of one by the presence of the other. There is growing interest in the co-existence of mental disorders and chronic physical disease.

Co-morbidity presents different problems, depending upon whether we are considering two psychiatric conditions or one psychiatric disorder and a general medical one — in the latter situation, the diagnostic boundary of the medical disorder is usually less ambiguous, making it easier to establish the presence of co-morbidity.

Co-morbidity involves the assessment and management of biological, bodily and mental considerations. The brain is the central terminal for these dynamics.

All mental capacities, including the ability to feel, be aware, recognize, remember, learn, or talk, depend on the 'programs' of the evolved brain. The brain's interconnections allow for differences among the structures and functions of the brain from one person to the next. The result is differences among people.

Science still knows very little about the storage and coding of memories and language and about how abstract ideas are developed. But according to Dr. Guze, "those of us who accept the central place of biology in mental functioning are confident that the brain is involved in all this."

Biological psychiatrists assume that many forms of psychiatric illness are the result of different responses of the individual's brain to the circumstances of his or her life — and that these differences in the way people respond to the cards life has dealt them flow from differences in the way the brain has developed and functioned.

Nonetheless, from a philosophical standpoint, consciousness, free will and "all the richness of mental life" are still largely beyond neuroscience and perhaps will always remain so. But to Dr. Guze, "it is a hopeful sign that modern biology and modern philosophy are reaching out to each other."

A second hopeful sign is the cross-current experienced in some quarters between leadership and spirituality. This bears upon mental states in terms not well defined by scientific doctrine.

For example, experts on leadership like Warren Bennis have stated that "by focusing on a vision, the leader operates on the emotional and spiritual resources of the organization, its values, commitment and aspirations."

Albert Schweitzer, one of history's great medical doctors and humanitarians, linked historic events to spirituality: "One truth stands firm. All that happens rests on something spiritual. If the spiritual is strong, it creates world history. If it is weak, world history suffers."

In practical terms — in the workplace, for instance — spiritual thinking (centred on the power within people, the role of feelings in human conduct, the influence of deeper motivations) can create hospitable spaces where working people can connect with each other in common cause and mutual respect.

This can have an up side in productivity terms.

The healing journey is made through channels forged by the elements of spirituality. They define caring. Leaders can help create environments where seeming opposites — can come together. Work and meditation. Leadership and empathy. Soulfulness and organization.

This convergence of compatible opposites creates a moral context in which productive people can function productively. Beyond that, returning to Dr. Guze's point, it augments "the richness of mental life" which so far lies beyond the reach of science.

Motivation and Cause
Conventional medical thinking centres on causes of disease. Psychiatry deals with the motivation, goals and intentions of the patient. Psychiatrists are "brought face to face with certain philosophical concerns linked to questions about cause."

At the same time, psychiatrists come face-to-face with mental experiences affecting bodily process, a dynamic we touched on earlier with, among others, Drs. Swenson and Lespérance of the Ottawa and Montreal Heart Institutes. There is vast literature demonstrating that mental experiences affect endocrine and the metabolic systems, the cardiovascular and gastrointestinal systems, the immune system and all other physiological functions. Dr. Guze, *verbatim*:

There is now evidence that deliberate efforts to think certain kinds of thoughts are systematically reflected in changes in regional brain flow and metabolism.

The only way all of these things can happen is for the mental experience to be based upon the brain's apparatus for interacting with the rest of the body.

Some have suggested that the mind interacts with the brain without having to obey the laws of thermodynamics. To many scientists, this is truly inconceivable and appears to be a way of introducing the concept of the soul into scientific discussions. A less radical view suggests that the mind and brain are inseparable but we must acknowledge the current limitations in our understanding of the details concerning the mechanisms for dealing with such concurrence.

Some who argue that the mind is inseparable will agree that medications can affect mood, energy, appetite, sexual drives, sleep, nervousness or anxiety, cognition, learning, memory and that mental experiences can lead to a wide variety of bodily changes.

But they balk when it comes to the content of thought, learning, memory or emotion. And they balk especially when it comes to intentions. They resist the belief that neuroscience can ever help us understand the content of our mental experiences. They insist that neuroscience will never be able to help us understand Shakespeare's insight into psychology, for instance, because such insights are different in kind from the insights of behavioural psychologists and both are different again from the neuroscientific correlates which may be occurring at the same time.

[In the study of the mind], metaphysical differences dictate scientific differences. [Nonetheless], the evident fact [is] that our mental states have both physical causes and effects.

On the question of free will:

Very few psychiatrists ignore the possibility, and even the probability, that many of our patients' thoughts, emotions and overt behaviours are determined, at least in part, by processes over which they have limited if any control. Most of us believe that this is the case when patients experience delusions, hallucinations, mania, depression, obsessions, compulsions, panic attacks, phobias, habituations and addictions. This contributes to our view that experiences constitute illness.

At the same time, most of us believe some patients can partially control some of these experiences with professional help. (We) assume some patients can modify behaviour, thinking, or emotional responses. In short, we seem to hold contradictory ideas. We often show the same apparent contradictions when it comes to patients' responsibility for their behaviour — some should be held responsible, some should not be.

Blunders of Linear Thinking

Earlier in this report, we forecast the decline and fall of linear thinking. The ways that information will be displayed and used within the architecture of 21st-Century computer technology are increasingly likely to alter how we perceive data, decision-making and life generally.

This has implications for the public media of entertainment and journalism, which historically simplify events into black-and-white, cause-and-effect symbols and portrayals. And to commercial and public enterprise. Maybe for the better. Linear thinking has periodically drawn wrong conclusions from the right facts.

In the 1960s, the shortage of housing for the poor led us to massive blunders in building high-rise apartments for subsidized families, when the solution for housing for people on low incomes was more likely to be found in jobs, education and health opportunity, as well as the dignity of community acceptance offered by the model of mixed-income, low-rise housing in well serviced middle-class and higher-end residential and commercial neighbourhoods of the City of Toronto. Admittedly a less linear and predictable concept.

In the 1980s, we began to move psychiatric patients out of institutions and back into the community, a rediscovery of self-worth that tended to be oppressed by the nature of institutional life. Here the linear conclusion was "de-institutionalization." Soon after, the problems facing ex-psychiatrics were those of suitable housing, which, as often as not isolated them in substandard rooming houses with no jobs.

As it turned out, the converse of dependence "inside" the mental institution was not independence "outside" the institution. The issues were too complex for the solution of one defined problem to be found in one trite solution. The product of linear thinking. Toronto's present-day homeless crisis is one result.

Former Health Minister Marc Lalonde, nearly 20 years ago, voiced the dangers of linear thought in healthcare. He said the healthcare system was only one factor in preserving the health of the population. He introduced then what has become faint gospel today — that social conditions, employment, the living environments we create for each other, economic opportunity and fairness, all determine health and contribute to disease.

Yet from Mr. Lalonde's call two decades ago for multi-dimensional thinking to the National Forum's repetition of that message last year, the limitations of a linear "cause-and-effect" healthcare system have pretty well held firm. Till now, at least.

But things are changing. "In a curious way," the University of Toronto's Dr. Harvey Skinner says, "escalating costs in healthcare are stimulating a realignment and even integration of two broad traditions that split apart at the beginning of this century."

"The first tradition, medical care, has focused on the diagnosis, treatment and rehabilitation of diseases in individual patients — the second, public health, has focused on the prevention of disease and promotion of health mainly at the community and population levels."

Describing these traditions as "two solitudes for most of this century," Dr. Skinner says new concepts of care are zeroing in on the needs of the individual and the population simultaneously.

Service integration is hot. And the sooner it generates light as well as heat in medical research, the better. Here again, we see the limitations of linear thinking historically, and the need to break with the past.

Eliminating Pump Handles

The discovery that the London water supply was the source of the Plague and the elegant but simple public health solution of removing the pump handles of infected wells defines modern epidemiology.

"This discipline focuses our scientific attention on removing pump handles," Dr. Heather Munroe-Blum, a prize-winning epidemiologist, told an audience attending the second Dr. Stephen Lett lecture at the Homewood Health Centre.

Stephen Lett was Homewood's first medical superintendent 115 years ago. A progressive advocate of holistic care, Dr. Lett, history has it, died a hero's death trying to rescue a drowning child in the swollen waters of the Speed River that flows through Homewood's gracious park-like grounds.

Dr. Munroe-Blum, the Vice-President of Research and International Relations at the University of Toronto, said in her provocative lecture that research in mental health has been defined in years past by a belief in a linear system of "cause and effect" that confined discovery and frustrated the application of knowledge to clinical practice. She told a story:

A young boy walked across a railway bridge. The day was sunny, with a slight breeze. As he looked down, he saw a fallen robin beside the track, the whistle of a train in the distance.

From that day to this, every time the man who grew from that boy sees a robin, he thinks of the whistle of a train that serenaded his sad find.

Human nature tends to correlate two events into a coincidence that can create a belief system and pattern of behaviour. Connecting train whistles to dead robins. We see it in business, too. First impressions stick.

A not-too-senior expert in drug pricing is hired by an insurance company and demonstrates his expertise in the early days of employment.

One day, in his first and only appearance before the CEO of the company, he struggles while answering questions and in his nervousness, gives what appear to be flippant answers.

The meeting ends and from that day until the employee leaves the company not long after, the CEO dislikes his manner and doubts his knowledge. Each time the CEO sees him, he hears a train whistle.

Dr. Munroe-Blum says belief systems in medical research have been forced to depart from a straight-line path of cause and effect self-prophesied by 'silo' funding arrangements.

The linear has given way to a "multifactorial" of what constitutes psychiatric illness and how to treat it.

The foundations of mental health research have been laid over the past century. Up to World War II, some 16 studies had aimed to establish a general prevalence of psychiatric disorders. But they underestimated the situation, because researchers took into account only those cases that had come to the attention of the medical establishment.

After the war, significant progress was realized in the classification of psychiatric conditions. This flowed from screening techniques developed for military purposes in wartime, a second generation of studies, and from a case study in Sterling County, Nova Scotia, one of the first investigations to document the prevalence of psychiatric disorders in a whole community.

It was in this period that degrees of impairment were objectively classified. In Dr. Munroe-Blum's view, this work is more relevant today than many of the clinical studies done since.

From 1980, some 18 studies reflected concerns for a system of diagnosis and treatment of psychiatric disorders and the "medical *sequelae*" which accompanied them.

Through the later 20th Century, from then till now, a new field of psychiatric research was born.

The ultimate priority of research in psychiatric disorders is to create the right complement of effective community and clinical interventions to detect and treat them.

In this we see the role of "psychiatric epidemiology" and the search for pump handles of a very different kind.

Light has been shed on the multiple risk factors associated with mental disorders. Despite its relatively small population, Canada has been in the forefront of scientific research linking psychiatric issues to internal medicine and psychosomatic questions — an example of the latter being a pain in the chest caused by the dynamics of a panic disorder.

Dr. Munroe-Blum saw advances in mental health research as "a cause for celebration," but she also saw its brittle underpinnings.

More Anomalies Than Trends

Despite the advancement and precision of screening methods, and technology, "we have yet to develop the receptor capacity" to adequately use in psychiatric practice the information new research is producing.

In the face of one of the greatest social transitions the world has encountered in centuries, the expectations, realities and possibilities facing clinical personnel are changing dramatically.

Cross-disciplinary leadership and ideas in the psychiatric community are called for, says Dr. Munroe-Blum. Good old fashioned "teamwork" among universities, researchers, hospitals and practitioners are key to the more effective deployment of the results of contemporary research in the treatment of the mentally disabled.

Departing from themes underscored earlier in this report, Dr. Munroe-Blum cautioned about an over-reliance on biological concepts of treatment in the face of overwhelming evidence that biological factors account for only a small portion of the variables at play in triggering mental disorders.

And even when they are found to be a root cause, successful treatments depend on a host of social, environmental and psychological considerations.

Calling for a "broadening of the framework" for mental health research, Dr. Munroe-Blum noted that clinical trials and research continue to produce more anomalies than trends in the understanding of mental illness.

Thus the critical importance of "an integrated approach" to research and treatment, taking into account questions of biology, psychology and social experience. Disdaining "clinical myopia," she cited the importance of promoting "cross-disciplinary collaboration" among new generations of highly trained specialists in psychiatric medicine and research. This improves the odds of creating "the receptor capacity" in the field that is needed to apply clinically what research is telling us.

What is mental health research telling us? Where is it headed? An examination of these questions will await part two of *Mindsets*. It is sufficient for the moment to note that dollar spending on other forms of medical research outstrips the investment in mental health research by a factor of 15 to one.

Given the stakes involved — socially, economically and medically — and in light of the newly discovered heft of mental illness as a source of work days lost through disability and premature death, that gulf must be bridged. First, though, we must find the public incentives needed to support the bridge structure. Perhaps this report, in "telling the story," can help.

The Maddening World

An 18-year-old student, writing in the *Toronto Star*, described a psychiatric ward of a large hospital in mostly optimistic terms, although she saw "experiences of infinite sorrow and shocking realism."

A troubled world she saw. And for many, a maddening one.

Researchers from the Harvard School of Medicine, after a two-year study in 1995 saw a similar world: "Mental health represents one of the last frontiers in the improvement of the human condition." They added: "In the face of widespread stigma and inattention, mental health must now be placed on the international agenda."

An international voice speaks up, former Canadian Finance Minister Michael Wilson:

"What is mental illness? It's a mystery to most Canadians. It is everywhere around us. At any one time, 10% to 20% of the population is experiencing a mental disorder."

As a result of tragic events that have been sensationalized in the media, we may think of the mentally ill as people who push strangers onto subway tracks. In our daily lives, we can see ill people who wander the streets talking to themselves. Sometimes they make us feel threatened.

But there are other faces of mental illness:
- The young professional who suffers from depression, the number one cause of disability in the world.
- The depressed, alcohol-dependent adolescent who has just tried suicide.
- The heroin addict who is trying to re-establish himself on methadone so he can care for his family again.
- The compulsive gambler who has lost everything and is now desperately calling for help.
- The young woman trapped in a foreign world, vomiting three times a day, barely able to establish a semblance of control.
- Or the woman who was taken into care after she had jumped in the lake — voices told her that this was the only way to save her children.

These are stories of private anguish and torment. They should remind us — all of us — that mental illness is never far away. Mental illness does not respect class or stature. We know that 16% of Toronto's residents will need psychiatric treatment at some point in their lives, but three quarters of these people will never receive any care.

For some groups, the prospects are even worse. Kids, for example — community surveys reveal that about 18% of Ontario's children need some form of care for emotional disturbance. Yet most of them never receive any help.

In another area, close to 90% of people with "concurrent disorders" — problems of both mental illness and substance abuse — don't get appropriate help.

And another: Alzheimer's. This deadly illness, which now affects more than 300,000 Canadians, will increase dramatically over the next 20 years as the population ages.

Also, there are between 40,000 and 90,000 Canadians abusing opiates, a family of drugs that includes heroin, among other killers.

Soaring Suicide Rate

Against this backdrop, is it surprising that the suicide rate in Canada has skyrocketed in the last 30 years, especially among the young? We now lose 3,500 human beings to suicide each year. The suicide rate among people with schizophrenia, one of our most serious illnesses, which typically begins in young adulthood, is about 20 times the national average. We lose about 300 young people with psychosis to suicide each year.

Mr. Wilson sums up:

Think of that. If an airplane were to crash at Pearson with 300 young people aboard there would be an epic outcry, and I would guess, a tremendous amount of study and investigation into the cause. Yet, something is wrong with our sense of priorities where the tripling of the rate of adolescent suicide causes barely a ripple.

Depression is overwhelmingly the chief cause of suicide. Of the 3,500 Canadians who die by their own hands each year, about 2,000 suffer from major depression at the time of death. What a waste in human, personal and economic terms!

Depression, which we noted earlier is the leading cause of disability in the world, costs the Canadian people about $12 billion in direct and indirect costs annually. Depression affects about 20% of women and 10% of men at some point in their lives.

Yes, the need is great. But today we can do more for people suffering from substance abuse and mental illness than ever before. There has been a revolution in the science of this field. We have learned more about how the brain works in the last 10 years than in the previous 2,000. We know more about the causes of illnesses, of the relevant cultural and social forces, the dynamics of the family, and interpersonal and individual psychology than we ever thought possible.

There has been an explosion in the development of new medications. Prozac is now part of our language and culture. And, with less fanfare, we have fostered the development of highly effective, targeted, psychological treatments — some of them very costly, to be sure, but not nearly as costly in the long run as ignoring and neglecting these ill people.

When you realize that the opportunities are great yet most people receive little care, you begin to think there is something wrong here. On the one hand, newer treatments can be very beneficial. On the other, most people who need care receive no help at all. If such a situation existed for heart disease, there would be an immediate public outcry and a quick remedy.

In no other field of medicine is the element of community support so important. In what other field could the demand have risen, and continue to rise so high, while it receives less and less public support? Mental health expenditures have fallen from 11% to 9% of the Ontario provincial health budget over the past 25 years. What a tragic waste of human resources in a nationnamed as number one on Earth for the quality of life.

Global Tragedy

The Harvard (1995) study, *World Mental Health* (not to be confused with Harvard's *Global Burden of Disease Analysis* cited earlier), was funded by the Carnegie Corporation, the Rockefeller Foundation and others. A 31-person advisory board consisted of major international scholars and experts. The study describes a "global tragedy," much of which could be avoided were we to commit ourselves to applying what we already know about prevention and treatment. The study sounds an alert:

> Unless we act now, the unprecedented gains over the past 40 years in reducing child mortality, improving physical health and increasing life expectancy, worldwide, are in jeopardy of being offset by a steady growth in mental and behavioural problems.

A major barrier to progress is stigma. Once again, the Harvard researchers speak forcefully: "We identify schizophrenia and depression as mental 'illness,' but stigmatize the individuals who suffer from it and fail to recognize that they can be treated."

Life expectancy is increasing worldwide, particularly in Western Europe and North America. But along with longer lives has come a surge in depression, schizophrenia, dementia and other forms of chronic mental illness, primarily because more people are living into the age of risk.

Along with economic growth and various social transformations has come a marked increase in rates of alcoholism, drug abuse and suicide. And while maternal mortality has been declining in countries around the world, the incidence of violence against women, young and old, has increased sharply.

"In other words, in many parts of the world, economic progress and gains in overall longevity have been accompanied by an increase in the social, psychiatric and behavioural pathologies that have become a part of daily life in North America and Western Europe," the Harvard report reminded us, as we said here earlier, that 34% of all disability is due to behaviour-related problems such as violence, sexually-transmitted diseases, automobile accidents and other injuries.

The Harvard study puts the number of women, men and children suffering from mental illnesses in the hundreds of millions, adding that the burden of illness represented by psychiatric disorders is "grossly under-represented by conventional public health statistics, which tend to measure death rates to the exclusion of suffering and dysfunction."

This distorted picture historically has stemmed from ascribing death to immediate causes rather than the behaviours underlying them. Liver failure, for example, may be an official cause of death, but alcoholism is the underlying cause.

Counting Deaths

National and international statistics have not reflected the enormous toll of misery from mental disorders because these conditions are not the immediate cause of death. For instance, even when suicide represents death due to depression or schizophrenia or drug addiction, it is generally baldly recorded as 'suicide.'

Until recently, counting deaths was the only way to determine if public health programs were working. Life expectancy is the converse. Having accomplished much in the way of reducing "excess death" and improving conditions of life, "society has been slow to appreciate that greater longevity has been accompanied by an increasing burden of chronic disease and social and behavioural health problems," according to the Harvard study on mental illness.

In part, the increase comes about because more people live to later ages when heart disease, arthritis, stroke, dementia and other diseases first appear; and in part because of change in diet, exercise, drinking patterns, drug use and changes in the way we live or progress economically.

Cost comparisons between mental illness and other disease categories have only recently been documented. They range from $148 billion for all forms of mental illness in the United States, to $99 billion for alcohol abuse and $67 billion for drug abuse.

"One yardstick for cost comparison," the Harvard study says, "is that the cost burden from depression is about the same in the United States as that from heart disease."

The number of people with major mental illnesses will increase substantially in the decades to come for two reasons, Harvard says. Demographics is one, and an overall rise in the rates of depression over past decades is the other.

As a result, the number of people with schizophrenia will have increased 45% between 1985 and the year 2000. This, because of a 45% increase in the population between age 15 and 45 the world over. "Similarly, there will be a substantial increase in the senile dementias — once again, by virtue of an increase in the numbers of people living to age 65 and beyond."

Depression (as noted earlier in this report) is now seen at younger ages and at greater frequency in countries as varied as Lebanon, Taiwan, Canada, the United States and Western Europe. The relative risk for depression increased for the population born between 1935 and 1944, compared to that born a decade earlier. The rate of growth was highest in the U.S. and Italy.

"In general, mental, social and behavioural health problems represent overlapping clusters of problems that, once connected to the recent wave of global change, interact and intensify each other's effects on [wellbeing]," the Harvard study says. "One cluster consists of substance abuse, violence, abuse of women and children, and the psychiatric *sequalae* of such aggression.

"Another cluster links health problems with biological causes, such as heart disease, stress and depression, to changes in social behaviour, interpersonal support and personal coping."

"These clusters," Harvard says, "are more prevalent in conditions such as high unemployment, low income, limited education, stressful work conditions, gender discrimination, unhealthy lifestyle and human rights violations. These social conditions are, in turn, influenced by the powerful global transformations of our era."

The Harvard report describes itself as the first systematic attempt to survey the burden of suffering related to these clusters of problems. In doing so, it describes mental health as:

> not simply the absence of detectable mental disease but a state of wellbeing in which the individual realizes his or her own abilities, can work productively and fruitfully, and is able to contribute to his or her community.

This definition is apt and appropriate for a global economy, in which human capital is becoming the major commodity of commerce, and mental health its underlying collateral.

In turn, mental health is underscored by what Dr. Graeme Cunningham, Director of Addiction Medicine at the Homewood Health Centre, describes as "the greatest source of human energy — hope." Hope is the converse of isolation. It is a determinant of health because it is a source of action and thought.

◈17◈
Epilogue

AGING IS NOT A DISEASE. NOR IS IT A DISABILITY ITSELF. ONLY A SMALL *minority of the elderly actually experience severe dependence on others. But the aging of our population has broad implications.*

For one thing, given the numbers of elderly parents living alongside *their baby boom children — sometimes literally — it carries a widening economic, social and emotional impact for millions of families, according to Dr. Olga Mallotte, head of the Alzheimer Research and Education Program at the University of Waterloo, Ontario.*

In the United States, 22 million households, one in four, are involved in *the provision of caregiving to elderly relatives or friends. The typical caregiver in the U.S. is a 46-year-old woman who spends an average 18 hours a week caring for her mother, who lives nearby.*

The 18-hour average is misleading in one sense. In fully one fourth of *those 22 million households the caregiving burden reaches 40 hours of commitment each week.*

Here again, men and women are differentiated by custom and proclivity. *Studies tell us 72% of all these informal caregivers are women and nearly a third look after two or more elderly people.*

Almost two thirds of those caring for an elderly parent, relative or *friend work full- or part-time, while 10% end up quitting work entirely, another 40% drop vacations or hobbies, half adjust their work schedule and half (the 'sandwich generation') also care for children under the age of 18 at the same time.*

For idealists with perspective, aging is a fact of life, not its price. None-*theless, it is helping shape the context and texture of the post-deficit society.*

Being alone is a growing fact of post-modern life — ironically in a hurried world that is getting smaller and faster (and more crowded in that sense) and convulsing with change.

Studies tell us that between 1970 and 2010, single-person households will have come to represent more than one in four of the total — many occupied by aging and lonely people, often women living in poverty. In fact, 30% of all women between 65 and 74 live alone.

According to some estimates, between 1970 and the year 2020, the number of people 65 or older will have increased 71% throughout the world, and between the years 1984 and 2001, in Canada, that same age group will have grown by nearly half and the 75-84 age group will have increased 73%.

By the year 2006, some estimates say that 20% of Canada's population will be 60 years of age or older.

A demographic shift is obviously underway, whatever the exact statistics may be. With that shift, five broad trends with significant implications for health and healthcare are emerging.

One is the rise in neuro psychiatric disorders, especially in consonance with chronic disease.

A second is the fundamental change in Canadians' health needs.

A third trend is the shift from communicable to manmade disease, the advent of behaviour as a major source of disease and injury, the principal weight of the global burden of disease, at least as we now perceive and calculate its impact. A cause of death may be listed as liver disease, but the underlying cause is heavy drinking.

A fourth trend will be growing knowledge of the human brain, pointing to social, environmental and behavioural influences as triggers in the onset of mental illness and suppression of the human immune system.

The fifth trend is captured by Harvard's exposure of disability as conceivably the health challenge of the 21st Century — with the role of mental disorders as a leading source of it.

Revisiting our Research and the Sweep of Mental Illness
Revisiting our earlier chronicles, we see what Harvard describes as an "unheralded crisis in mental illness" worldwide.

We see depressive and anxiety disorders accounting for one quarter to one third of all visits by individuals to primary-care physicians.

We see depression emerging as the leading cause of work days lost through premature death and disability in the developed world by the year 2020. It is number four now.

We see psychiatric illness growing faster than cardiovascular disease as a proportion of the global burden of disease. Mental illness in the 21st Century will mean more productive years lost to death and disability than AIDS or suicide.

We see mental, neurological and behavioural disorders together becoming the single largest cause of quality years lost through disability and death.

Around the world, we see 300 million people, equivalent to the populations of the U.S. and Canada combined, suffering from mental and neurological disorders.

We see chronic physical disease and mental disorders intimately connected, and heart patients who are depressed several times more likely to suffer death from a second heart attack inside six months after the first.

According to a study commissioned by the Homewood Health Centre, we see more workers absent from work because of stress and mental anxiety than because of physical illness or injury.

We see the possibility of stress as an independent complication in the treatment of cancer.

We see more than three quarters of all Americans being worried about job security, the greatest worry of Canadians as well. We see sustained economic prosperity paralleled by the absence of a celebration of it, by what Time magazine calls the 20th-Century Blues and another observer, the Age of Melancholy.

According to U.S. surveys, we find job and financial satisfaction, and overall happiness, lower than at any time in the past 20 years.

In Canada, we see anxiety levels climbing to the extent that some experts are assessing the impact that economic uncertainty of parents has on children.

We see strings of uncertainty in millions of lives tied to "a loss of control" (or the sense of it) that has accompanied globalization — where even profitable companies have laid off thousands of employees in apprehension of global competition or to consolidate whole industries.

The number of major mental disorders will increase substantially in the decades to come for two reasons, Harvard says.

Demographics is one, and an overall rise in the rates of depression is the other.

The number of schizophrenics will have increased 45% between 1985 and the year 2000 because of an increase in the population between the ages of 15 and 45 the world over. The Harvard report on disease globally: "Similarly, there will be a substantial increase in senile dementias — once again, by virtue of an increase in the number of people living to age 65 and beyond."

Depression affects nearly a quarter of workers surveyed in some 200

U.S. companies, yet only about a third seek or receive treatment. Fully 25% of those same people abuse alcohol and other substances.

Stress disability claims in the United States have increased dramatically and will lead all other disability claims through the rest of the 90s. U.S. labour experts and psychiatrists are calling for comprehensive epidemiological studies of American corporations to better understand stress-related disorders in individuals and organizations.

The Impact of Disability

The burden of mental illness has been severely misunderstood because of the failure to measure the impact of disability on quality of life.

The leading causes of disability are not the same as the leading causes of death.

Harvard concludes this: "There is serious doubt in the value of judging a population's health from its mortality statistics alone."

Life expectancy is increasing worldwide, but with it has come surging growth in depression, dementia and other forms of chronic mental illness, primarily because people are living into an age of risk.

In major parts of the developed world, economic progress and gains in longevity have been accompanied by social, psychiatric and behavioural pathologies in daily life.

Step by step, we are winning the war for longevity. But are we advancing the quality of life along the way? We will live longer in the next century, and in some respects, we will live sicker. This is the legacy of demography, and the result of an incomplete vision by one generation to the next of the kind of society we want to create for future generations.

Clusters of psychiatric disorders intensify in times of high unemployment, low income, stressful work, and limited education. We know, for example, that education in the first two decades of life can help prevent Alzheimer's Disease — believed to be related to synaptic density in the part of the brain dealing with learning and memory.

The Yearning for Identity

The projected growth of Alzheimer's Disease is, itself, a fearsome reflection of demographic trends. It has become a metaphor for the times. And for 300,000 Canadians, it is a form of human development in reverse.

It implacably unravels a lifetime of neurological connections, starting with those governing higher cognitive functions and moves back from there.

It is a disease of paradox. It strips its victims of identity. At the same time, there is something in that experience that causes its victims to yearn for and express their individuality.

There is great sadness and frustration embedded in this disease. As the familiarity of close faces and places recedes, it becomes a search for familiar things. In that sense, a search for home.

It becomes a version of the scary dream many of us had when we were kids — where we keep running and running from strangers to get back home. Those with Alzheimer's Disease live the nightmare.

In this context, long-term care — another hot issue in the public policy and funding debates — is, however, not just another stretch of highway on the real estate of healthcare reform. It is a question of values that resonates for millions of informal care providers.

In the eyes of Dr. Olga Mallotte, head of the remarkable Alzheimer's education program at Waterloo University founded by Homewood Chairman, Ken Murray, long-term care in an aging society is a matter of basic human consideration.

The aged, the demented, the confused must have a voice, and an ear. Not listening or talking to them presumes they can neither speak nor hear and that, Dr. Mallotte says, "is one short step to believing they cannot feel."

The year 2020 stands out as a summit of some kind. It represents the time that Harvard projects as the pinnacle of rising depression and heart disease as partners in the destruction of lost work years.

It is the year that Peter Drucker sets out as the end point of the industrial transformation now underway, if not its culmination.

It is a frame of time within which the former Primate of the Anglican Church of Canada, Ted Scott, seemed to reach for as he forecast a deepening of "our yearning in this world to help each other."

"People today," he says, "are being hurt by too much and too little." The Primate, one of Canada's earliest and most articulate spokesmen on corporate social responsibility in the 1970's, worries that we have created a culture that is not reflective enough, where people are occupied by doing one thing after another.

"We have no daydreaming time, no time for fruitful idleness, we are losing touch with ourselves. So many of us are completely and utterly alone, losing sight of the eternal realities that form a backdrop to temporal crisis."

"We seem self-conscious of our feelings, self-conscious of our power to make choices. Canadians have adopted a more punitive sense of things, a lower order of meaning." Calling for a benediction of trust, Dr. Scott says the opposite of love is not hate. "It is selfishness. Most of us need a sense of community, we need to experience love and not be content with what divides or threatens to conquer us."

In the spectrum of images evoked by one of Canada's most revered religious leaders, we find an essential point of reference in defining the core issue or contest between opposite forces in the post-deficit society. Human connection versus human isolation.

On this pivots the quest for empathy and search for peaceful, not lazy minds. A big part of that quest — and that search — must be undertaken in the world of the economy and work.

For it is in the economy that we find the means we rightly seek to live our lives. And in work, we experience fulfillment, we engage the essential contract of being useful, we satisfy the need for association and validation. Without the means, our health will suffer; with it, our health can prosper. Without usefulness or associations — as Dr. Bob Swenson reminded us — we grieve for both.

These are business issues in that they touch the central chord of what entails the productive capacity of human beings in the information society, where human health is linked to the promise of economic prosperity, and where mental health is a strategically critical transporter of that promise.

Part IV

Mindsets

⇜18⇝
Mental Health and the Global Business Agenda

THERE IS A NEW MANAGEMENT AGENDA TAKING SHAPE IN THE GLOBAL economy. It links health and economic performance. It drives to the heart of why and how businesses should value the resilience and wellbeing of their employees as the vector of productivity and profit.

This new agenda is defined, in part, by an awakening of how illiterate we really are in the recognition of mental illness as a powerful deterrent to sustainable business and economic performance — and conversely, what a major asset healthy mental states are in the work and market place.

The Washington Business Group on Health has led the charge in trying to get a handle on this new agenda, fleshing out a health-based productivity model.

The process of developing the agenda extends the meaning of the terms "health and safety" beyond the physical standards of accident prevention that have historically governed the efficacy of the workplace in most parts of the industrial world.

Today, potent intangibles are beginning to get the attention they deserve. Fairness is one. Surveyed workers mark it at least as high as compensation as a decisive influence on healthy employee outlooks.

Absenteeism is linked by studies to problems in people's work environment. Respect, meaningful work, trust and openness, and the opportunity for personal growth, all temper or tamper with the capacity of people to remain motivated on the job.

Remarkably, rates of disability and absenteeism, sickness and accidents can be forecast by drawing signals from employees' own perceptions of their workplace in light of values that are acceptable to them. These "predictors" of disability take the form of a lack of understanding by employees about what the company is trying to achieve — its goals and objectives. Or the lack of mutual respect and self-respect among co-workers and their supervisors.

Disability rates can be predicted from a lack of opportunity for workers to develop their skills in their *current job*. Opportunities for promotion are not the main motivator of every worker. People want to be productive in what they do now.

Employees are emotionally nourished by a belief that the management of the company has a sense of direction and knows what it's doing. They are starved emotionally by ambiguity or doubt about the prospects of the company and their role in it. This is a predictor of disability.

Autocratic management styles, meaningless, repetitive tasks or even too little to do, create tensions and insecurity, and signal a rise in accelerated costs associated with absenteeism, low productivity and disability — all of which are often driven by emotional distress.

Insufficient coping skills to manage stress and conflict drain the productive capacity of employees and the dollar value of their performance. And coping skills have molecular *and* mental roots.

Fraser Mustard, founder of the Canadian Institute for Advanced Research, and a leading world authority on the determinants of health, says one of the key findings in recent years "has been the observation that the nervous system and the immune system are in direct communication with each other."

"Thus changes in the nervous system, including one's psychological sense of wellbeing could affect an individual's host defence status through changes in the immune system and the body's hormone system — influencing susceptibility to cardiovascular disease, cancer and allergic reactions," Dr. Mustard said.

"One of the factors that would influence an individual's host defence system through the nervous system is how well he or she copes with the demands of where he or she lives and works, as well as major life changes," he said. "This is sometimes referred to as 'coping skills.'"

More Than A Question Of Lifestyle
'Work' is more than a job, it is a community. Deteriorated social alliances and support at work can interfere with employee wellbeing and eventually cut into sustained productivity. Isolation in the workplace can have the same disabling impact as isolation on a deserted mountaintop.

Some of the largest corporations in the United States are pulling out the stops to address issues of this nature.

The 3M Company, for example, a $15 billion enterprise with 74,000 employees worldwide, now has a human capital measurement tool that integrates employee health and productivity.

The company is using this tool to analyze the non-medical drivers of ill health, including the use (abuse) of prescription drugs, adverse work climate, troubled personal relationships within the workplace, management practices that undermine the emotional state of people.

3M introduced a strategy not only to bring down the costs of disability through improved health but to improve productivity. From these seeds scattered more widely may flower a health-based productivity model, and ultimately, a health-based economy.

Contemporary disability management schemes tend not to take into account "best management practices" (or their absence) in assessing the causes of disability or ways to reduce it. Health promotion and employee assistance programs have focused principally on the lifestyles of working people and less on the health of the organization itself , less on the culture it has spawned or the atmosphere it has created, and their impact on people's wellbeing.

But that is beginning to change. For context, we turn to Dr. Jack Santa-Barbara, President and Chief Executive of CHC-Wellness, the largest behavioural health service company in Canada.

In the 1940s, he reminds us, EAPs centred mostly on alcohol and drug abuse problems. Over time, this base broadened. Insured health benefits emerged. Wellness schemes took hold. The integrity of EAPs — based on employee confidentiality at all costs — came to be accepted. Use of EAPs grew steadily in ensuing decades.

But these companion initiatives had one common limitation. They were also seen by companies as cost centres and were vulnerable, as a result, to the exigencies of cost reductions on a period basis — at the quarter, the year end or in the business planning process. They were (and are) left unprotected because they offered no tax advantage.

Dr. Santa-Barbara sees occupational health reaching a new plateau in mental health and human behaviour. Organizational health — and organizational behaviour — are central features of that equation.

Dr. Santa-Barbara says there is "lots of confusion and lots of energy" among employers to come to terms with behavioural health issues in the workplace, issues that have been largely neglected. They are still stigmatized. Yet it is enormously important to help people manage normal workplace stress. He cites a "need/demand dichotomy" in the under- or over-use of medical resources for just this purpose.

Dr. Santa-Barbara paints this picture. It will be crucial going forward to manage behavioural health demand more effectively — the present dichotomy impairs the capacity of employers *and* employees to intervene profitably before stress-related problems make the employee eligible for a disability claim, for example. By then, the health disorder has begun to take root.

"Psychosocial drivers of long-term disability are increasing," Dr. Santa-Barbara says. "If employees fail to recognize and deal with their early symptoms, a disability claim becomes inevitable." Which is not productive.

"The big priority is to help people understand the early signs and symptoms" of behavioural disorders and then take action on them." This will set into motion an important variable: early detection.

One of the most enlightened and effective EAP executives in North America is Tom Reynolds, the International EAP Director for the Bank of Montreal and a member of the Advisory Board of the famed Clarke Institute of Psychiatry.

Interestingly, Mr. Reynolds synchronizes the detection of mental disorders in the workplace with the broader quest of "making them normal" in public perception and acceptance.

Others in Mr. Reynolds' field are thinking the same way.

A November 1998 peer conference on disability management involving many of Dr. Jack Santa-Barbara's colleagues and companies ranging from the Toronto Transit Commission and Carlton Cards to the management-consultant giant Price Waterhouse, tackled these very issues.

Broad Structural Issues

A substantial part of their agenda focused on "time and money" questions associated with stress related disorders in the workplace. Subtext for this probe was drawn from matters such as the role of upper management in returning the "stressed-out" employee to work.

Dr. Bruce Rowat is a physician-educator who teaches at the University of Toronto, and serves as the medical officer for two of Canada's largest financial service organizations — Sun Life and the Bank of Montreal. He applauds any trend in which problems of employee health are scrutinized against the backdrop of "the broad structural and macro issues" facing corporations today.

He's right to do so. Physicians must be concerned about the tendency of employers *and* employees alike to medicalize emotional problems — raising fundamental questions asked in one forum by one of the authors of this report (Pérez): "Can we medicalize issues that are plainly issues of life?"

Some physicians see EAPs as "band-aids," and employee confidence in these programs has trailed off somewhat after considerable growth in the 20 years previous.

Nonetheless, psychological problems, including stress, are one of the 10 leading work-related disorders. They represent more than $100 billion dollars in annual costs to North American business, according to researchers at Brigham Young University. They say "many illnesses and diseases may be prevented by appropriate stress management." The immune system "link" once again.

There is no doubt that work and health issues are complex. Contemporary EAPs must respond in kind, not with blind complexity but with an eye for recognizing the "integrated nature" of behaviours and disorders. It has been found repeatedly that "multi-factorial" programs, which recognize "the diversity" of the prevalent sources of disability, are the most successful.

Issues such as child care, elder care, substance abuse and psychological problems, domestic violence, and their impact on job performance, are a common part of the EAP agenda today, like it or not. At the centre of all this is the question of performance, by both the individual and the company.

In this light, we might ponder the question posed by researchers at the University of Baltimore's Merrick School of Business. Does EAP stand for *"employer"* or *"employee"* assistance plan? The paradox can be resolved this way: both.

"The New Crying Game"

The Employee Assistance Society of North America met in Toronto this year. The Society's agenda mirrored the crosscurrents of employee health as a business issue.

These include gambling addictions — "the workplace's new crying game," organizational health as a "precondition" for employee wellness, AIDS and chronic illness in the workplace, and cultures of cooperation in the face of employee pressures "to do more with less."

Mutual support is paramount in a healthy workplace. We return to this point again and again throughout this report. We might do well to take instruction from none other than Albert Einstein, as he weighed the consequences of human behaviour for a larger universe he helped define.

In that universe, he mused, we experience ourselves, our thoughts and feelings, as if they are separate from the rest. This amounts to a kind of optical delusion of consciousness and that "delusion is a prison for us, restricting us to our personal desires and to affection for a few persons nearest to us."

He continues: "Our task must be to free ourselves — by widening our circle of compassion to embrace all living creatures and the whole of nature in its beauty."

Now, Einstein might be expecting a lot more than most of us can deliver. But his point about expanding our consciousness has striking relevancy for contemporary society.

In that context, a word from a Canadian, Dr. Richard Bucke, author of *Cosmic Consciousness*, written when North America had reached the end of its geographical frontier and was about to travel another one — technology.

He saw mankind stepping closer to a true identity and destiny to the brink of failure to discover either one. Dr. Bucke's question, posed earlier this century, seems just as appropriate to the closing days of this epochal period.

It is not our eyes and ears or even our intellects that report the world to us; but it is our moral nature that settles at last the significance of what exists about us. The human moral nature, in turn, includes many faculties, such as conscience, the abstract sense of right and wrong, sexual love as distinguished from sexual desire or instinct, parental and filial love, and love of our fellow man as such, love of the beautiful, reverence, sense of duty, responsibility, sympathy, compassion, faith.

✒19 ੨੧
The Metrics of
Human Capital

CORPORATE PRODUCTIVITY IS SIMPLY A SUSTAINABLE CONTRIBUTION TO AN organization's success made by one or more people. Productivity that cannot be sustained isn't productivity at all.

The capacity of any company and its people to achieve higher and higher levels of performance — by producing products or delivering services at a cost less than the net income from customer sales — obviously resides in the resilience of employees who build on today's success and create momentum and profitability — both of which are recognized and rewarded.

This contrasts with another notion that productivity is a relentless, statistical quest where employees are pushed to new limits one day to the next with "no end in sight" and a steady rise in expectations placed upon them by their supervisors — whether actual or perceived.

In fact, this more oppressive version of productivity dominated many corporations throughout the recession of the early 90s. It produced a short-term acceleration of productivity statistics, but at what cost?

The essential strength and durability of the information age will likely be found in the answer to that question — in a kind of corporate productivity that has the effect of nurturing employee wellbeing and inducing employee commitment as companions to its basic purpose of measuring and installing — within the company itself — the level of competitiveness needed to survive and grow in a tense and intense global economy. In some respects, we may find this is the central goal of the 21st Century business agenda now taking shape.

The Upsides are Mutual

The relationship between health and a "nurturing" form of productivity centres on the capacity of people to perform in a manner that produces mutual benefit to them and their employer. But that's not always a clear-cut task.

The process of industrial productivity and the human condition are drawn together by a complex pool of currents: among them the disposition of people flowing from a basic psychological makeup often at odds with their job or their expectations; or the relationships they experience at the worksite plus the employees' own control over their personal work "space."

Personal control of one's own hour-to-hour workload as an element of preserving employee emotional equilibrium — is important in mitigating stress as a negative force. Studies have linked a lack of personal "play-by-play" control at work to the kind of distress that employees are more likely to take home, polluting home life while undermining their resolve or capacity to function productively at work.

Conversely, corporate productivity is enhanced by the degree of support that employees receive at work in the form of personal encouragement, validation of their efforts and reinforcement of the values they bring to their jobs.

Uncertainty at work is a source of terrific grief and can lead to oppressed resilience, anxiety and even depression. Depression is probably the "devil's favorite" disease because of its invasive and insidious nature — and the mask it often wears.

Under some circumstances, stress can trigger depression. But it is probably best to visualize stress as neither a state nor a state of mind. It is a process, a constellation of issues in an unusual galaxy of human experience and predisposition. This murky path can deepen and corrode the human spirit when a person lacks the ability to cope with the lights and the buzz that intense stress may produce.

In 1983, the U.S. National Institute of Mental Health defined 'stress' as a relationship between a particular person with certain characteristics and an environment with certain characteristics, much like the biomedical definition of 'disease.'

Unsettling stress can become distress when individuals are faced with a steady and indigestible diet of ambiguity in the expectations placed upon them at work or in their job mandate, or when the business prospects of the company itself are (or feel) perpetually unsettled.

Deeply personal conflict can sap our productive strength. Things such as fear of the boss, fear of making a mistake because of the likely reaction of our immediate superior, the pressures of coping with obligations at home and work at the same time are increasing, especially among women.

Perhaps one of the most combustible forms of stress undermines the health and productivity of working people. It stems from unpredictable or ineffective management amid enormous worksite change, common during the recession of the early 1990s.

The National Institute of Mental Health, by way of its benchmark report, *How to Define and Research Stress*, says "Stress is a rubric. A *system* of interdependent variables."

This "system" effect is crucial. And a person's reaction to the system depends on how he or she appraises the significance of the encounter to his personal wellbeing and his "possibilities of managing it."

"Stress and emotion are overlapping concepts — emotions (their intensity, their quality and the internal human processes that generate them) tell us more about what is important to people and how they think they are faring in their daily lives than any one reaction to any one encounter of a stressor."

No single circumstance or event can be called a source of stress, the Institute's report says, without us understanding how and why certain people react to it.

A modern-day example of the Institute's point might be electronic voice mail. Some people hate it. Some depend on it. Some find it useful and others want to outlaw it because it minimizes human interaction. Based on that collection of evidence, voice mail cannot be pilloried as a source of stress. Its guilt depends on how and why we individually react to it.

Except, probably, in one respect. Callers who speak normally when they leave messages, bolt through their phone number so fast that the recipient can neither write it down nor note it mentally, probably should be convicted as crazymakers on that ground alone. But even then, the person, not the phone system is guilty as the source of stress.

Seriously, the point is an important one. Business is becoming aware of the negative impact of stress. Disorders related to stress take a toll. For managers, the question nowadays is not *whether* to find a way to reduce workplace stress, but *how*. The answer may be found in the essence of being human. We are all different. Our stressors are varied because our reactions to circumstances, pressures and people vary so widely.

Stress-reduction strategies, in that light, settle like the knowing butterfly on the petal that is most accommodating — in the case of stress, the accommodation is probably found where we should have looked all along: in relationships, in how people treat each other, in how we consider each other's needs. Next time you leave a message on the voice mail, when you come to your phone number, the best stress reduction measure possible is to slow down and say it twice.

Emotional Resilience and Physical Wellbeing

The kind of work climate we create for our employees is every bit as important to good health as good health insurance or generous disability rights. Even more so.

One of the best predictors of the way a person will respond to serious injury or illness is the degree to which they have been able to adjust to the circumstances of their life and work. Emotional resilience is not merely a factor, but a determinant of physical wellbeing, as we discussed at some length just above.

Co-morbid conditions in the workplace are complicated deterrents to productivity — that is, the co-morbidity of mental illness and physical disease, especially those of a chronic variety; the co-morbidity of emotional distress and economic uncertainty playing off each other; the co-morbidity of behavioural disorders like drug and alcohol abuse and clinical depression; the co-morbidity of unhealthy work environments and human genetic predisposition to vulnerability in the workplace itself.

The Washington Business Group on Health, in its *Health Agenda 98* conference in March 1998 reported that there are significant psychosocial incentives to curbing rates of disability.

Across a range of large companies in the United States, researchers found that the strongest predictors of disability days lost, absenteeism for minor illness and on-the-job accident rates are psychosocial work climates. Most powerful among these powerful predictors of disability may well be the employee's own perception of the company's financial prospects, its values, and top management's performance and style.

Disabled employees can be deterred from returning to work by the hangover of a sour perception of what it's like to work for a boss or management team they don't trust or believe in.

Not surprisingly, the new management agenda of the 21st Century will struggle to contain organizational climate "variables" of this nature. They are connected to the health of the organization and therefore to its productivity.

In papers delivered by Dr. Michael Scofield, Chief Science Officer for Solution Point Inc., a U.S. health technology company, and a member of the Faculty of Medicine at Pennsylvania State University and Seton Hall, the "key metric of productivity and organizational health" is said to be the total cost of illness, including its economic impact, through lost workdays and lost productivity. It is here where depression — singly and co-morbid with heart disease — will have its most telling impact in economic terms.

These costs multiply when mental disorders are neither diagnosed nor quantified in the course of managing a physical disability. Low back pain and soft tissue injury, the leading cost drivers in the Canadian Workers' Compensation System, are prime examples of physical disorders that are compounded by emotional distress.

One example used at the Washington Business Group conference compares a coronary artery bypass and an episode of depression in measuring the respective cost effects of a physical and mental disorder. For example, the bypass may cost the healthcare system thousands of dollars in medical expenses and require about six weeks of lost work time. At the same time, an episode of depression may be treated with medication and psychotherapy, a relatively low up-front dollar cost, but the disease results in lost work time of three or more months.

The imperative, in the case of depression, is not spending money, it is spending time — the time and learning necessary for people to recognize the signs of depression in order to facilitate early detection.

In the most troublesome categories of worker disability, the impact of psychiatric illness appears most vividly.

At one corporation in the United States, behavioural disorders and neuro-psychological ailments triggered the second-highest rates of disability across the entire company. Minor back pains and neck disorders were the source of the highest rates — and they too contain a major emotional component.

The Dawn of Life and Work

Disability and employee health issues have had the attention of business managers for a long time, but so-called "life issues" have not. This theme has a certain powerful inevitability — in part because of the greater number of women in management and self-employment.

And because of the surging number of women who must provide for children *and* an elderly person at the same time they work, this is another kind of co-morbidity effect that results when those realities collide to injure the working mother/daughter.

The U.S. Department of Labor projects that by the year 2005, for every 10 men in the work force there will be seven women. There were less than six at the start of the 90s.

Nearly one in four of 22 million U.S. households is involved in family care-giving to elderly relatives or friends.

That caregiver typically is a 46-year-old woman who is employed and spends about 18 hours a week caring for her mother, who lives nearby. Typically, the person receiving the care is a 77-year-old woman who lives alone and has a chronic illness.

Fully three quarters of the care-givers are women and in 30% of the cases, the care-givers are looking after two or more elderly people while one quarter are looking after someone who has dementia. Ten per cent eventually give up their job and about the same number take a leave of absence from work.

Work and life issues are assuming a significant place in the new business management agenda, particularly when one notes that the replacement costs for employees who quit their jobs in order to manage these responsibilities are 75% of the annual salary costs of the departing employee, on top of the incoming person's salary.

The financial and emotional burden associated with eldercare has an economic impact that places it high on the list of priorities awaiting the new management agenda.

The costs of absenteeism are part of this burden — reaching beyond the threshold created by the one in five employees who takes a leave of absence or quit work altogether as a result of the pressures of being squeezed in the 'sandwich generation.'

It has been estimated that employers in the United States pay out nearly $900 million a year because of absent employees who are meeting home-care obligations, including those who arrive late for work or leave early, take extended lunch breaks or experience upwards of 50 hours a year of distractions and downtime. Workday interruptions alone cost U.S. employers nearly $4 billion a year. This calculation is based on the median weekly wage paid to those employees providing elder home care.

The aggregate cost of elder care-giving — as measured in lost productivity to U.S. business — is estimated by one care-giving survey at more than $11 billion per year.

The nature and proliferation of these costs are an expression of the times in which we live, a time of aging, a time of family distress, uncertainty — multiple pressures from varying sources, at the speed of life in the rapid-fire information age. There simply isn't enough time to do the things we have to do. "Time poverty" rattles the emotional equilibrium of millions of otherwise productive people.

Health as a Competitive Advantage
Studies in the United States tell us that corporations, on an impressive scale, are turning to human health as a competitive advantage globally. At the same time, healthcare costs continue to rise at rates that exceed the Consumer Price Index. Employers, however, remain essentially unaware of the magnitude of the health-related costs they pay.

The U.S. and Canadian healthcare systems differ fundamentally in how they access, pay for and fund healthcare. But the issues of work and health are transnational in nature. The experiences of the two countries are pretty well parallel in the degree to which public ignorance about mental illness confounds our national capacity to detect, treat and contain it.

The basic objective of the newly formed Institute for Health and Productivity Management in the United States is to make employee health a "sound investment in business success." This means a greater understanding of the consequences of poor health on productivity and, conversely, the benefits of good health on work performance and profitability.

The bottom line is to give productivity a new face in the information economy. As we noted earlier, corporations have generally relied upon statistically measures associated with a production-line economy. Clearly, that is no longer adequate.

The new agenda for management will require the measurement of productivity to be re-ordered in order to quantify the return on investment in employee health.

A new research agenda is needed not only to design the metrics for this purpose but to deepen our insight into the conditions of work and health that commingle to create the most prevalent forms of mental and chronic physical disorders.

In the United States, studies show that 5% of employees account for 80% of the costs associated with chronic disease. These include cardiovascular illness, cancer, diabetes, asthma, arthritis, muscle and bone injuries, and mental illness as defined by depression and stress-related disorders.

In Canada, the newly formed Canadian Business and Economic Roundtable on Mental Health is helping to illuminate the business stakes tied to the dual impact of depression and heart disease in the same person, a state that predicts sudden death from a second heart attack inside six months of the first.

The new management agenda is also about the concept of organizational health. What is a healthy company? What corporate values are coincident with the values of human health and employee wellbeing? What commitment must companies be prepared to make in order to foster health as the underlying collateral of human capital?

How will employers feel about workplace designs that foster mental health in much the same way as the ergonomic revolution has reduced low back strain and repetitive muscle and bone injuries?

As one observer noted, mental ergonomics is destined to become a thing of the future: "We work in environments where the hard skills have become easy and the easy skills have become hard." We will return to this point later.

Studies point to what has been described as "toxic workplace syndrome," where relationships are buried under values and behaviours at all levels of the company, undermining the economic and emotional cornerstones of trust, respect and fulfillment.

These "environmental issues" are emerging like the ecology involvement in the 60s and 70s, only faster.

The ultimate design of organizational health strategies is still unclear. What is less unclear is the growing urgency of heading off the escalating pattern of work days lost to mental disorders, principally depression and anxiety disorders, including panic attacks — all of which are far more common in the workplace than we have recognized up to now.

The "co-morbidity crisis" shows up in a variety of studies that illustrate the complicating effects when more than one disorder is present but only one is diagnosed or treated. This may help explain the length of illness and injury especially for soft tissue and low back problems — the principal drivers of worker compensation claims. Both entail emotional dimensions that often go untreated except passively through drugs.

Productivity and Judgment
Through the industrial age, increases in productivity were realized through mechanical means — automation being one, the redesign of production lines being another.

Productivity gains produced by machines centre on speed, frequency and blind efficiency. In a future framed by the information economy, productivity will be measured by the capacity of human beings to manage information where speed is a given, thanks to new computer technology, but creativity, innovation, judgment, predictable quality and empathetic customer relationships will make the critical difference.

This is the basic transformation now taking place as we move from an industrial society to an information one. This illustrates the meditation of Pepsico CEO, Roger Enrico, who says "mindsets" will grow business.

Organizational health has been described by some as the sum of the number of healthy people inside the workplace. That is a limiting and narrow definition, and insufficient for the purposes of defining the challenge it reflects. In fact, organizational health gives expression to the composition of values, enlightened management practices and working relationships among people based on respect, empathy and trust. The Bank of Montreal's Maria Gonzalez says organizational health and work climates are synonymous — and both are pre-conditions to the sustainable financial performance of the company promoting them.

These are the most fundamental and often the most elusive characteristics in the practical design of a healthy organization.

Texas Instruments is one of the largest corporations in the world. Its vision says that competitive advantage "is a culture that optimizes performance through work and life quality." This is one way of describing "balance" between the personal and job lives of working people.

The people at Texas Instruments seem to believe that individual performance is the result of health and wellbeing at two levels. One level is physical well-being, mental health and a sense that the lives of their employees are headed in the right direction. On another level, there is the individual's search for a deeper satisfaction with life, emotional intelligence and social harmony.

The company has introduced a variety of devices to support the expression of these values: programs to manage time lost, travel policies that minimize fatigue, strategies aimed specifically at reducing corrosive conditions such as hypertension, on-site flu vaccination and personal counselling to avoid unnecessary and destructive stress.

In all of this we see corporate efforts to contain the cost of health benefits and improve productivity intersecting with efforts to meet employee needs.

One U.S. study revealed that in one large U.S. corporation, fully 30% of all disability claims were lifestyle-related and $40 million of cost was attributable to poor lifestyles of employees. At the same time, the question that went unstated — and unresolved — was how the work climate contributed to these lifestyle issues. Inevitably they did. These findings showed that stress-related disorders were by far the leading category of health-related expense. Alcohol abuse and drug abuse were second and third. Others ranged from smoking to high blood pressure to a lack of exercise.

That same study uncovered a drop in those same disability statistics when the company and the individual worked together to identify conditions in the organization that produced pressures triggering such behaviours, while at the same time, seeking ways to modify the behaviours of the employees themselves.

Decline of Paternalism

Times are changing. Some management groups are gravitating away from decisions based on rules and regulations inside the workplace to decisions based upon values and the views of employees who take part in the decision-making process. One example is the incremental movement away from paternalistic corporate policies. Employee responsibility, accountability and job flexibility reflect the newer order of things.

Another shift is moving companies away from mass recruitment practices to targeting people with specific skills and attributes. The Bank of Montreal has established personal effectiveness and emotional intelligence as characteristics they will hire for and not train for. The goal is to improve the success rate in matching people with jobs they are best suited for. One objective worldwide among corporations of all stripes is to reduce termination and turnover costs, among the highest costs facing business today.

Another transition now under way will rescue business from narrow and self-destructive efforts to control healthcare costs by reducing access to supplementary health benefits or services. This knee-jerk approach has been replaced by recognition that an investment in health means access to needed benefits, raising the odds of an early return to work by a disabled employee.

Compensation and reward systems have changed. Incentives based on the performance of the company now reach much farther down into the employee ranks. New union contracts, workplace flexibility and job-sharing have all contributed to the remaking of work environments where health is a common cause of employers and employees alike. The health of the individual is reflected in the health of the organization.

In fact, the health of employees is being seen as a differentiator as companies seek new ways to sharpen their competitive edge. The Texas Instrument experience gives us an important insight.

In the late '80s and early '90s, the focus of that company centred on "how to manage this building" — referring metaphorically to the immediacy of a plant or production line.

In this light, human affairs — including health — were more or less incidental. And frankly, often a distraction to the process of managing the building and the "things" that happened there.

Texas Instruments changed its focus. It invested in the prevention of disease, promotion of values and creation of a hospitable workplace. An interesting perspective emerged. They invested this way in 92% of their work force at a rate of $1,100 per employee, or about $1 billion dollars. A mere 1% improvement in the productive capacity of the active work force annually yields $11 million in productivity gains.

Meanwhile, 8% of TI's workforce is disabled and off work, representing about $18 million a year, an expense of $11,000 per employee. A significant 10% improvement on those base costs — in terms of reducing the disability — yields only $1.8 million in savings.

The strategic investment in the active work force has dramatic potential. As part of that, a *strategic investment* in health may be the biggest single contributor.

Delta Airlines seems to agree. It tries to match investment in human resources to the company's strategic business objectives, saying "health-related expenditures create value." Delta introduced a model equating the dollar value they put on their employees to the dollar value they hoped to realize through the operating performance of their business and the shareholder value they aimed to create.

The "Value Game"

Value has become a big word in business. It centres on the question of financial capital and human capital as two sides of one very important strategic coin. A *Globe and Mail* supplement published by the Richard Ivey School of Business at the University of Western Ontario chronicles the growth of "value management" systems.

One model centres on the measurement of economic value, another on shareholder value. We are cautioned, these "financial systems are not magic elixirs, but can be effective tools to ensure that management remains focused on creating value".

Central to these concepts is the efficient use of available *financial* capital. Economic value added is calculated using an equation of net operating profit after tax, minus the cost of capital. In an age of information and *human* capital, a new construct might inject the value of human effort into the front end of the calculation — before tax.

The Xerox Corporation, famous for having reinvented itself in the 1980s, concludes that the productive workplace of the future will require management groups to attain a greater understanding of what it takes to make people want to come to work in the morning. The question is one of attitude — the attitude of the organization, the attitude of its leaders and the attitude of its workers. The company has established a direct link between the climate of a hospitable workplace and the level of employee motivation. The Bank of Montreal in Canada is forging a similar link through a new initiative it calls "shifting the performance curve."

Xerox found that customer satisfaction and business results were linked to the same underlying qualities of the environment it expected its people to work in. In a study at its Customer Administration Centre in Dallas, Xerox found that employees had a feeling of no control over their schedules, their work and therefore their lives. The objective, therefore, was to build employee teams to come up with working schedules and set priorities as a means of improving business results.

Xerox found, as have many other corporations, that morale sinks when employees view their management as having no idea of the time it takes to do things or how much time is wasted by unclear expectations, shifting priorities and plain work interruptions. For every manager and employee, time is especially scarce in this day and age. Wasting other people's time is a corporate health issue.

Emotional Work Hazards

The Xerox study found that the day-to-day reactionary nature of the corporation created a sense of crisis and disorganization that undermined the sense of place and usefulness they expected their employees to have.

The "work hazards" they uncovered ranged from constant interruptions and lack of any sense by the employees that they had enough time to get their job done. The remedial measure that Xerox introduced was to give people a sense of greater control over their time and make managers more conscious of the time constraints that the employee groups worked under.

For Generation X and the Baby Boomers, time, not money, is often the most precious commodity of all. Xerox began scheduling parts of the day when managers could not interrupt their engineering staff, for example, and when a person working on an assignment could be assured they would not be randomly interrupted even by their peer group.

The Xerox experiment found that when time itself — a non-renewable resource, so to speak — does not seem important to senior people, the result is a more densely harried and less innovative workplace, which isn't unique to this company.

In the days when automation produced efficiencies that in turn defined progress, such issues were moot. The quality movement changed all that. Like other companies, Xerox saw that its productivity goals had to be balanced with the needs of employees in the task of managing their work, in short giving them a chance "to have a life" as well as a job. Even in a tight job market, having one without the other fast becomes no loaf at all.

This study essentially expressed the importance of empathy as a management tool — through empathy, the impact of work processes are seen through a "personal lens." Empathy-based leadership recognizes that people have a life outside work and that to get work done, supervisors, co-workers and people up and down the hierarchy had to respect that "other life."

In this light, the self-interest of the corporation is served by the search for things that satisfy and motivate the staff. This search produces something else, a legitimate expectation that the company will receive employee commitment in return.

PepsiCo is one of the world's major corporations. When its Chairman and Chief Executive Officer, Roger Enrico, said "mindsets grow businesses," he may have been referring to the mindsets of those who make the sale. Selling takes optimism. But the wider implication is doubly relevant at a time of enormous change when the so-called "exclusive contract" between employer and employee has become something of an artifact.

Measuring Intangible Assets

In its promotion of healthy mindsets, PepsiCo deployed "a balanced scorecard," to take a picture of the organization. Scorecards supplement standard financial measures with operational metrics that assist managers to monitor progress in building up "the intangible assets of the company."

Scorecards are not new in business. They have been used to measure how a company looks financially to its shareholders, to its customers in terms of service and quality and to its employees. Scorecards help illuminate what the company is really good at, what it excels at, how the internal processes work. Scorecards have helped companies learn where and how to grow. PepsiCo's *balanced* scorecard brought a broader dimension and the company established four main benchmarks. Mr. Enrico and his colleagues would measure employee enthusiasm, financial performance, customer experience and how consumers generally felt about the company.

Historically, the profit and loss statement was the only benchmark that mattered. PepsiCo stepped beyond that perimeter and introduced what they describe as the "marketplace P&L" to act as headlights for the company, to complement the rear-view mirror effect of financial reporting.

Metrics of this nature not only *do not* obscure "tough realities" a company must always deal with, but tend to help management recognize and deal with them. Pepsico is a case in point. Over the past 19 months, according to published reports in the *Wall Street Journal*, the company has spun-off its $10 billion fast-food operations, shaken up the international beverage business and taken on its arch-enemy Coca-Cola in the orange juice market.

Recently, the company moved closer to publishing a share offering of its bottling operations. If that happens, the company that emerges will be half its former size, with higher profit margins.

Profitability and Human Health

The point is, measures to deal with the emotional health of employees are not designed to alter the basic premise upon which businesses function — to make money. Without profitability, a company will not survive. What *can* change, what *is* changing, is the way organizations go after bread and butter goals.

Large corporations in Canada and the United States — as a result of intensified global competition and the spectacular advent of new information technology — have sought to become more flexible, adaptable organizations. At the same time, new skill sets are urgently in demand and there is a growing shortage of employees who have the know-how needed in the new knowledge economy. This is an essential point about human capital.

In the information age, machines will depend on people more

than people on machines — a complete reversal from the industrial era we are now exiting. And employee needs are changing, because of enormous alterations in social and economic norms.

For example, studies tell us that 62% of employees in the United States have dependent care responsibilities; 64% of women who work have family responsibilities; 51% of men have wives who work outside the home; and fully one fourth of working parents also have responsibilities for an aging relative. Single-parent homes have become increasingly common.

More than a third of all employees surveyed feel their productivity has declined because of child care problems. And more than half of the absenteeism in the United States is attributable to family-related problems. These are signs of a dramatically changing workplace.

We noted earlier in this report that companies that realized improvements in their bottom lines through straight cost reduction — without revenue and market growth — did less well in share value than those who led their industry through a combination of bottom and top line excellence. The topline is an expression of the human factor at work, validating the PepsiCo CEO's "mindset mandate."

One of the challenges facing business is helping employees to manage productivity "distractions" and reduce absenteeism.

In a series of studies sponsored by some of the best known company names in the United States (Johnson & Johnson, Chase Manhattan Bank, AT&T, Motorola, Xerox, Marriott Hotels and the Merck Corporation) we see clear evidence of the dramatic business up-sides of investing in employee health.

The study said corporations that help their employees balance work and life — principally through the resolution of time conflicts — will attract a more qualified and committed work force, and in the process realize a distinct health-based competitive advantage. The bottom line enhancements that flow from an investment of this kind are distinct and impressive: higher morale, reduced absenteeism and lateness, lower turnover, improved workflow and, crucially, an increase in the perceived value of the employees themselves.

New Ways to Value People

In today's environment, work/life programs are not exclusively for women, but clearly the "sandwich generation" is heavily populated by working mothers and single parents who are juggling work and home responsibilities at a feverish pace.

Corporations such as IBM, Johnson & Johnson, Corning and

AT&T are among those making fundamental changes in the way people are valued — this, in the face of some enormous pressures flowing from competitive disadvantages that AT&T, for one, is facing in the wake of huge layoffs.

Again though, the point should be underlined. Enlightened policies tying human health to business performance are not in conflict with tough business decisions that must be made to sustain the survival or profitability of the company itself. The opposite is true: they are aimed at sustaining corporate performance. Such initiatives may range from the redesign of work processes to rewards for innovative practices and work/life strategies.

The recognition of "balance" in merging work and family priorities may take the form of flexible arrangements for work schedules and work locations; the creation of career paths that accommodate both professional ambitions and family responsibilities; innovative leave programs and time away from the workplace; mid-life technology training; and a corporate commitment to fairness in all things.

In this, equal access to opportunity or personal growth is all-important and is exhibited in many of the programs that were discussed at the Washington Business Group on Health conference.

The Washington Business Group tells us that leaders across industry are rethinking workplace systems, work processes and the nature and impact of organizational culture on financial results — all in the face of new evidence about the effect these factors have on employee health and satisfaction and, along that route, the productivity of the company itself.

The search is on for ways to value "people factors" and tie them tightly into business planning. Xerox Corporation is participating in a Ford Foundation study rethinking life and work using a variety of catalysts for organizational change and work practices that treat the sensibilities and emotional needs of employees respectfully.

The PepsiCo balanced scorecard illustrated the merits of a conscious business decision taken by one leading corporation that is attempting to advance its position in a globally competitive workplace where human capital is assuming greater currency each passing day.

The experience of the Dupont Company also illustrates the point. Dupont introduced a range of return-to-work plans and, in Canada, has been a leader in this field. At the same time, General Electric introduced a "one-stop shopping" form of disability management for its employees. Such initiatives come straight from the head, not the heart. They make business sense.

Low Hanging Fruit All Picked

The Washington Business Group on Health notes that "even as the stock market soars and confidence in the economy is at an all-time high, the 'low-hanging fruit' of business cost-cutting and restructuring has been picked." In fact, despite the massive cost reductions in North America, business productivity has shown little, if any, improvement. Canada faces a productivity gap between its competitors and the world.

At the same time, the demands on business are substantial. Globalization has made it absolutely imperative for companies to have access to people, ideas and products from any part of the world they need to draw from. Sustainable performance is more than a buzzword. It will be a way of life for corporations in the 21st Century.

The Morality of Practical Thinking

One of the premiere business organizations in the world, Canada's Bank of Montreal certainly grasps the point.

The Bank of Montreal has won international awards for its human resource practices, and now has embarked upon a bold and comprehensive "people initiative" to prepare itself for the 21st Century.

Vice-President of Strategic Initiatives, and architect of the Bank of Montreal's "Shifting the Performance Curve" initiative, Maria Gonzalez tells us that "what we knew morally — creating a work climate supportive of human effort — was critical to business success, is now something we can demonstrate and prove. That's new." The process of creating and measuring a high-performance culture is now a much more scientific process than it ever was in the past.

Ms. Gonzalez spoke to the authors of this report about re-profiling the concept of human performance at the Bank of Montreal, pointing to organizational health and emotional intelligence as two of the heartbeats that will fuel the program's success, and energize its potential.

Q: *First, let's start with terminology. How do you define organizational health?*
Gonzalez: Organizational health is synonymous with work climate. Both are key to the success of this initiative.
Q: *What prompted the Bank to decide to shift the performance curve, as you call it?*
Gonzalez: About 18 months ago, we began to ask ourselves, "What will differentiate this bank from other financial services institutions

in a world where new technology is a fact of life and where financial products, in time, can be replicated, sometimes overnight? In the face of all that is happening in a global economy," we asked, "what will make us different?" And we answered that question by creating what our President, Tony Comper, describes as a "high performance culture — a culture, when all else is said and done, of best practitioners fully engaged in best practices."

Q: *The first step?*

Gonzalez: Recognizing, first of all, that the true difference we offer our customers is the people we employ — and in turn, the belief of our employees in themselves and in the organization's purposes. Profitability and human performance are inextricably linked — something we now can scientifically prove.

Q: *What did your research tell you?*

Gonzalez: One of our initial findings was that people were a leading indicator of financial performance as much as two to three years in advance of the results an organization the size of the Bank of Montreal can hope to achieve. We also found that if we tap into what the customer is thinking, we are about a year away. So this is a long-term strategy.

Q: *Was there another critical fact that stood out in the early going of your research?*

Gonzalez: Yes, the role of the **manager** in the Bank — and by manager, I am not just talking about reporting lines. I am referring to anyone with responsibility for the work of others.

The manager, in this sense, has a great impact on employee performance — and as we move increasingly to projects, work committees and task forces, and less traditional reporting lines, the manager of the future, as we define the term, will have responsibility for these outputs as well.

Q: *Did your research include an historical assessment of management practices?*

Gonzalez: Very much so. We reviewed literature over the past 25 years and did best practice work with other organizations. Through internal interviews, we also identified "role models" for managers and in this way signalled the importance of the manager in the successful implementation of this initiative.

Q: *Was the "performance-shifting" initiative introduced on a bankwide basis?*

Gonzalez: Yes. And we are looking for differences and commonalities at all levels that will enhance and sustain performance. In this respect, sustainable performance does not mean short-term results. We are in this for the long term.

Q: *What are some of the practical or operating implications of this initiative?*

Gonzalez: Well, for one thing, we will now hire for specific attributes or characteristics (as opposed to competencies). Personal effectiveness is one — the ability to get things done and communicate a vision for people at any level of the organization. Emotional intelligence or self-awareness is another — how you impact other people through your own behaviours or how you are affected by the behaviour of others — these are critical underpinnings of the kind of people we will look for in the future.

Q: *Did you consider the question of personal values?*

Gonzalez: We saw values as another component of the hiring criteria in addition to personal attributes. It is vital to have the right match between the culture of the organization and the values of the people.

Q: *We have heard you distinguish between what the Bank will "train for" and what you will "hire for." Explain that for us a bit further.*

Gonzalez: Well, for example, we will hire for emotional intelligence. It will form part of the hiring criteria at the Bank of Montreal in the future. We don't believe we can entirely train for that. It is learned early in life and, in fact, there is an ethical question as to whether an employer should even try.

On the other hand, we believe we can train for management skills — the technical knowledge and basics required to function as a good manager — conducting interviews, doing performance evaluations, managing compensation issues. If the person's personal effectiveness and emotional intelligence are already in place, we can train for these other skills.

Q: *Have you developed a tool for this purpose?*

Gonzalez: We are in the process of developing a mandatory curriculum for managers that will serve as a pre-condition for attaining a position from the most junior to the most senior.

Q: *What are some of the performance levers you have identified so far?*

Gonzalez: A critical one is making sure the skillsets of people and their jobs are the right match. All of us come to this world with certain gifts and the question is "do we use them or not?"

Positive results arise from people who are in jobs where they use their skills. But when there is a mismatch, they experience a very destructive fear of incompetence, of being "found out."

For example, when a person is in a position they are suited for, but still must learn aspects of it, they have a very positive learning experience. When that's not true, the learning experience becomes a source of stress. Where people and their job are a fit, they will perform better.

Q: *In your terms, what constitutes organizational health?*

Gonzalez: An environment that is supportive, where opinions count, where voices are heard, where people are recognized for their efforts and their accomplishments.

An environment too, where teams are supported. This brings us back to the importance of the manager. As much as 75% of an individual's performance is attributed to the manager. Organizational and individual needs reinforce each other. While that's obvious, I suppose, sometimes in the past, across many organizations, it didn't always seems like it was.

An Issue of Billions and Millions

Ms. Gonzalez, in a speech to the Employee Assistance Society of North America, said the principles of organizational health were tied to another major question linking business and health generally: mental health.

"It is important to acknowledge the fact that we need to demystify mental health and mental illness in business terms. We come to work as human beings and we don't become something different when we walk through the door at work."

She said the containment of mental illness is a "billions and millions" issue — billions of wasted or productive dollars and millions of wasted or productive lives. That's what's at stake. Those are the choices.

"This," Ms. Gonzalez said, "has enormous repercussions for the conduct of business, for the realization of sustainable economic performance broadly, and for the sustainable performance of the Bank or any other corporation."

It is remarkable, she said, "how much we *leave on the table* by not maximizing the efforts of people, because of under-productivity and lost opportunity costs."

The question of sustainable mental health — as an ingredient of organizational health or as an outcome of it — is relevant to an earlier point raised by Ms. Gonzalez — that is, employee-job matching.

"Employees who are not well matched with their job are not very healthy — the problem is fear, fear of otherwise competent people being discovered as 'incompetent.'"

"A healthy organizational climate," she said "is a pre-condition of sustainable high financial performance."

The Bank of Montreal's organizational initiative is a profoundly important milestone in the industrial transformation we are witnessing worldwide — a shift away from a preponderant reliance on financial capital as the measure and tool of corporate performance, to the advancement of human capital as a strategic tool to achieve concrete, bottom-line, competitive ends.

A health-based economy may be less than a generation of business leaders away. And in saying that, we might recall, as people live longer and get older, the corporate lifespans of business leaders at the top are getting shorter. So a generation in these terms is not such a long time after all.

Interconnected Forces of Change

Aside from the need for flexibility in the workplace, flexible attitudes, flexible work arrangements, the capacity of employees to adapt to change, and the refashioning of competencies from one discipline to another — aside from all this — is a growing demand for ways to measure investment in health and disability. Without these metrics, the efforts to forge health-based productivity models will take on a desperate and ill-focused form.

Three interrelated forces confront business strategists in the early dawn hours of the 21st Century.

One is the global demand for knowledge-based workers and a capacity for self-initiated change by working populations. A second is the need to rely on incentives to marshal non-exclusive employee relationships to retain employee loyalty. A third is the shift to looking at the future through the valuation of human capital.

The Washington Business Group on Health picked up the challenge and recently introduced, at a June conference, a new model for making and measuring the investment in people as a channel to "corporate growth and success."

"A decade ago," they said, "few human resource professionals thought it was possible to demonstrate the value of dollars spent on employee health beyond program-cost containment and [certainly not] in terms meaningful to business performance. Healthcare and disability benefits were seen as costs of doing business, and rapidly rising costs at that."

Times have changed, thanks to new information technology and advances in disease prevention, new knowledge about human behaviour, advances in scientific understanding of the brain, break-throughs in understanding mental illness as a biochemical disorder and progress in devising management practices that deploy the strengths of the work force and reduce blind reliance on automated production equipment (thanks to the information revolution). The financial and asset value of people is becoming a measurable part of corporate planning and success.

♨20♨
The Lengthening Shadow of Mental Disability

NOTABLY, DISEASE AND INJURY ARE COSTING CANADA MORE MONEY in economic terms — through lost productivity, for one thing — than we spend on the healthcare system itself. In other words, the effects of disease cost more than its diagnosis and treatment.

The single fastest-growing cost within the healthcare system itself, prescription drugs, is paid for in Canada mostly through private insurance. And coverage is not as widespread as a lot of people thought. Hence the push for some kind of national pharmacare program.

Considering the understated impact of mental illness, and our collective illiteracy on the subject, it isn't hard to conclude that business is facing a very sharp learning curve in order to get a handle on the influences inside and outside the workplace that affect the resilience of its employees. In the face of Harvard's forecast of the devastating future impact of depression, the case for mental illness as a business issue seems indisputable.

A second feature of the Washington Group's new model for health and productivity centres on work time lost. Throughout this report we have referred to the impact of mental illness on the productivity of working people through work days lost.

The Washington model returns us to the whole question of disability as a prominent health concern of the 21st century. Certainly, it is a major economic issue that will be resolved as much through non-medical means as through the healthcare system itself. The economic incentives differ.

When disability and not just life expectancy is taken into account as a measure of the health of working populations, the profile of psychiatric illness sharpens and its shadow lengthens.

Let us re-examine the indirect costs of clinical depression in the United States. The annual cost is an estimated $44 billion. Of that amount, only $12 billion is spent on direct treatment. The rest is expressed in lost work time and lower productivity.

Compared to other fairly common conditions, like diabetes, back pain and heart disease, depression is often the most tenacious, its length of disability longest and the probability of recurrence greatest. In fact, as we noted earlier, more than 80 percent of depression cases can be effectively treated, but three quarters of them are not even diagnosed.

Lost work time is relatively easy to measure, and it is used by many employers as a yardstick for the success of programs such as disability or disease management. It is also "a window through which to look at relationships between work force health, work climate and productivity," in the words of the Washington Business Group on Health.

In one example, 199 of Bell Atlantic's 5,700 U.S. employees were absent each day. The company estimated the total cost of lost time, including wages, lost sales, overhead costs, out-sourcing services and the costs of managing short-term disability, training and other related costs, at $45 million each year.

A 2% decrease in turnover, meanwhile, would save that company $14 million over five years. Reducing absenteeism by two days per employee per year would yield nearly $6 million.

After two years, through dollar incentives to improve work climate, increased employee control over their hour-to-hour, day-to-day work agendas, and introducing proactive return to work and disability support measures, the company reduced lost time by 55%, the average short-term disability duration rate by 40% and new disability claims by 15%.

The return on this investment in the health of the Bell Atlantic employees was realized not only in reversing growth of absenteeism, but in new sales, higher productivity and improved employee morale.

The third phase of the new model advanced by the Washington Business Group on Health establishes health and productivity as two sides of the same coin. That said, there are few tools or metrics available to measure the impact or value of health in these terms. Such metrics await further investigation.

The authors of a Michigan State University study comparing workers' compensation costs for 50 companies found that work climates in which teamwork, open communications, and the profit-sharing with employees were promoted, by and large correlated with lower disability expenses per employee.

In another study of 30 business units by Solution Point Inc. researchers found that a number of work climate factors, such as understanding company goals and objectives, respect and employee satisfaction with the company, were found to predict rates of disability, on-the-job accidents and absence due to sickness.

These findings point to a new role for human resource professionals in business. That is a timely point of reference for many who worry that the HR function has either lost its way or should be abolished altogether.

HR Obsolence

Earlier this year, the *Harvard Business Review* confronted that question rather directly. "Should we do away with HR?" author Dr. Dave Ulrich asked in an article for that distinguished journal. A teacher at the University of Michigan's School of Business in Ann Arbor, he calls for an entirely new role and agenda for practitioners in this critical field, characterized by:
- Moving to a strategic level
- Becoming an expert in the organization and execution of work
- Becoming a stronger champion and voice for employees
- Becoming an agent of continuous transformation
none of which, Dr. Ulrich says, is happening now.

The urgency of the issue is self-apparent. Forces abound: globalization, profitability through growth, the infusion of technology and the management of intellectual capital, topics discussed thoroughly in this report.

The author says human resource practitioners should identify the underlying organizational model of the way companies do business, plan an architectural role. Dr. Ulrich cites six characteristics that the human resource architecture should embrace.

One is the shared mindset that must exist in a company for it to meet its goals, the question of culture. A second is the competence of the organization — its knowledge and skill base.

A third is the competence of the organization — the incentive and reward system it needs to motivate its people and get what needs doing done. A fourth is governance — the right organizational structure, communications systems and policies. A fifth is capacity for change — to what extent, Dr. Ulrich asks, does the company have the ability to improve, change and learn? And, finally leadership — the critical engagement of people in pursuit of goals within a strategy beneath a vision. Dr. Ulrich cites a prominent example of HR working on this level. Let's listen in:

HR played an important part in changing the culture at Sears, which underwent a transformation of its business beginning in 1994. In facilitating that change, HR first took on the task of getting the organization to define and clarify the concept of culture. It helped lead the top 100 managers through discussions and debates of the questions: What are the top three things we want to be known for by our customers? And what do we do that is world class in those things?

Ultimately, those conversations led to a consensus that Sears would define its culture as "the identify of the company, in the minds of the best customers." In addition, HR at Sears took on the responsibility of making the business case for a transformation of the company's culture. It compiled data showing that even a small increase in employee commitment led to a measurable increase in customer commitment and store profitability. The data illustrates conclusively that Sear's transformation affected employees, customers, and investors.

HR at Sears guided the company's culture change in numerous other ways. The specific details, however, are not nearly as important as their implications. HR can be the architect of new cultures, but to do so, its purpose must be redefined. Virtually every imperative of the new mandate for HR requires such a redefinition. For that to happen, senior managers must lead the way.

The Washington Business Group on Health goes on to say that the central challenge facing corporations today is the development of human resource policies to measure the connections between the company's financial performance and values associated with human health. But there is little research available to use in designing these new metrics.

The basic task remains to define the contribution that people make to corporate values and financial results. And, in the same light, to assign concrete values to the underlying collateral of productive human behaviour, which is human health. Going one immediate step further, to recognize the value of mental health as a productivity weapon in an environment where the mind has replaced the back as the principal instrument of labour.

The Duration Crisis

Having awakened to the effects that disability has on human and economic performance, we are then able to see the eventual role of mental illness in forming and forging the most troublesome forms of disability, those of long duration.

There is a certain amount of "obvious truth" to all this. And the fact is that in the 21st Century the most successful companies will be those that invest in people to build human capital, which means preserving and protecting the mental health of their employees, through, among other things, resiliency and mid-life renewal strategies.

The fact also remains that the most successful companies demonstrate an ability to attract and hold onto talented employees. In the latest survey by *Fortune* magazine of "the most admired companies in the world," this single fact stood out most boldly as the most reliable predictor of overall excellence.

The Washington Business Group's health and productivity model links a variety of conventional, less conventional, and new concepts to help measure return on the investment in employee health.

Three main components revolve around the concept of health management. One is improving the work climate. The second is hiring the right people for the right job. And the third is fostering new skills among employees in their present jobs, not just holding out the carrot of promotion or job change as the necessary precursor to personal development. People want to do what they are already doing — only better.

The Washington model embraces an integrated approach to healthcare services, disability management, health promotion, disease management and employee assistance. While this is not a new idea, it becomes one when it is connected to the creation of new value systems that sculpt the relevance of employee efforts to the company's financial results. They produce a new corporate constitution where human health and corporate productivity are aligned as "strategic partners" in the success of the business.

Near Perfect Quality

In the case of General Electric, 'near-perfect quality' is a principal value. In turn, the company includes in that definition the health of employees and sets out employee health as access to medical care, work satisfaction measurements and best management practices.

At the centre of all is a single word: 'leadership.' Business leadership can inspire employee commitment and job satisfaction, and has everything to do with the clarity of expression that employees need to do their jobs and to know what is expected of them and what, in their own minds, they expect of themselves. Leadership, grounded in empathy, is telltale. A company's vision must be a shared experience and the attitudes of employees invariably influence the decisions senior management makes.

The Hay Management Consulting Group in Toronto recently published an "integrated consulting model" rooted in the premise that investing in good practices in treatment, encouragement and support of individuals in the workplace has a direct impact on reducing employee turnover, improving productivity and, in fact, the financial performance of the company itself.

Hay reports on efforts to quantify this investment per employee. Some of the results are quite stunning. In one case, turnover was decreased by more than seven per cent a year; in another, sales, market value and net income per employee were increased by more than $27,000 (U.S.), $18,000 and $3,000 respectively.

Hay reported that a study of 30 American steel mini-mills shows that those with human resource systems based on an articulated commitment to employees enjoy higher productivity, lower scrap rates and lower employee turnover than mills using "control" human resource systems.

The latter is based on employee compliance with rules and procedures; this forges psychological links between the goals of the organization and the needs and aspirations of the employee.

"Commitment systems" are marked by higher levels of employee involvement in managerial decisions, by formal compensation programs with incentives and participation in the financial returns of the company, group problem-solving, training, and higher percentages of skilled employees and average wage rates.

The Hay paper also reports that an agricultural production company with a number of worksites found that the way employees perceived the fairness and accuracy built into the company's pay for performance and promotion system were important predictors of how committed those employees would be to that organization.

In fact, the study showed that these issues were more important in fostering employee loyalty than demographics, the characteristics of the jobs they performed, the "social environment" inside the company or the quality of supervision they received.

In a study of 25 work areas of large unionized manufacturing facilities over four years, researchers found that worksites marred by traditional poor labour management relations — rooted in adversarial attitudes towards "the other side" — had higher costs; and more scrap materials indicated wasteful manufacturing practices and lower profits. The study showed that co-operation in the workplace is more productive and more profitable.

Through the lens of these studies, we see the importance of enlightened recruitment practices and an absolute need for drawing out the highest motives and best instincts on both sides of the employment contract if the emotional ties between the employee and employer are going to be healthy and conducive to productive behaviour.

At the heart of this proposition is the acknowledgment of individuals as a composition of physical and mental characteristics which are influenced by predisposition, biochemistry, value systems, and environments in which they work and the expectations they work under.

Where Mental Health Begins
"Building on the strength of people" makes fairness an easy doctrine to apply. Getting the right person into the right job is where mental health in the workplace begins.

The Canadian Mental Health Association assembled a team to examine mental health and the workplace environment. The team found that there were two important sources of employee stress — job demands and the amount of control a worker has in meeting those demands. We visited this point earlier. It is reinforced here.

The team said that "without risking productivity, job-related mental health can improve by increasing employee autonomy, regardless of the workload involved.

Mental health is affected by the organization of work, including how tasks are defined and assigned. "When employees feel they have little influence over the organization and design of their work, they are less likely to enjoy good health."

One of the members of that team, a leading Canadian authority on organizational health was Dr. Martin Shain, Head of the Workplace Program, the Centre for Health Promotion at the University of Toronto. Dr. Shain will be a guest lecturer at the Homewood Centre for Organizational Health in late 1998 as part of the Lett series.

In a paper he co-authored with Helen Suurvali, Dr. Shain says health in the workplace "is increasingly seen less as a state and more as a dynamic, an ever-changing product of transactions between individuals and their social, physical environments." This is reminiscent us of the National Institute on Mental Health definition of workplace stress as a process.

"Mental and physical wellbeing are intimately connected" by the relationships that the people experience, characterized by mutual respect, trust, personal regard — or a lack of them. The presence or absence of these factors can yield health or illness. Either way, the physical and mental self are tied. The organization of the workplace itself is an influence on health, Dr. Shain and his colleague say, referring to the physical layout and design of the work environment as well as the psychosocial aspects of how work is planned, managed and executed. People bring their values, attitudes, beliefs and practices to work; but once they are there, the workplace exerts significant influences upon them — and the effects are never neutral. They either promote health or defeat it, sometimes in combination.

Examining the same theme, Dr. Raymond Fowler, CEO of the American Psychological Association, relates "quality and fairness" to the efficacy and hospitality of the workplace. He says they are a major factor in the health and wellbeing of working people. The APA's newspaper, *Monitor*, examines the links between psychology and work. In doing so, it describes the 1990s as "like a trailer for a Hollywood film, previewing the coming attractions of what we can expect 'more of' as we emerge into the re-engineered fast lane of the 21st Century world of work."

Monitor says a "better understanding and nurturing of the human side of business" is on a par with streamlined advances in information technology in creating a workplace that functions to the advantage of those who invest in it — and those who work in it. Recognizing personality as a factor of job performance is part of this "other" side of business.

In one study, Hewlett Packard Corporation found growing numbers of "isolated" employees achieving a new sense of belonging through a "process of engagement."

Dr. Kevin Murphy, President of the Society for Industrial Organizational Psychology, says 20-year careers in one company are less likely with fewer large corporations, and more flexible, less exclusive and more changeable job arrangements.

Employee and even executive training, as we noted earlier, will become a way of life in this kind of environment. One expert predicts that by the year 2010 it will take 50% of a workday simply to catch up on the information you received the day before. The challenge becomes how to prepare organizations and individuals for the change that this portends in worklife.

Imprisoning Disability

From a different pole, we see the other part of the human relations challenge facing business in a post-deficit society: the spreading effects of psychiatric disability.

Nearly three fourths of employers responding to a recent survey on the place of the mentally disabled said that the reluctance of employees to come back to work is perhaps the biggest obstacle of all that employees face after a term of disability. Stigma is one reason. The melting away of self-esteem is another. Fear of the unknown, can they perform their job again? is another.

In 75% of cases, the employer said in a U.S. survey by the William M. Mercer Company, it was more difficult to return mentally disabled employees to work than it was those who were physically disabled.

The issue that face employers is uncertainty about how to create a supportive environment for employees who must return to work in order to get better.

Nearly a third of the employers polled pointed to this as question number one. But there was another: did they even want this person back?

The Mercer study said behavioural disorders are on the rise as a source of disability, but remain difficult to nail down in terms of how to manage them in the workplace. In this light, the question of comorbidity raises its head once again. Mercer consultant Colleen McMurray: "These types of problems are often masked by concurrent physical problems that may underlie a behavioural disorder."

An article in the *Journal of Commerce* noted that headaches, backaches and stomach aches "can all be a manifestation of behavioural health problems" but the question for employers is which is the problem and which is the symptom?

The Mercer consultant said the changing nature of the workplace is partly to blame. "Look at the things now going on in organizations: downsizings, restructurings, more stress, people having to do more with less, and layoffs in the ranks of white collar employees as well."

The National Mental Health Association in the United States recently launched a campaign on clinical depression that described it as one of the four most costly illnesses, along with cancer, heart disease and AIDS. It cited the $43.7 billion impact on the U.S. economy, noting that the annual economic cost of depression in 1995 was $600 per depressed worker, with only one-third of those costs relating to treatment. The findings are similar to those noted earlier.

The Association said depression ranks among the top three workplace problems, following only family crises and stress. All three, in fact, affect the emotional dimension of human capital.

The Association also reported 3% of short-term disability days in the U.S. are due to depressive disorders, three quarters of which involve female employees.

An estimated 200 million workdays are lost each year to employee depression. At any one time, one out of every 20 employees in the United States is suffering from this disease.

According to the Employee Assistance Professional Association, a recent survey says that there are four basic reasons why employees with depression seldom seek treatment: 1. they believe they can handle it on their own; 2. they are unaware they have it; 3. they are concerned about the word getting out; and 4. they worry about the cost. The last point is uniquely American because the question goes to the heart of private versus public insurance and universal access to physician care.

The symptoms of clinical depression point to a pattern of suffering for the afflicted person that is both recognizable and definitive: emptiness; early morning awakenings; sleeping too much; reduced appetite and weight loss; increased appetite and weight gain.

Restless Souls and Irritable Minds

The faces of depression, restlessness, irritability, loss of interest, persistent physical symptoms such as headaches and chronic pain that don't respond to treatment, fatigue, guilt, hopelessness, and difficulty concentrating, making decisions or remembering things.

Detection of depression can only happen if these symptoms become apparent. In the workplace, they become apparent in ways that often fail to point to the disease itself, especially when supervisors or co-workers and the community itself are as unaware as we are about depression and mental illness generally.

In these cases, an individual's symptoms can become the company's symptoms. Decreased productivity, morale problems, lack of co-operation, unexplained aches and pains, or alcohol and drug abuse typically bleed into each other.

Productivity, in its own depression, relentlessly saps dollars and output, impairing the company — often without identifying the root cause: that the person's depression and the non-medical work climate contribute to that condition.

Supervisors who spot warning signs can help employees seek treatment. But they seldom do, because their eyes don't see what their mind's eye can't.

Thus the importance for employers and co-workers to learn about depression and understand the role that a friend and colleague can play in the process of detection. The economic and human stakes for doing so are enormous and growing in light of Harvard's findings about depression as a source of workyears lost.

The Chairman of Trilon Financial Corporation, Tim Price, puts it interestingly this way: it is fairly common today for people to take first aid training in order to help drowning, choking or bleeding people through critical moments prior to a professional taking over. Why not do the same thing for mental illness?

A clear picture of the impact of disability was cited by Harvard as critical to a clear understanding of the scale of disease and injury in our society. This is particularly so with psychiatric disorders which, in the context of disability, rise to prominence as five of the 10 leading causes of workdays lost through premature death and disability by the year 2020.

A study by the University of Pennsylvania notes that severe disability in the United States has increased by some 70% in the past 20 years, a stunning figure. Estimates of the size of the working population disabled by serious psychiatric disabilities are "similarly disconcerting."

Functional Depressant

The U.S. National Mental Health Association estimates that some 42 million Americans have psychiatric impairments that limit one or more major areas of human functional performance. The National Institute of Mental Health, meanwhile, says the annual prevalence of all mental illness in the United States is in the order of 45 million people, of whom 10% are considered seriously afflicted; among the latter, 70% to 90% are unemployed or have a hard time finding a job.

According to the University of Pennsylvania study, mental illness, unlike physical illness, presents no clear pattern of symptoms, background, diagnosis or course of development. Usually we only deal with its boundaries or chase its shadows.

"We attempt to describe it, classify it, count it, contain it as best we can because we really don't understand its origins or essential nature and we are only partially successful at treatment and rehabilitation, and much less so at prevention."

People with psychiatric disabilities often have cognitive, perceptual, affective and interpersonal deficits intrinsic to their disorder. The symptoms affect their thinking and functioning. Most kinds of mental illness come and go, episodically and unpredictably. This complicates even further the whole notion of recovering from this form of disability. There is no clear beginning, middle and end employers can reliably depend on for a recovery process that will return their worker to work.

Psychiatric disorders are unpredictable and can't be planned for or actuarially forecast, unlike most chronic ailments.

Barriers to work facing the mentally-distressed are built by the lack of coordinated treatment offered among practitioners, who are looking at the problems of long-term and short-term disabilities from varying perspectives — some of them vocational, some medical and some economic.

At the same time, hope flowers from new medications that improve the odds of returning to work successfully. When combined, one day, with the training of supervisors and managers to help facilitate re-entry, and the prospects of using "return to work" productivity enhancements as part of the recovery process, then mental illness could become a beast tamed. Other studies tell us that depression is a significant precursor to the entrenchment of disability for up to one year. And contrary to some earlier thinking, even people with relatively mild symptoms face a serious risk of disability when mood changes or behaviours become unacceptable in workplace relations.

The Downtime of Depression

We have referred several times in this report to employment or unemployment as a determinant of health.

Studies in the United States indicate that depression is three times more likely among people who have been unemployed six or more months in the past five years.

It is estimated that the "downtime cost" of depression in the U.S. is more than 172 million person-days a year, based on six-month prevalence rates for major depression at 3% to 5% of the working population. Kinds of impairment range from absenteeism, to basic performance and interpersonal problems to poor overall functioning and, ultimately, incapacity to work at all.

Job loss often ensues because the source of the impairment — depression — is masked by plain worker failure on the job. The disability is interpreted as an inability to do the work the job requires. It has been found in studies that the reduction of symptoms through treatment outpaces the recovery of the person's capacity to do productive work. Once again, the critical importance of early detection.

In understanding depression as it impacts work, researchers draw a distinction between the functional and "affective" dimensions of the disturbance.

For example, the affective aspects of depression often take the form of shame or disinterest and distress when the sufferer is at work. While the impact of "affect" and function are not independent of each other, they can often progress at different rates and influence the work re-entry process quite a bit.

The distinction between these two components of the disease in lay terms is important because reducing the affective symptoms can mislead the depressed person or his family into believing he is ready to function at work, when often he is not.

Here we encounter a clash of the standards that define the person's pace of recovery and those that measure work performance. One may present good news, the other may not. And the sufferer and his or her family may have trouble knowing how one relates to the other. Thus the critical importance of the employee and the medical practitioner having a clear picture of what constitutes real progress on both fronts. When they converge, the return to work becomes a conduit for fuller recovery.

Health and business planners must also consider the links between this disorder and chronic ailments usually treated in the general medical sector. One study, for example, found that after two years, patients with depression still tended to be worse off than those with general medical conditions such as congestive heart failure, diabetes, arthritis and other chronic disorders. The question is why.

Prime Targets
To answer that question — why the prolonged disability associated with depression — two prominent U.S. organizations — the Washington Business Group on Health and the National Institute of Mental Health — embarked upon the construction of a strategy to manage the impact of depression in the workplace. They noted that depression often strikes during the prime *working* years — between the ages of 25 and 44. Left untreated, it becomes chronic and disabling.

As noted earlier, 75% of depression cases go undiagnosed. It is estimated that 72% of the 17.6 million American adults who experience clinical depression each year are in the work force. And in 1990, it was estimated that U.S. employers spent more than $3,000 on each worker with depression, which comes to about $13 billion if those calculations are correct.

As noted earlier, studies tell us that depressive symptoms are associated with abnormally high utilization of the general medical services, and efforts to contain the disease become an important tool to contain the rise in the cost of healthcare generally.

According to the Washington Business Group on Health and the National Institute for Mental Health, compared to other chronic medical problems such as diabetes, low back pain and heart disease, depressive disorders represented the longest average length of disability — 40 days — and had the highest probability of recurrence within one year.

A remarkable study of the experience of the First Chicago Corporation, discussed earlier in this report, is one of the most comprehensive corporate initiatives towards understanding and containing the effects of depression in a workplace.

The tenth-largest bank in the United States, with 18,000 employees, First Chicago examined its short-term disability data over a four-year period between 1989 and 1992 and discovered that depressive disorders accounted for more than half of all employees absent from work on short-term disability.

First Chicago Corporation expanded employee benefits and redoubled its efforts to ensure early intervention, timely treatment and on-the-job support for depressed employees. It adopted an integrated approach to managing the disease along with chronic health disorders, striking the co-morbidity theme again.

The components of their "Defeat Depression" campaign ranged from employee education, including wellness seminars, to management training and work re-entry initiatives to ensure that employees returning from short or long-term disability because of psychiatric disorders received the support they needed.

These and other initiatives, the study showed, led to a 2% reduction of First Chicago's behavioural healthcare costs as a percentage of total medical expenditures under its employee health plan. Even a 2% gain is a promising step forward when cost containment alone is an important goal.

Targeted Attack on Depression

The Washington Business Group, having researched this case history, urged its clientele in the United States to establish integrated benefits and service plans to manage depression. It customized its disability and employee assistance plans to rein in this disease.

The Washington Business Group on Health also placed emphasis on managerial, EAP professional and employee 'rank and file' training to help identify the symptoms of a deepening depressed state early as a first step in the detection and treatment.

The question of accommodating workers with psychiatric disability has been addressed in law in the United States under the incentives established by the *Americans With Disabilities Act*, and in Canada, by way of a Supreme Court of Canada decision in 1996. In both cases, accommodating the psychiatrically afflicted in the workplace is a question of human rights as well as reasonably-expected corporate conduct.

The high court decision in Canada is notable on a couple of levels. It precluded the need, apparently, for an industry guideline recognizing the inherent rights of the mentally ill in the composition of disability insurance; and, it established the precedent (some argue in a limited way) to protect those rights in the future.

The case revolved around a woman in Saskatchewan whose disability benefits at work were discontinued under the terms of a company insurance policy which said that if the employee's disability was mental illness, the replacement income would terminate after two years — even if the person was still unable to resume her job.

There was one exception or condition: The benefits would continue beyond the two years only if the mentally disabled person remained in a mental institution. On the other hand, according to court documents, had this employee's disability been physical in nature, the benefits could have continued until age 65.

The employee complained that her human rights were violated under Saskatchewan law. The province's human rights board agreed, as did the provincial Court of Appeal.

The insurer, The Co-operators, and the employer appealed further and the matter reached the highest court in the nation. The employer and insurer essentially argued that the question turned not on distinctions between mental and physical disability, but between the generally disabled and the (generally) "able-bodied".

The Supreme Court rejected the insurer's view. The undercurrent beneath the decision is worth measuring.

Institutional Illiteracy About Mental Illness

By drawing a distinction between "disability" and "able-bodied" for purposes of the insurance policy, the employer and insurer were exhibiting the kind of institutional illiteracy about mental illness that has plagued society for generations.

The "able-bodied nature" of the mentally ill person in this case — even if she could be described in those terms — does not mean she is free of the disease causing her disability. It is a false measure, in fact, a dangerous one. We learn elsewhere in this report that the "affective" or external improvement in a condition of mental illness often deceptively precedes the recovery of one's capacity to function in a work or social setting. We also noted elsewhere that:

- depression is, in a significant way, a bio-chemical experience and so-called "able-bodied" sufferers experience as much or more incapacity as people who suffer from chronic physical disease.
- mental illness is often co-morbid with physical disorders, triggered by them or as a cause of them.
- outpatient treatment in the United States is found to be just as effective in many cases as inpatient treatment, and is certainly less expensive — so to define mental disability for insurance purposes by keeping the insured person in a hospital — as in the Saskatchewan case — is an uninformed view of the subject.

Writing for the Supreme Court, the late Mr. Justice John Sopinka said the Court's decision was influenced by the appropriateness of directly comparing the insurance policy's treatment of the mentally and physically disabled and by the historical disadvantages faced by persons with mental disabilities. He said the question of discrimination should be settled by examining the "true purpose" of the insurance plan.

The Court's decision did inject one qualifier, which produced a minority report. The Court said the employer and employee may in some cases define the purpose of disability benefits narrowly, and the result may be to condone the exclusion of otherwise entitled employees, including the mentally ill.

In a letter to its member companies, the Canadian Life and Health Insurance Association Inc. wondered aloud if the Court's decision applied to benefits other than long-term disability and to individual insurance as well as to employee group plans.

The Association called it a "very significant" decision for Canada's insurance industry. It interprets the decision this way:

- Distinctions between mental and physical disabilities (and apparently between any disabilities) violate human rights legislation if the plan or contract has a broadly defined purpose.
- There is some scope for limited-benefit programs if the purpose is defined in a narrow way. (An example is a pianist insuring only his hands and receiving benefits only when one or both are injured to the point where he can't play his instrument.)

In turning on the question of the purpose of the insurance plan, the Court's decision was especially significant:
- *...it is understandable that insurance benefits designed for disparate purposes will differ. If, however, benefits are allocated pursuant to the same purpose, yet benefits differ as a result of the consequences that are not relevant to this purpose, discrimination may well exist.*
- *If the true character of the plan in all circumstances were simply to insure against particular injuries, it may be appropriate to compare the benefits for different injuries. However, given the true character of the plan in the case at the bar, and given the particular disadvantage faced by those with a mental disability, a "disability-to-disability" comparison is appropriate.*

The insurance industry may well seek legislative clarification in light of the minority report in the Saskatchewan case by Mr. Justice McLachlin who effectively disagreed that insurance plans could be written in any manner to exclude mental illness.

Another point made to the authors of this report by Charles Black, a socially conscious senior advisor to the Canadian Life and Health Insurance Association, is worth recording here.

He says that as a matter of common practice, the built-in differentiation in insurance policies between physical and mental illness has pretty well been eliminated as a matter of general practice, the Saskatchewan case notwithstanding.

"Even in the older contracts that have not been formally amended," he said," such differentials have been largely eliminated through administrative practices." He felt the Court decision clarified the matter in any case.

Mr. Black also noted that the industry is populated by activist companies seeking to raise awareness and understanding of mental illness and its consequences. In one campaign two years ago, Mutual Life of Canada teamed up with the Canadian Mental Health Association for an information campaign about depression in the workplace. The CMHA also launched a "Work and Wellbeing" program to highlight the changing context of employment, a fact that will have as much defining impact on the acceptance of mental illness as an authentic source of compensable disability as any court decisions past or future.

Accommodation of Mental Disability

In the U.S. legislation, the accommodation of mental disabilities at work may mean flexible scheduling and time off for medical appointments; being given an enclosed office to minimize distractions when and where that helps; allowances for telephone support and counselling during work hours; and resolving the source of negative stressors that exacerbate the disability.

In one case, a general office clerk developed an anxiety disorder following a work-related injury that affected her ability to tolerate stress. Under her accommodation, when she felt anxious, she was permitted to take a ten-minute time-out during which she could play relaxation tapes.

She kept a log of her time-outs each day and made up the time if it exceeded 40 minutes. Meanwhile, selected coworkers were asked to help her adjust to the workload and generally provide the support she needed to move through the work day and the recovery process simultaneously.

Under the headline "Putting Troubled Minds to Work," the *Palm Beach Post* ran an article in the spring of 1997 that asked if every employer has to provide "a little wheelchair access" for the mentally ill, and concluded that is exactly what the new U.S. legislation intended them to do.

"Underlying the new set of rules is the assumption that physical illness and mental illness should be treated as one and the same. But can they? Are diabetes and schizophrenia akin to diabetes and deafness?"

"Does a troubled mind heal the way a broken leg does?" the article asked under the byline of *New York Times* writer Sheryl Gay Stolberg.

The U.S. legislation, driven by two U.S. Senators, one Republican and one Democratic, both with mental illness in their family, will require U.S. insurers to set the lifetime and annual reimbursement caps as high for mental illness as they are for physical illness. The concept is called parity. In the U.S., as in Canada, it breaks new ground.

Dr. Kay Redfield, a psychiatrist at Johns Hopkins University, chronicles her own manic depressive condition in a book entitled *An Unquiet Mind*. In anticipation of a feared backlash to the new American statute, she says "psychiatry has brought this on itself in some respects by making everything a diagnosis and by being sort of absurd — not really making clear-cut distinctions between very serious illnesses and things that are part of the human condition."

There has been considerable debate, according to observers, about whether health insurance coverage should be limited to certain major mental illnesses — such as severe depression, obsessive-compulsive disorder and generalized anxiety disorder. "All are extremely debilitating and all can be diagnosed and treated."

If nothing else, the *Palm Beach* article suggests, the new U.S. legislation is likely to raise awareness of how many people actually are mentally ill. That's progress.

Dr. Arthur Caplan, head of the Centre for Bioethics at the University of Pennsylvania, sums up the prospects of that discovery this way: "There are very few people who are completely mentally well. I think we are going to realize through this kind of policy that our workforce is much more like Woody Allen than Marcus Welby."

The Homewood Health Centre has embarked upon a series of clinical and non-clinical initiatives to help employers rein in depression in the workplace, by aiming to reduce the periods of incapacitation and accelerate a return to work.

The Homewood initiative operates on two levels, the remedial and the preventive. On the first front, Homewood is employing tele-medicine techniques not only to treat less severe cases but to help identify employees who are at high risk of becoming depressed and are still at work. The key to this, according to Homewood's strategy, is the introduction of emotional intelligence as a means of developing or reinforcing attributes of people which, in turn, decrease vulnerability to depression.

≈21≈
Vulnerability and Globalization

EXECUTIVES AND RANK-AND-FILE EMPLOYEES ARE DEALING WITH PRESSURES unique to a globalized economy. *Toronto Star* columnist David Crane says dangerous stress flows from a "period of unprecedented competition, as trade and investment barriers tumble around the world and new competitors emerge on all sides." He cites a report from the World Competitiveness Council that says companies are under "intense pressure from financial markets to constantly improve their performance — with performance measured by the current year's profits and return on equity."

This source of pressure mirrors the intensity built into a global information economy. For instance, thanks to new forms of information technology, financial money managers anywhere in the world can shift billions of dollars with the touch of a computer key and, as Crane points out, when companies don't boost earnings, the effect can be immediate. That can influence the behaviours and anxieties of people within those corporations. In turn, the writer says, "finance has thus become a kind of referee for the competitive economic performance of companies and whole countries alike."

In these circumstances, he says employees are under as much pressure as their bosses to perform. And it appears today the younger population is more disillusioned and skeptical than ever. It tips a work/life balance (which often means rejecting extremely long hours of work) toward independence and mobility.

Quoting a report of the Competitiveness Council, Mr. Crane says, "Employee loyalty and management credibility are in tatters, making it easy to understand why there is a growing gap between employee trust and employer expectation."

In Canada, the United States and many parts of the world, two manifestations of stress and pressure are high youth unemployment — young people struggling unsuccessfully to enter or stay in the workforce — and the phenomenon of "burnout."

New studies show that young people, contrary to myth, are experiencing abnormal distress because of high unemployment. Jobless youth have twice the mental distress of their peers who have jobs, according to scores determined by a study entitled "Unhappiness and Unemployment."

This research, done in the United Kingdom, found that mental distress is disproportionately evident among women who are unemployed, among people in their thirties and among those with higher levels of education.

The link between the jobless rate and the average loss of wellbeing from unemployment appears to be established in this study. It also found that unemployed people are not indifferent to their plight — disputing a view often held by critics of unemployment and welfare programs.

We recall the observations earlier in this report by Ottawa psychiatrist Dr. Robert Swenson, who said that disabled workers often "grieve for work" even when their disability has prevented them from working all their life.

All of us must find a place of usefulness. The U.K. study found that being unemployed is worse than divorce or marital separation in its effect on mental stability.

The Emotional Burden of Caring

Earlier in this report we referred to the cost of neglecting the value of investing in the mental health of working people, managers and executives. In a study by the Washington Business Group on Health, the First Tennessee Bank itemized the cost of neglect and reported that 71% of employees' productivity was negatively affected by work/family issues. This produced approximately 21,000 workdays lost. The company cited the primary cause to be "dependent-care issues" and personal distractions in the working population. Employee turnover also produced replacement costs as high as $50,000 per employee on average.

Conversely, a 1993 study by Johnson & Johnson said employees who had supportive supervisors in managing work/family concerns, and access to family programs at work, were among the highest performers in the company and were the best providers of internal and external customer service; least likely to leave the company; least likely to have disciplinary problems; and more likely to make what David McQuaig of the AON Consulting Group in Toronto calls "discretionary efforts" to support the organization's goals and objectives.

The First Tennessee Bank also reported significant productivity gains in specific parts of the organization, including their loan operations and account processing departments, both of which functioned with flexible work schedules.

Overall, First Tennessee experienced a six-fold improvement in productivity between 1990 and 1997 which delivered $1.5 million to its bottom line.

In companies where supervisors welcome the concept of supporting employees in their struggle to manage conflicting obligations of work and family pressures, employee satisfaction was up 69%, employee retention was twice as high as in companies where the support was not offered. Quality standards were 18% higher, and customer service and retention 6% and 7% higher respectively.

Work and family issues are an emotional load for employees to bear. If borne alone, they will have emotional implications — negative ones — for the business performance of the company.

One of the principal goals of "work and life" programs in corporations is to "de-hassle" the circumstances under which employees function day in and day out.

Alternative work schedules, flexible work hours, job sharing, telecommuting, compressed work weeks, a gradual return to work for new parents and a range of services to provide support for those who must care for dependents — including both the very young and the very old, all these can be very helpful.

Company support systems also include referral services at work for child or elder care, assistance to help defray dependent care expenses when they grow dangerously in the family budget, and services to assist employees in arranging for emergency care-givers or sick child day-care.

Intergenerational Daycare

The provision of on-site child day-care centres for both emergency and non-emergency purposes is becoming increasingly common. But there is some movement in the United States for employers to examine the possibilities of providing "intergenerational day-care" for children and the elderly alike.

Inside the workplace, behavioural healthcare services can be discreetly advertised to the advantage of those who are conflicted by family care problems or experiencing personal distress through eating disorders or substance abuse. Given the sense of community that people attach to the workplace, it is inevitably one of the places where working families can access advice around family violence or anxiety and panic disorders — all increasingly present phenomena in a high-stress society.

The definition of employee health assistance is deepening as well as broadening as a corporate value. Women's health services is an example of both dimensions. In one case, Merck & Company has introduced a breast cancer detection and awareness program.

Studies tell us that workplace services relating to reproductive healthcare, mental health and substance abuse can have a decisive impact on the productivity of female employees.

What employees expect they will get out of their work often becomes a question of what they themselves decide to ask of it.

Employers, to their own benefit, can help employees sort out their purpose and personal goals as a way to instill value in the nature of the work they do, often in tightening time constraints.

Author Richard Leider, who wrote *The Power of Purpose*, said working people today run the risk of becoming "tranquilized by the trivial" and sedated by the small stuff of life.

Whole books have been written to great acclaim on how to keep little things from swamping our capacity to cope. Dr. J.P. Pawliw-Fri, Director of the Stress and High Performance Centre at the King's Health Centre in Toronto, has introduced something he calls the "Aliveness Questionnaire," which aims to help working people determine what energizes them, how they use their own skills to create value in other people's lives, their adherence to truth, their capacity to understand and express their sense of purpose clearly and succinctly, and the likelihood of whether they can see each day as well lived.

The themes espoused by Dr. Pawliw-Fri are reminiscent of the principle of "mindfulness" advocated by others in the psychiatric field — which in turn relates to the broader concept of emotional intelligence. That is, being mindful of the present and what we are putting into and getting out of it.

The ideas driving the theory of 'emotional intelligence' are gaining currency in business, and at the heart of EQ is the concept of self-efficacy. This in turn centres on emotional energy.

The EQ Mantra

EQ ('emotional quotient'), as we discussed earlier, is said to rival or surpass IQ ('intelligence quotient') as a determinant of success in relationships at work or elsewhere.

Dr. Robert Cooper, author of *Executive EQ: Emotional Intelligence in Leadership and Organizations*, says studies have demonstrated that emotional intelligence and "practical creative intelligence" underpin many of the best decisions, the most dynamic organizations and the most satisfying and successful lives. The key, however, is to be able to value and acknowledge the role of feelings in arriving at decisions, building relationships or choosing the most useful way to go about doing things.

For many in business, all of this is foreign ground.

According to Dr. Cooper, research tells us that people with high levels of emotional intelligence tend to experience more career success and lead more effective lives while enjoying better health. They are motivated and motivating people, he says.

The good news, according to some indications, is that emotional intelligence is learnable at almost any age. The powers of EQ range from strong intuition, and a capacity to trust and be trusted, all the way to integrity, constructive discontent and making sound decisions. Not a bad definition of leadership.

Dr. Cooper underlines three driving forces that shape — from within — competitive advantage for business organizations. One force centres on trust, the second focuses on high levels of energy and effectiveness inside the organization, and the third is what he calls "creating the future."

In each case, there is an emphasis on developing people's skills — and practical strategies to get things done in a meaningful way — from day to day. In each case, there is a premium on people's attentiveness to each other.

The capacity to listen. The instinct and ability to respect feelings and express them in a constructive and strategic way. These forces centre on words like "commitment" and "vision" as staples that animate and feed the working environment — all of these things being skills that Dr. Cooper says are teachable.

The Power of Divergence

Creating the future, he says, means building these essential skills and tapping into the power of divergent views to make the most of the core talents and strengths of people, and at the same time helping them recognize their own innate strengths. The development and application of skills like this, he says, leverages the talents of individuals into the power of employee teams — both in solving technical problems in the work process and in promoting better customer service.

One of the principles upon which the EQ theorem is based is described as emotional literacy — clear and useful ways to respect and value the feelings of people in the workplace.

Dr. Cooper describes the commitment to EQ by Colin Marshall, Chief Executive of British Airways who has made it a point to promote people with emotional honesty and who challenged 'the system' constructively. Robert Galvin, CEO of Motorola, "oversaw the transformation of his company from a sleepy appliance-maker to a high-tech powerhouse." In doing so, he drew upon what he called the greatest discipline of all — the capacity to trust people.

"Trust is a key characteristic of emotional intelligence and emotional fitness," Dr. Cooper says. It includes resilience, personal renewal and constructive discontent, qualities that illuminate character, and feelings that enliven and drive them."

On the other hand, trust is often a "casualty of our unwillingness or inability to face up to emotions." In the global economy, management theorist Tom Peters says, "technique and technology are important, but adding trust is the competitive issue of the decade."

Meanwhile, Dr. Cooper cites the experience of leading corporations and their CEOs in building market strength and profitability on a foundation of trust. Among these corporations are Southwest Airlines, Nordstrom and Ritz Carlton Hotels. He says Wal-Mart's founder Sam Walton has been able to correct mistakes largely because he has had so much trust in others.

In 1993, Edwards Deming, the architect of the principles of continuous improvement that formed the basis of Japanese models of management, said, "trust is mandatory for the optimization of any system, and without trust there can be no cooperation between people, teams, departments or divisions."

"Without trust," Dr. Deming said, "each component of the business will protect its own immediate interests to the long-term detriment of the entire (business) system."

In his book *Beyond Reengineering*, also quoted by Robert Cooper, business strategist Michael Hammer says that the dollar overhead of distrusting relationships represents an enormous business cost.

Dr. Cooper once again: "Trust is more than a good idea or attitude, it's an actionable emotional strength." Without it, innovation is stillborn inside a company. A recent survey of multinational corporations, published in the prestigious magazine, *The Economist*, concluded that many firms are beginning to resemble networks of farflung alliances. That being the case, trust is becoming a pivotal business issue of the global economy and one's success in it.

Supremacy of Ideas Over Hardware

Robert Cooper reminds us that unless people working in the same company trust each other, "leaders feel compelled to draw up regulatory procedures in great detail even for simple transactions — unlike some Japanese companies that ensure agreements are limited to one or two pages."

In today's global world, "many successful leaders are unwilling to compete in the future based on solely incremental change and the mind-sets and limitations that go with it." They seek transformational change. This is more the rule than exception in the information economy as we are disconnect institutions and individuals from a very recent past characterized by obsolete notions of productivity and dominated by production hardware over ideas or intellectual software.

A new balance of nature in the business world has begun to materialize — its roots planted in 1991 when industry worldwide spent, for the first time, more money on communications than on traditional production equipment.

Michael Eisner is Chairman and CEO of the Walt Disney Company, a firm known for motivating people and expressing its employees' dreams as individuals and as members of Disney's working family. In an article written by Robert Cooper, Mr. Eisner says "being in connection with our emotional depths is critical to releasing our most powerful and creative forces."

"Denying this deeper level," Mr. Eisner says, "leads to disconnection, and people lose touch with aspects of who they are. The result tends to be vulnerability, fear and denial, as well as superficiality, falseness and a mistrust of intuition — all of which can get in the way of deep creative expression."

He goes on: "Fear of criticism and lack of acceptance are primary reasons people censor their feelings and intuitions and shut down their depths — trusting our deepest intuition and instincts may mean overriding contrary research, peer pressure, conventional wisdom or intimidation."

In the same article, management expert Peter Drucker describes the practice of relegating the best people to simple problem-fixing as a "deadly business sin," pre-empting the creative pursuit of opportunities for personal and corporate growth.

The CEO of 3M Company conceded that 40 years ago his company stumbled onto some of its major products and services, but reminded the world of that day, that "you can only stumble if you are moving." As a result, 3M is known as a creative, forward-moving company, not only tolerating but encouraging constructive discontent, to the point that current CEO Desi De Simone was said to have repeatedly tried and failed to kill a project that ultimately became successful as "Thinsulate."

Dr. Cooper reminds us that by training and experience, managers often feel they need to push for closure in meetings and tend to believe that it is necessary to compromise or forego discontent to reach consensus in order to realize progress. That notion of progress is "largely illusory," he says. It doesn't actually create anything.

The EQ Map

The Homewood Health Centre became one of the earlier employer organizations in Canada to use the *EQ map* designed by Q-Metrics of San Francisco, a company owned by Robert Cooper and Esther Orioli.

Travelling the course defined by the EQ map is no lighthearted adventure. It poses questions to managers and employees that are probing and direct. It seeks to illuminate how strongly employees believe in the security of their jobs. How strongly do they believe their service to the customer is as good and as sure as it could be? How strongly do they believe their own skills will keep them employable? How strongly do they believe their level of work satisfaction is improving? How strongly do they believe their employer really wants to grow as an innovative organization and a provider of (in the case of Homewood) specialized healthcare services.

The map leads its traveller into other fundamental realms of inquiry about ourselves, our feelings, our company and our view or vision of what this business relationship — our job — really amounts to. It asks how strongly we believe that building trusting relationships will actually increase the likelihood our company will be successful. Do we trust our superiors in management? Do we really believe that when the president tells us that we can make a difference that matters, it is the truth? How ready are we to keep an open mind during times of disagreement and uncertainty at work, and are we managing our "life pressures"?

The EQ map probes our capacity to express ourselves, the personal pressures we face, including those associated with raising our children, being separated from our wife or husband, living in dangerous or unsafe neighborhoods, our loneliness or lack of intimacy. It probes how satisfied we are with our life and our job, including whether I like or trust my own supervisor. Am I respected by people I associate with after work for the job I do at work? Can I name my feelings, can I accept them? Would my co-workers say that I appreciate them and let them know that fact? On the other hand, would I do anything to avoid looking foolish in the eyes of my peers or my supervisor?

Do I have a pretty good instinct as to when ideas will succeed or fail? Do I run away from defending them instead of fighting for them? Do I finish things I start? Can I focus myself on the task I need to do? Do I seem to regret things later on? Can I postpone personal gratification for some greater goal? And when I am in a bad mood, can I talk myself out of it, or do I get angrier, especially when I am criticized, and do I know the source of my anger when that happens?

The EQ map looks further.

Can I bounce back after I am disappointed? Do I appreciate there is sometimes not a right or wrong answer, just beliefs? Am I able to see the humorous side of things from time to time? When I encounter a problem, do I try to solve it or do I cave into it? Do I get uncomfortable when I see someone else experiencing emotional upset? Do I doubt that my colleagues really care about me, and do I have difficulty making friends or letting my emotions show, even at times of great stress, like when I go to the funeral of someone I have cared about?

The Q-Metrics questionnaire — the EQ map — goes on: Do I take the feelings of others into consideration? Am I able to forgive myself for not being perfect? Do I look on the bright side, or do I see the darker side more instinctively? Am I willing to admit a mistake when I make it? If I lose the passion for my job, do I have the courage to change the job? Do I exaggerate my skills in order to get ahead, and do I do things on the job that conflict with my beliefs?

These are the paths that Dr. Cooper and his associates asked Homewood people to travel, paths of uncertainty, paths of intimidation for some, but a journey intended to help them discover whether the organization, and their place in it, are based on job satisfaction and trusting relationships, or whether work pressures are creating a negative flow of energy; whether colleagues are emotionally aware of others' needs; whether they are resilient and able to take the good with the bad; whether compassion is commonplace or rare; whether there is a quality of life or just a quantity of things in the Homewood workplace; whether they intend to do good work or just get through the day; whether, in fact, the organization, in these terms, is healthy.

This journey is aimed at discovering whether opinions count, or if senior people just say they do. Are there opportunities to really learn and grow, or do senior people just say there are? Do Homewood people get recognized for their contributions, or not?

Are they given a chance to do their best by using the skills that they are most confident in, or are they channelled into work they neither like nor feel very comfortable with? Do they see in their place of work evidence of fairness and honesty? Does their work just put food on the table at home or are they nourished spiritually too?

These questions represent a bold stroke of inquiry essential to the advancement of emotional intelligence as a management practice and company strength. And perhaps as a tool to combat stigma and promote enlightenment in our quest to understand and contain mental illness.

A Sense of Being Heard

For a long time, business managers focused on financial operating results. Understandably so. For a long time, they said of employees that they got a decent day's wages for a decent day's work: why aren't they happy? implying that's all that matters. For a long time, business enterprise drew sustenance from the macho pride of having an exclusively bottom-line focus.

Studies are telling us that working populations require more than a decent wage for decent work. They need to experience a sense of what's right, a sense that the company itself is headed in the right direction, a clear sense of being heard.

Economists have assumed, by and large, that people focus solely on outcomes. According to the *Harvard Business Review*, "that assumption has migrated into much of management theory and practice. It has become embedded in the tools managers traditionally use to control and motivate employees' behaviour all the way from incentive systems to organizational structure."

It is an assumption that needs to be re-examined.

While people do care about outcomes, they also care about process, how those outcomes are achieved in business. They want to know that their point of view was considered, even if it was rejected. They want to understand that the process of things inside the company is on balance fair, intelligible and reliable.

The *Harvard Business Review* tells us that "never has the idea of fair process been more important for managers than it is today — fair process is a powerful management tool for companies struggling to make the transition from a production-based economy to a knowledge-based economy in which value creation depends increasingly on ideas and innovation, and where fair process profoundly influences attitudes and behaviours critical to the performance of the company and the people in it."

Fair process, *Harvard* says, builds trust and unlocks ideas. "With it, managers can achieve even the most painful and difficult goals, while gaining the voluntary cooperation of the employees affected."

The question becomes: what is fairness? A question that has echoed through the ages. In a recent study of 19 corporations published by the *Harvard Business Review*, researchers found a direct link among internal processes, attitudes and behaviours.

For example, managers in the surveyed companies who believed that operating processes of the company they worked in were fair, displayed a high level of trust and commitment. This, in turn, engendered active co-operation. The opposite was also true. When fair process was not self-evident, managers and senior employees alike — not to mention employees further down the pecking order — tended to hoard ideas and drag their feet when asked to do something.

The study concluded that companies seeking to harness the energy and creativity of committed managers and employees must make fairness visible. Like justice, it *must be seen to be* in order *to exist* in perceptual terms. Employees are likely to trust and co-operate freely with whatever system or process is in place when fairness is apparent, even when they don't personally benefit.

Studies reviewed by these authors cite three principal features of fairness in the workplace. One was what they described as "engagement," which means involving individuals in decisions that affect them by asking for their input and allowing them to debate the merits of ideas and the assumptions behind them. We referred to this "engagement" concept earlier.

"Engagement" shows management's respect for people and their ideas. Like EQ, it encourages constructive discontent.

The second feature was "explanation," meaning that everyone involved and everyone affected was given a chance to understand why a certain decision was ultimately made.

For example, an explanation of management's thinking behind a decision tended to reinforce the confidence people had not only in what was decided, but why, the motivation factor.

Beyond the *Harvard* study, the work done by a crisis communications company co-founded by one of the authors of this report, The CorpWorld Group, repeatedly found that in times of company distress, the capacity of executives and managers to explain "uncertainty" clearly and explicitly was a pivotal part of engaging the belief of the working population in what management said and did. We will visit a simulated example of this later.

In the recession, downsizings and layoffs occurred frequently. When employees were told, especially in the face of rumours, that decisions about the future were going to be made but couldn't be announced for a number of reasons, they perceived that a process was underway and that they would have an opportunity to hear the information when it was ready. In short, the company was trying to do the right thing, not necessarily the easy or happiest thing.

The *Harvard Business Review*: "Fair process, therefore, responds to a basic human need. All of us, whatever our role in the company, want to be valued as human beings and we want to be treated with respect for our intelligence. We want our ideas to be taken seriously, we want to understand the rationale behind specific decisions, and we are sensitive to the signals conveyed by a company's decision-making process because in that process we see whether or not the company itself is willing to trust people and to seek their ideas."

A third principle is 'explanation clarity'. Even when the rules of the game have changed inside the organization, and things may be less or more than before in terms of what is expected of us, we want to know up front what standards we will be judged by, and what goals we will be asked to support, and why.

"To achieve fair process, sometimes it matters less what the new rules and policies are and more that they are clearly understood and who is responsible for what," the *Harvard Business Review* says.

"Fair process" may sound like a soft issue in business terms. But it has hardened considerably. Gaining the active co-operation of employees, says Nobel Laureate economist Friedrich Hayek, may well turn out to be one of the key managerial issues of the coming decades.

Interpersonal Burn-out

The question of fair process reaches into human psychology, a mostly unexplored frontier of conventional management theory or practice. It suggests that trust in the workplace is near the heart of corporate, competitive progress, and that human capital now takes its place alongside financial capital as a currency in corporate management in the global information economy. According to Steven Stein, President of Multihealth Systems Inc. in Toronto, some 600 North American companies have tested or are now using his version of a tool to assess the level of emotional intelligence in their organizations. Among his clients are Ault Foods, Canada Life, Chase Manhattan Bank and the Canadian Armed Forces. The U.S. Air Force is also said to have found emotional intelligence testing a helpful tool for nailing down the personal characteristics common to senior officers at a volatile time in the management of military operations.

One of the most important human management studies in recent times, a 1983 ground-breaker produced by the Centre for Creative Leadership in Colorado, found that corporate "stars" tended to burn out more often from interpersonal flaws than technical failings.

In his bestseller, *Emotional Intelligence*, Dr. Daniel Goleman says impulse control is an essential skill, and while that skill doesn't show up in IQ scores or even some personality tests, one's predilection for it has value in predicting future behaviour.

At AT&T's Bell Labs, the top technical performers were found to be not the ones with the highest IQ's but those researchers who had their e-mail answered, in other words, those who could count on help from their colleagues. On the other hand, E-mail requests from disagreeable types generally went unanswered, and they were left to sink or swim on their own, according to the U.S. magazine, *Training*.

One of the fundamental shifts that must occur in management thinking, according to emotional intelligence advocates, is to move away from rigid reliance on purely rational thought. Brain research shows that the instincts of people dealing with rapid change, and fast-breaking, often surprising events, are less developed than those instincts we have historically relied upon to think things through at such times.

When change seems overwhelming, people turn to their survival instincts. This often produces aggressive or defensive behaviour. According to Dr. Goleman, this is the "feeling part" of the brain in action, the part that is far less developed than the "thinking brain" we all cultivated from one generation to another, leaving us more vulnerable as a society to behaviour which responds to unplanned events. This is the side of us that needs more attention and development.

Up to now, it has been unclear if negative reactions to rapid-fire events can in fact be managed, let alone unlearned. Both may be possible, according to the concept known as emotional intelligence. But unless we learn this kind of intelligence, people are more likely to confront the exigencies of the post-deficit society with an emotional repertoire that Daniel Goleman says has been shaped by an undeveloped side of our personality.

ᴥ22ᴥ
The Emotional
"Dollar Value" of Employees

WHETHER CONFRONTED THROUGH EMOTIONAL INTELLIGENCE OR SOME other believable management practice or theory, the challenge remains. Companies that aspire to success must come to understand the dollar and emotional value of employees who are motivated, trusting and clear on what is expected of them and what they are likely to get emotionally from their efforts at work.

A *Fortune Magazine* survey of the world's most admired companies, conducted by the Hay Group makes the point vividly.

Atop one page in the Hay/Fortune report is a line stating that the "key to success is people, people, people." Legendary General Electric CEO Jack Welch says, "all we can do is bet on the people we pick, so my whole job is picking the right people."

Mr. Welch: "Making your numbers but not demonstrating our values is grounds for dismissal at General Electric." GE, according to the Hay Group, uses a clear and specific list of values aimed at keeping everybody pulling in the same direction.

Bruce Pfau, Managing Director of the Hay Group in the United States, says, "most companies have created a sketch of the culture they want to build, but by contrast, the most admired companies have something closer to a detailed architectural blueprint and are constantly referring to it."

The Hay study found that the most admired organizations still use intensive psychological testing in recruiting of new employees. Federal Express, for example, looks for what that company calls "risk-taking and courage of conviction." The Hay-Fortune report says "you probably won't land a job at Disney unless you have an 'up' personality." Procter & Gamble aims to hire the best young people now and develop them over their entire careers, something CEO John Pepper describes as the "lifeblood of our future."

The computer giant Intel spent 6% of its total payroll, or $160 million in 1996 on an in-house university that all senior managers must attend as teachers every quarter. The 34,000-person Bank of Montreal is planning a mandatory curriculum for its managers.

CEOs of the most admired companies call themselves "coaches" and commit to supporting the most promising talent.

The most successful companies, whenever possible, promote from within, and most have a far greater percentage of the work force that is eligible for stock ownership, options and bonuses.

They measure work force satisfaction, frequently using "360-degree evaluation schemes" as an expression of genuine interest in what their employees think. The underlying feature of their success is the degree to which they put real muscle behind the rhetoric and human beings into the asset column of the share value plan, if not the balance sheet itself.

The Fortune-Hay study says employee motivation is the underpinning of "stretch objectives" being realistically adopted by organizations, according to Hay Vice-President Melvyn Stark.

Human Health: Logical 'Next Step'

Companies on the cutting edge of performance, like the Bank of Montreal, also seem to use information better than their peers. JP Morgan today earns more than half its revenues from outside the United States. This company, like increasing numbers of others, "plays hopscotch" across national boundaries.

The *Fortune* report says there is evidence that corporate concerns for the environment and the community are being upgraded strategically by the most successful companies in the world. It is but a short step to putting the question of human health on the same plateau. Indeed, it is the logical next step.

One example of this is British Petroleum, the most admired company in Britain, which also happens to be ranked as the number one environmentalist in its industry. The company's CEO says that companies must perform well for their shareholders if they hope to be equally responsive to the communities they live in. There is the link between business interest and the public interest, between financial and social integrity.

Studies reinforce the notion that best management practices boost productivity at a time when powerful realities like these converge.

Health and disability costs are soaring and the idea of wringing out more elusive cost savings through downsizing and restructuring has largely run its course.

MEDSTAT Group, in Ann Arbor, Michigan, a healthcare consulting firm, did a benchmark study of 16 Fortune 500 firms to identify those practices that contribute most to worker health as a way of boosting productivity.

The study concluded that employers can lower their disability costs by as much as 31 per cent by focusing on the wellness of their employees. This is feasible when the company adopts best managerial practices that centre on five key areas — group health, unscheduled absences, turnover, non-occupational disability and workers' compensation. In a nutshell, these categories delineate the principle known as "health and productivity management," the theme so ably advanced in the United States by the Washington Business Group on Health.

As reported earlier, PepsiCo independently surveyed its workers to determine their feelings about the corporate climate, managerial style and work environment they found themselves in. According to published reports, the company discovered a correlation between job satisfaction and accident rates.

In a study at a Boeing factory in the State of Washington, researchers found much the same thing — employees who said they "hardly ever" enjoyed their job were two and a half times more likely to report back injuries than those who liked their work. Dr. Ron Goetzel of MEDSTAT says the trick is to connect employee satisfaction directly to the corporate bottom line.

Texas Instruments, which manufactures semiconductors and employs 43,000 people worldwide, has introduced the concept of a "health excellence team" led by its Worldwide Director for Health Benefits.

In an article in the March edition of *Business and Health*, a U.S. publication, Sue Nelson said, "We provide resources to manage chronic illnesses correctly and create an atmosphere which promotes the vitality and energy of the people working there." She links health excellence to business excellence. Dr. Goetzel tells us:

> When indirect costs associated with maintaining the productivity of absent employees and lost profits due to absenteeism were added to the direct costs of the health benefits provided by the company to employees, the health cost per employee jumped 47% to nearly $12,000 per employee.

On the other hand, firms would save an estimated 31% in employee health costs if they were able to show improvement in unscheduled absences, turnover and non-occupational disability through best management practices.

The MEDSTAT study was commissioned by a number of Fortune 500 firms with household names, including Citibank, Delta Airlines, Motorola, General Electric, Federal Express, Honda, Bechtel and the Travelers Insurance Group.

One of the most powerful best practices that emerged from this benchmark study was what has been commonly referred to in Canada and the U.S. as "a continuum of care" — bringing together services and disease detection standards that capture the health risks associated with the 'whole person' — physical, emotional, psychological and social states. This way, companies can identify patterns of expenditure and the use of health services, including prescription drugs, as well as patterns of disorders that foretell the kinds of preventive strategies needed to contain costs measured in human suffering, absolute dollars, and painful disability.

There is, of course, no question about the economic importance of productivity among competing corporations. Corporate consensus is also settling on the proposition that human health is, in turn, an essential component of productive industrial output. When the two issues of health and productivity are twinned, other issues can be considered in a different light.

Take the performance of the Canadian dollar, for example.

According to distinguished newspaper columnist Richard Gwyn, the current state of the dollar "signals an underlying major economic problem." The world simply doesn't think Canada is as productive or competitive as the United States.

He suggests that the most reliable long-term solution to supporting the Canadian dollar rests with Canada becoming as economically productive as our neighbour to the south. But to reach that level would require fundamental shifts in a number of areas that Canada has yet to come to terms with, one of them being the promotion of motivated entrepreneurial behaviour across the economy and within large corporate organizations.

Mr. Gwyn's proposal for protecting the dollar takes us directly to questions of human motivation, resilience and, of course, health — and on that premise, to issues such as mental health and its affiliation with chronic disease.

Predictors of Success

David Sissons is the Vice-President of Marketing for Hay Canada. He says in the afterlight of the study his company did for *Fortune Magazine*, that a key predictor of corporate success is an ability to attract and keep talented people. This seems reasonable enough. But within that key determinant of success is another — that is, the degree to which organizations can build a strong *human* capital base and not just a strong financial capital base.

Mr. Sissons also sees the need for companies to link the interest of employees to the financial interests of the company. The most admired companies in the world invest huge amounts of time and money in selecting and recruiting people and in determining how they will mesh with the company's culture and working environment.

These companies practice motivational techniques, among them job rotation and promoting a better balance between work and family life. The latter, according to Mr. Sissons, is becoming one of the bigger issues of the times. We saw evidence of that earlier in this report.

In a separate study to determine the best companies to work in, versus the most admired, *Fortune Magazine* sent more than 200,000 questionnaires randomly to employees in 238 companies and found, as "their most striking discovery," that these elite employers are "desperate to retain their best workers." And they are coming up with inventive ways to make the lives of their employees easier and more fun.

At organizations such as General Mills, Johnson & Johnson, Xerox, and the Homewood Health Centre, the employer has introduced dry cleaning services for employees, and at Honda, Starbucks and AlliedSignal, personal concierge services to alleviate the stress and strain of getting things done when your obligations mount both at home and at work.

Fortune Magazine: "A few companies (Kodak, IBM, Phillip Morris) are still making headlines with layoffs, but at most U.S. corporations, downsizing jitters are becoming a memory. Indeed, recent studies reveal that companies that downsized a few years ago are now realizing they cut too close to the bone and are frantically rehiring."

A recent survey by the American Management Association found that more than half of U.S. companies said they had recently lost so many talented people that their ability to compete had been severely damaged, *Fortune* reports.

This led *Fortune* to find out why certain companies can attract and retain people, and what exactly employees are looking for, at least those who know they are in demand.

One thing they found was that nobody mentioned money. The reason: people expect to be paid, but most of them need a better reason than that to get up in the morning. While that probably describes people who are already pretty well off, it also represents a wide swath of middle and upper middle income management people who have struggled through more than a decade of terrific uncertainty and have come through with a sense that life and work must possess values beyond the purely economic considerations.

Among 74% of the "star managers" of the more than 1,000 "peak-performing companies" in the United States, the most important thing to them, the thing they would be most reluctant to give up, was the "close working relationships" they enjoyed with the people they worked with.

Fortune magazine: "Over and over again, people at the 100 best companies talk about how much fun they are having, about the people they are very comfortable with, about the team-oriented approach, about coming to work in the morning as fun."

Procter & Gamble's policy of promoting from within has produced new job experiences that in turn promoted personal growth and fulfilment. Next to fun and pleasant relationships, the best employees at the best companies talk about flexibility.

One senior manager at the consulting firm Deloitte & Touche in Dallas started to look a little frazzled at work soon after the birth of her second child. Her boss, an HR person, convinced her she could work fewer hours and still remain in line for a partnership. Generation X cares about balance.

Many of the 100 best companies in the world care about having a strong vision and a powerful spokesperson to articulate it: the CEO. Successful companies frame their work as part of a deep and purposeful experience. Employee fulfilment, not just job satisfaction distinguishes these leading organizations.

One of the offshoots of inspiring, empathy-based leadership is what employees take from their proximity to these qualities embodied by others, especially their own leaders. The effective leader, *Fortune's* report tells us, not only inspires employees to work hard and succeed, but also to become "mini versions" of themselves. This enhances their own self-esteem.

Shareholder Value in the Right Place

One of the insights drawn from this work is how to put shareholder value "in its rightful place." To employees in an emotional sense, it is often an abstract notion. While obviously basic to the well-being of the organization, it will neither stimulate nor motivate the employees within it.

In fact, in the era of downsizing and restructuring, shareholder value became an unhappy catchphrase rationalizing hard decisions that led to the severance of tens of thousands of people. So the objective for many companies is to turn their employees' attention toward the human service they provide through the products they make.

One health equipment company, for instance, downplays shareholder value (while returning about 34% annual growth in share value over the past decade) and plays up the fact that employees' research and products help sick people get well.

At a holiday party in a private session without publicity, employees of that company, Medtronic of Minneapolis, met with customers who related their stories about how they used this equipment and what it did for them. Parents spoke of how some of the medical equipment kept their kids alive. Motivation was drawn from the end result of what these workers had done.

Thirty years ago, a U.S. astronaut was said to have stood in front of 10,000 employees of the company manufacturing the booster rockets that were to fly him into space. The company was under severe duress to meet a production deadline, and the CEO asked the astronaut to come to the huge production plant and speak to the employees, who were gathered in a nearby airplane hangar. The company was virtually shut down for one hour in order to do this — and the purpose justified that very big step, motivating the employees to meet the looming deadline.

As the story goes, the astronaut stood on the stage, himself a nervous speaker, looked out upon the sea of faces, and asked those employees, simply to "do good work."

The phrase was greeted for an instant by silence. And then a huge roar. The assembly of employees rose as one to take the challenge and applaud the challenger.

In an instant, and in simple language, this astronaut, according to legend, who had the courage to fly to distant worlds but not to make a speech to a big audience, embodied the purpose and goal that these workers were asked to serve. Just by being there, and talking directly about what he needed from them to survive a flight to the stars, he won an emotional commitment from them, and they took emotional nourishment from him.

Do high-minded stories like this reflect a true picture of how working people will respond tangibly to intangible stimulus? It depends on the underlying values that fuel the inspiring words with the one essential ingredient — truth.

Motivation and Money

Fortune Magazine found evidence among the world's 100 best run companies linking employee motivation and goodwill to financial results. The editors of this very prestigious and conservative publication believe the link must be examined more carefully, understood more clearly, and used more widely.

Among 61 of the best run publicly traded firms, 45 yielded higher shareholder value than the performance index measuring the average yield among large and small companies in the United States. Over ten years, companies on the "100 best run list" — emphasizing best practices promoting employee emotional ties and wellbeing — have realized annual share growth two-thirds greater than companies that failed to make the list.

This is a huge distinction, one that *Fortune* calculated in dollar terms. As an example, $1,000 invested in the non-100 best run companies, over that ten-year period, would produce a return of less than $4,000. The same amount invested in their opposite number — those companies most evidently committed to promoting trust, employee well-being and values centered on the mutuality of the company's interests and those of the people working in it — would have returned more than $8,000 — exactly twice as much.

Share value, it seems, is one return on an investment in the emotional health of working people.

Attitudes Aligned With Profitability

The Gallup organization surveyed 55,000 workers earlier this year in an effort to match employee attitudes to company financial results. The survey found that four attitudes, taken together, correlate strongly with higher profits; workers feeling they are given the opportunity to do their best every day; believing their opinions count; sensing that their fellow workers are committed to quality; and seeing a direct connection between their work and the company's mission.

A recent report from management consulting giant Ernst & Young in the United States says that institutional investors are now more likely to buy stock based on a company's ability to attract talented people, literally betting cash that human relations inside a competitive organization make a material difference in the prospects and performance of that organization.

According to a study for the U.S. Department of Labor conducted by Harvard and the famous Wharton School of Business, "a company's surest way to profits is to treat employees as assets." A recent survey by the American Management Association finds that fewer than half of organizations that downsized since 1990 went on to report higher operating profits in the years following the layoffs, and even fewer saw improved productivity.

Research by the U.S. consulting firm Monitor found that nine out of 10 firms that had out-performed their industry over a 10-year period had stable structures with no more than one reorganization and no change in the chief executive. A considerable number of downsized banks, insurers and retail chains have all seen customer satisfaction plummet.

One in every five employees who lost their jobs through downsizings were supervisors. But this level of management had often acted as the synapses within the firm's institutional brain, linking shop-floor workers with senior managers. Thus the dilemma that we noted earlier about how excessive firings and terminations had the effect of depleting human capital.

It has become apparent that current depressants on productivity stem from a lack of critical mid-level leadership or effective co-ordination of efforts across the company. There is insufficient evidence, even now, in the wake of the downsizing era, that companies recognize or promote the value of knowledge and experience among middle managers — until after they leave. As a result, ex-employees are frequently rehired as consultants or subcontractors.

According to studies by management consultant Towers Perrin, expectations expressed by 550 employees of Canadian companies encouraged their management to cultivate an organizational culture that allowed them to have an influence on the company's financial success. Employees not only want to succeed personally, they want the company to succeed. This represents a correlation of positive factors that, if disconnected, undermine the emotional ties between the organization and the people in it.

Workers say, "Give us the tools to do our job, and trust us to do it." The question in managers' minds is, "Do they mean it? Can they do it?" Thus we return to our earlier theme of culture and the fit between the individual, her job and the company.

Strains of Resilience

Success in the global economy will increasingly mean tapping into the resilience and energy of employees. Both of these qualities are contingent upon the mental health of those individuals, and both are sapped by the absence of it.

One of the casualties of the downsizing era, all these studies tell us, may well be the sense of shared destiny between employer and employee — destiny in the sense that the company's success and the personal security of the employee are inextricably linked. In this compact, the sense of security comes from contributing to the company's financial progress. But the compact has been shaken by the downsizing wave and perhaps the most fundamental question of all gnawing at the modern marketplace — does hard work pay off?

Management experts are developing measures of employee feelings on such issues to give management the insight and the tools to reconnect employees' emotional interests to the company's financial interests. Towers Perrin refers to a career security index, a business alignment index, and a customer focus index, all tallying employee performance and expectations.

The Towers Perrin study tells us that employees are realists. They are more than familiar with the economic uncertainty of business today. More than two thirds have seen their company downsize or significantly restructure in the past two years.

Employees also know the business climate is improving, and believe the company they work for is more financially secure than it was a year ago. But they want to know how management intends to keep that trend going and how they can share in it.

Towers Perrin tells us that these findings suggest employees may be "a bit shell-shocked by events of the recent past, but are at least cautiously confident about the future."

"More interesting though, is the source of that confidence: not the company's efforts to streamline and restructure for growth, but rather a strong belief in their own work ethic and a commitment to their customers and the quality of what they do."

The survivors of downsizing, according to the Towers Perrin survey, generally believe little good has come of the efforts over the past number of years to chop headcounts and cut costs. They have been shaken by the loss of "family givens" such as homes and a reliable paycheque which became the dramatic residue of the job reductions they have seen around them.

Two thirds of those surveyed in this study maintained that their company's restructuring efforts either hurt or had no impact on the organization, and less than half believe their companies were successful at eliminating waste and bureaucracy, one of the most commonly stated objectives of the productivity quest that was such a driving force in the downsizing era.

Towers Perrin says that employers currently have "a vast reserve of excellent raw material in the form of a willing and able work force. But their ability to fully leverage this resource depends largely on how they approach the task."

The consultants also turn to the word "engagement," saying it is critical to engage employees if companies hope to have a productive work force that makes them more competitive.

The tools to do this are in the development stage as human resource and management consultants rally to find the best ways to use the revealing data flowing from a vast reservoir of contemporary post-deficit work and health studies.

Indices of the kind Towers Perrin cited are one such tool, emotional intelligence is another and a range of 'character measures' are a third. For these, we turn to Dr. Len Sperry.

The Imprint of Character

Dr. Len Sperry is a Professor of Psychiatry and Behavioral Medicine at the Medical College of Wisconsin in Milwaukee. He serves as a Director of its Division of Organizational Psychiatry and Corporate Health. He is a prolific author, having written 24 books and more than 200 professional papers.

In an interview for this report, and through the pages of his 1996 book, *Corporate Therapy and Consulting*, Dr. Sperry guides us into the realm of character and organizational health.

On the question of character as a measurable executive strength or weakness:

Q: *In a nutshell, how do you define character?*

Sperry: Essentially, it is what you do when no one's watching — but, beyond that, it represents the enduring component of personality based on learned, psychosocial influences. Character reflects the capacities of the self, the exercise of good judgment and the display of moral development.

Q: Can character spell the difference between success and failure among those who hold executive positions?

Sperry: [Indeed it can] — there are a large number of candidates for executive positions with superior knowledge, technical abilities and skills who will derail in the workplace because of their inability to function effectively with others consistently.

Q: Even after they've gone through a demanding selection or recruitment process?

Sperry: While they may have interviewed well, and scored well on standard measures of 'normal' personality, they cannot seem to sustain effective interpersonal functioning over time and under specific conditions.

Q: To understand this, should we draw a distinction between character and personality?

Sperry: Character can be differentiated from temperament, the biological influence on personality. [In the case of the failing executives just described,] they are said to be charming and good interviewees. In short, some executives have the capacity to present themselves as more promising during the job interview process than their actual performance after they have been offered the position.

Q: Are there signs or markers of character in a work setting?

Sperry: There are tangible markers of character — one is the capacity of the person to take responsibility for himself in meeting expectations; a second is the ability to be co-operative and collaborative with others, and a third, the capacity for 'self-transcendence' — that is, to step outside oneself to connect to a higher purpose for his actions, to see larger needs versus "my needs."

Q: Can these markers be picked up by psychological testing?

Sperry: 'Paper and pencil' psychological tests will not pick them up.

Q: How relevant is character to a healthy, competitive working environment?

Sperry: I believe it is the question of the 90s — a question of the Millennium. Leadership literature is replete with books and articles [on the subject] and it may well be that the recent spate of moral scandal in both the business and political arenas is fuelling this interest. Whatever the explanation, [in the U.S.,] corporate clients have begun prevailing on organizational psychiatrists and psychologists for advice.

Q: What, specifically, are they asking for?

Sperry: These clients want to know if a specific executive is a 'good fit' for working with a given manager or a certain team. They want to know if what they observed about a prospective executive during the interview process will hold up over time. And most importantly, they need to know if this executive will demonstrate sound judgment when threatened, tempted or when taking appropriate action that may or may not be in his or her own best interests.

Q: *This seems to extend the 'playing field' for psychiatrists and psychologists into the occupational arena?*

Sperry: Well, clients do expect [those disciplines] to be able to understand and deal effectively with the 'dark' as well as the 'bright' dimension of personality — in other words, they need to know about basic character dynamics of executives and other employees.

Dr. Sperry went on to note that 'character markers' were signals of some personality disorders. He said that executives who make 'bad hires' should not necessarily see themselves as having failed because these markers are often masked by an appealing external facade during the candidate interview process.

Having said that, "bad hires are killing business" because of the proliferation of job candidates who interview well, score high, look the part, are great actors and then bomb in the job.

When these new hires show themselves to be duds and troublemakers, the CEO will often just buy his way out of the difficulty. As a result, these people not only do well financially, they usually leave the company after a short time with a "socially lubricated letter of reference."

Dr. Sperry cited a class of executives who specialize in 'serial severance' packages — living handsomely, in effect, on their ability to win the job, only to then lose it too early for his or her boss to do anything other than to buy their way out of a "bad hire" for the sake of everyone who had a hand in it.

In short, their 'character deficit' pays off very well for them.

The non-performers Dr. Sperry talks about are familiar to anyone who has ever had responsibility for the work of other people. They take on new work eagerly but don't meet deadlines. They agree to meetings but regularly cancel at the last minute for 'unchallengeable' reasons [eg, family problems] and they are terrific note-takers, scripting every detail of every conversation with their boss. Dr. Sperry says they are very litigious.

These 'players' are consistently inconsistent and often prone to indiscreet disclosures. They may seek early or premature intimacy with their boss (talking about family concerns in the first week on the job) as they smoke out a kind of bonding with a personal dimension (not sexual in nature) so, in their minds, their boss will protect them.

People with character deficits like this have fine-tuned 'detector systems', picking up the boss' longings, and they are adept at making strong eye contact. They are 'high-functioning borderline' cases on the edge of a diagnosable personality disorder.

The Mask of the Inner Self

Dr. Jacques Bradwejn is Psychiatrist-in-Chief at the Royal Ottawa Hospital and Chairman of Psychiatry at the University of Ottawa. He is an expert in anxiety disorders. In an interview for this report, Dr. Bradwejn moves to a related front in business-emotional health: anxiety disorders. A spectrum of everyday people, powerful executives, politicians, doctors and lawyers are "suffering like hell."

Obsessive-compulsive disorders, he said, represent the fifth highest cost of the medical system. Those with this disorder suffer a merry-go-round of disorientation. While at work, at their desk, they will rewrite one letter 25 times before sending it out, part of the ritual phenomenon associated with this disorder.

The sufferer is extremely anxious, teetering on a sense of doom. Dr. Bradwejn says otherwise rational people will spend three hours washing their hands before going to work, an agony they suffer alone, held prisoner by the 'shame' they feel.

That same person may drive to work captured by the fear of having a fatal accident. They may pull over 10 to 15 times before they get to work and experience the same ritual on the way home. Before reporting for work, an obsessive-compulsive woman might take seven hours in the morning applying her makeup. While at work, she is always well-prepared, articulate and organized. "Suffering a great deal — alone," Dr. Bradwejn says.

Many who suffer this form of anxiety disorder don't know that it can be diagnosed and treated. They are subsumed by the great flaw in character or personality that the disorder has come to represent in their mind.

"Letting them know that the anxiety they are experiencing is a known entity is a big first step," Dr. Bradwejn says — adding, at the same time, that even when some people come to that realization, they often continue to deny it.

Eventually, obsessive-compulsive disorders become chronic. The employee just stops functioning, goes on long-term disability or simply fails to progress in the job, while co-workers and supervisors in the company look on understandably bewildered about why this person's performance has fallen so precipitously.

Sarcasm Born of Insecurity

A manager stands before a staff meeting seeming 'full of himself' and says a few things to his colleagues that verge on the sarcastic. "Full of himself" is not the way it is. Full of terror and anxiety is more like it. Hostage to a social phobia that Dr. Bradwejn says plagues the workplace largely undetected.

The attitude this person displayed was the compensation he used for the fear he felt. Typically over-prepared for meetings weeks in advance, his sarcasm and outward over-confidence were driven by 'low self-worth.' He drank alcohol before every meeting and was like the phobic truck driver who took five drinks in the morning just to calm down. His problems would grow bigger.

Anxiety disorders, including panic disorder, post-traumatic stress disorder and generalized anxiety, bleed into other conditions, including alcoholism and depression.

Dr. Bradwejn says those who suffer an anxiety disorder are often diagnosed with depression but it proves secondary — the real problem is anxiety, a different condition or set of conditions which are "well defined, well studied, and preventable, but difficult to detect even by a family physician."

Anxiety pervades daily life. Sufferers continue to function but are clearly affected, lose concentration and lose energy at work, and experience a serious decline in their performance on the job.

Howard Hughes was obsessive-compulsive. "Unfortunately for him, he was so rich, he was able to arrange the world for his compulsion," Dr. Bradwejn observed. So he did not get appropriate treatment.

Elusive Reasons

Anxiety disorders can strike out of the blue. One Bradwejn patient suddenly developed feelings of anxiety three times a day, sometimes watching a football game. He had no money or family problems — so why the anxiety? His condition worsened. He developed a fear of being confined in a large plane. He panicked when he couldn't get off so he stopped flying. He avoided anywhere he felt trapped.

Anxiety disorders can have physical implications — irritable bowel syndrome can flare up. The whole body can become hyperactive. Migraine headaches may occur.

The symptoms of panic disorders can replicate those of a heart condition. Often in emergency rooms, that is what the person exhibiting these symptoms will be treated for.

Dr. Bradwejn points up the differences between anxiety and depression: the first represented by generalized worrying all the time, can't sleep, can't relax, overall a poor quality of life; the other characterized by an inability to concentrate, very negative, hopeless and helpless feelings, no appetite or energy, can't work. The two disorders engage different biological systems.

Dr. Bradwejn says the symptoms of an anxiety disorder are often "so concrete that the person experiencing them will go to the emergency room, feeling faint or severe pain. Told nothing is wrong, he goes home, but the next time it happens, returns to the emergency room again." Emergency physicians are not trained to recognize [anxiety] when there is no heart pathology.

Personality disorders are a member of the anxiety family ranging symptomatically from the mistrustful, dramatic and histrionic to the highly narcissistic and self-centred, a class often populated by high achievers who "become sick for the company."

Anxiety is an expensive disorder — in part because of its elusive and masked nature and the instincts of people, including some health professionals not to look for it or to deny its existence. Anxiety disorders are treatable, Dr. Bradwejn says, and, as for depression, the principal weapon is early detection. The alternative is to see sufferers slide into long-term disability, depression and often addictions.

The Economic Cost of Anxiety

The Centre for Anxiety and Related Disorders at Boston University tells us one third of the patients it treats for panic disorders are chronically unemployed; they are off work at twice the rate and generally use medical services seven times as often.

In a report issued by the Centre this year, Drs. D.A. Hope and C.N. Carmin note that while anxiety disorders are very common mental illnesses, only a few studies have investigated their financial burden on society. Yet one fourth of the 'normal' population reports at least one anxiety disorder in their lifetime and nearly one in five, over the preceding 12 months. Anxiety disorders last a lifetime for more than a quarter of those afflicted.

The Boston Centre study goes on to say that the indirect costs of panic disorders spread in all kinds of directions: 58% of female and 63% of male patients seek help for emotional, alcohol and/or drug-related problems, and significantly, 33% of male anxiety patients and 15% of females received disability payments in the previous six months.

"The highest rates of substance dependence were observed in patients with panic disorders. Compared to patients with other psychological problems, those diagnosed with panic disorder use the emergency department for emotional problems most often."

"Compared to the general population," the Boston University paper said, "people with subclinical panic are at higher risk for other co-morbid mental disorders, especially alcohol and other drug abuse; at risk for increased use of healthcare facilities for emotional problems, and for more use of psychoactive drugs."

A recent study from France documented the impact of co-morbidity on the direct and indirect costs of treating 1,042 patients with generalized anxiety disorder. The co-morbid conditions included gastroenterological, gynecological and rheumatological problems, as well as psychiatric diagnoses such as depression and addictions.

The estimated total costs per patient for three months was $1,208 among sufferers of generalized anxiety disorders co-morbid with other disorders compared to $733 for those without a complicating "second presence."

Lost productivity at work equalled the cost of hospitalization as a further indication of the huge cost of mental disorders.

Offset Effect

Dr. Beth Reade, a psychiatrist at the Homewood Health Centre says "it is cheaper to treat panic disorders than not to treat them". This is particularly true if indirect costs are high and the treatments are cost-effective. Her point was drawn from a study by Boston University that examined what it called "the offset effect" — essentially how direct spending on the treatment of mental disorders offsets the indirect (productivity) costs associated with them.

The offset effect was documented in Spain where direct spending on psychological and drug treatment of panic disorders went up from $30,000 to $47,000 in the cases under study, while the indirect costs of the disorders, lost productivity, went down from $66,000 to $14,000. Direct spending offset the indirect cost of the disorder.

The Boston University study found that outpatient settings are less expensive and just as effective as inpatient services. Yet inpatient care still takes 70% of mental health dollars in the U.S., although that trend may be changing. Still, this finding is notable in the context that one Canadian insurance policy, ruled discriminatory by the

Supreme Court of Canada, stipulated in 1996 that the only way an employee could retain her disability benefits for mental illness was to remain hospitalized.

The Emotional Pollution of Office Politics

Returning to our discussion with Dr. Jacques Bradwejn, he describes the behaviour profile of what we call office politics, a source of emotional wreckage caused by mental disorders which go unchecked and flow from some corporate cultures.

Office politics are often crafted (and played) by psychopathic personalities, the type of individual who can be charming and, on the surface, supportive of others but who is driven by massive self-absorption and who "has no problem screwing somebody else." In fact, this kind of person exhibits a pattern of behaviour that is often encouraged by the corporate culture in which he or she works.

Dr. Bradwejn describes this psychopathic personality as living by a "self-serving morality." Often, he runs whole departments of people who suffer beneath him and experience a take-and-no-give operating style.

Office politics of this brutal variety are played skillfully. Those who are victimized by it have given themselves and their ideas to their employer, only to see both translated into the personal ownership of the practising office politician. Eventually, they feel used and grow demoralized. Their values seem to take on a fool's gold quality in the atmosphere created by psychopathic office politics, and they become cynical.

Dr. Bradwejn says the issue often turns on the mental health of the people who exchange their destinies in this intimate working context. He says that corporate environments where these disorders play out with impunity are those where the values of the company, and the people working in it, are 'not aligned', "a system," he says, "that is sick, and one that loses money."

The mission of the company or department, and the people in it, degenerates into deep-seated doubts about the long-term prospects of the company. No stability. No loyalty. High levels of sickness in the workplace. Conflicted workers unable to concentrate and functioning below par, knowing that "this is not the right place for them, but they need the money."

The homes of the employees who work under these conditions are ultimately invaded by this emotional pollution, which is carried like the flu from the workplace to the home in the form of stress and anxiety. Kids suffer emotionally and at school. Marital breakdown is a direct by-product of the pathologies of a 'sick system' at the office. Employees who are victimized by psychopathic politics can develop "a pathology themselves."

Dr. Bradwejn describes the "sick system" as one characterized by hypocrisy. For example, employees are sent to seminars to learn about how to be heard, to be empowered, to work in the 'new economy'. But they learn from their experience in the sick system that this is all talk and no action. The values that the company pays for them to learn are never made use of.

The Cloud of Uncertainty

Uncertainty faces all companies. One telltale sign of the state of health of the organization is the way the company works to minimize the emotional casualties of that uncertainty.

Dr. Bradwejn says the problem is how we perceive uncertainty. Does it produce a sense of personal or corporate failure? Does it project the worst in likely outcomes and morale?

The CorpWorld Group — a company that one of the authors of this report, Bill Wilkerson, co-owned with Fraser Kelly, formerly one of Canada's leading journalists — worked with large corporations that were facing uncertain times.

One of the keys to navigating those churning waters was the capacity of leaders to articulate the reasons for the uncertainty with clarity and precision, but without making false promises about how the uncertainty will work out, and without engaging in speculation or conjecture.

The CorpWorld experience found that employees who may be reacting to layoff rumours, or to conjecture about the acquisition of their company, to depressed operating results or to sudden changes in senior management, are not looking for what management can't deliver to them.

What they are thirsty for can be summed up in one word: the truth. Conversely, for the senior management group, truth doesn't mean making inappropriate or unclear disclosures. Neither does it mean silence rationalized on the premise that if you can't tell everything, you tell nothing. In uncertain conditions, the former is hazardous; the latter is unreasonable.

Employees will take uncertainty as a "fact of life" if it is imparted clearly. Let's listen in on a hypothetical general manager speaking to his supervisors and line superintendents:

Q. (Employee): Mr. Franklin, we've heard rumours for days that there will be layoffs in the plant. Can you clear this up — are layoffs being planned?

A.: I won't be able to clear it up as much as you would want me to — and while I can tell you we haven't planned specific headcount reductions, clearly we will have to bring our costs down if our sales don't harden up.

Q. (Employee): Can you tell us when you will know for sure?

A.: I can't say, for sure, but I can say this: when I do have the information you require, I will talk to you about it fully and completely. I understand this kind of uncertainty is very difficult to live with. I really regret that. And I'll tell you what I can, when I can. In the meantime, the best thing all of us can do is to carry on with our jobs the best way we know how.

Just let me add this. You know that I believe very strongly in being as open and as fair as I know how when it comes to things like this. That won't change. When you hear rumours, remember what I've just said, or come and see me in person and I'll tell you at everything I can.

There is a catch in all this. This fictional dialogue ended on a note that can only be struck in a tense situation if the employees **believe** their manager. Only if he is believable, and only if his track record substantiates his claim to being open and fair. **Only then**, will he have the trust of his people when he needs it most.

Our hypothetical general manager didn't promise what he *couldn't* promise. He didn't speculate or emptily sympathize. He didn't clear up the uncertainty, but he did talk about the fact that it existed, frankly and openly.

Remembering Dr. Bradwejn's point about "how we perceive uncertainty," the result of this general manager's talk was to help his employees perceive this uncertainty. First, as a fact of life, not as a metaphor for some kind of failure on their part, and second, as a question of business performance. Unless sales improved, costs must come down, but that was not presented as a threat.

In fact, he held out the possibility that by doing their jobs the best way they knew how, they could, in turn, help impact the outcome. His words were not laced with rhetoric. His only obligation was the truth.

Dr. Bradwejn says that "how people use words" can have a defining impact on the state of mind of people who are on the receiving end of them. Words like "sharing" and "empowerment" and "commitment" (used a lot in this report) may have lost meaning because of their frequent use and because they are often used by people who don't practise the values the words describe.

Treachery With Trust

Trust is earned, the cliché says. Not always.

Some people are trusting by nature and give of themselves, in this sense, quite freely. When they are misled, the fall is particularly steep. Often, they are the victims of narcissistic empathy exhibited in the workplace by managers and colleagues who use this insight and instinct to get to know the trusting person they intend to manipulate.

Rather than earned, trust is defined in the workplace by the capacity of people to *return* it. In effect, one person recruits evidence that another person *can* be trusted to do what they said or believe what they said they believed in.

A capacity to *illustrate* trust, Dr. Bradwejn says, can go a long way in fostering the core values of an organization. If the values of the company are not conflicted, then the inevitable disappointments and stresses of daily working lives can be managed in a more straightforward way. More often than not, the company that illustrates trust — whatever its problems and promises — will also be a healthy company to work for.

♨23♨
The Loyalty Effect

FREDERICK REICHHELD IS DIRECTOR OF BAIN & COMPANY, A LEADING STRAT-
egy consulting firm in Boston, and has been widely published in business journals. In 1997, the Harvard Business School Press published
his bestseller, *The Loyalty Effect*.

Certain themes articulated in Dr. Reichheld's book are worth visiting here, given the emphasis we have placed so far on human relations and mental health as productivity issues.

Companies that downsize mainly to outperform their competitors tend to lead by a slight margin for a six-month period, but then
lag badly, typically netting a negative 24% rating on the Standard &
Poor's 500 by the end of three years.

Historically, business managers have under-invested in retaining
the loyalty of their people. Apparently they know the cost of this
kind of investment but not its value. The metrics, up to now, have
had a face value. Laying people off saves money. This seems clear
enough. At the same time, though, the ongoing cash flow consequences of diminished loyalty are less obvious.

HR departments have tried to quantify the price of employee turnover by tracking costs of recruiting, training and even lost productivity. But, Dr. Reichheld says, these numbers have failed to convince
managers to change course because they are not tied to familiar accounting numbers or to cash flows.

Cash Flow Impact of Unhappiness
"The true cash flow consequences of employee turnover far exceed
most managers' intuitive estimates," Dr. Reichheld said. "In fact, the
turnover tax on corporate earnings, although invisible in most ac-

counting systems, is larger than any state or federal tax. At one trucking company, one of our consulting teams carefully quantified the economic penalties of excessive employee churn and found that the client could increase profits 50% by cutting driver turnover in half. At a stock brokerage, those same consultants found a 10% improvement in broker retention (from 80% to 90%) would increase the value of the brokerage by 155%. The economics of agent retention in the insurance field are similar.

Dr. Reichheld says the key to quantifying the cash flow consequences of employee turnover is essentially the same in any industry: that is, recognizing that employee retention is not only critical for cost efficiency but important to revenue growth. It links directly to the acquisition and retention of customers.

Hard evidence of this can be found in the auto service business. People feel more comfortable doing repeat business with the same individual, if their experience justifies it, regardless of the employee's technical finesse.

When one chain of stores ranked its operations on the basis of both loyalty and productivity, Dr. Reichheld found, the employees in the top third of length of service were also in the top third of the productivity ranking, they had sales per employee 22% higher than the bottom third.

Dr. Reichheld says U.S. business has invested billions in enhancing technologies to improve productivity, from mainframes to PCs to information networks, and from copiers and faxes to cell phones. They have re-engineered processes and laid off millions of workers. But he disputes the apparent logic of it all.

Why hasn't productivity skyrocketed? Its growth in the United States has lagged behind that of other major economies. In Canada, the productivity rate is the lowest in the G-7 nations. Since 1960, U.S. productivity has inched ahead at a glacial pace, according to Dr. Reichheld, with the service sector showing the weakest performance. The size of recent investments in technology to enhance productivity, should have set productivity rates into orbit. But it didn't. The reasons aren't clear.

He cites telephone and real estate companies that spent heavily on technology for years, but realized marginal productivity gains, then began to invest heavily in their human capital — nearly 3% of revenues, in one case, or on about a million hours of training, plus new work and pay policies designed to keep the best people. The turnover rate among the companies surveyed dropped by more than 40%.

Frayed Conventions

'Convention' is often just a worn-out truth. The quest to improve productivity often meant big investments in automation. The thrust of those investments was to displace workers, not empower them. Resulting layoffs and policies meant to minimize the growth in salaries often led to reduced employee loyalty and soaring turnover.

The truth is that revenues and costs are inextricably linked, and decisions that focus on one but not both usually misfire.

The manner in which productivity is measured also merits reconsideration. The number of transactions each employee can do is just one of the ways that companies have attempted to manage productivity rates more effectively. Dr. Reichheld argues for a different measure: revenue per person, a topline characteristic of business in the post-deficit era. This is a theme we discussed earlier in the report.

In the retail sector, many companies measure sales per square foot. Nordstrom uses the yardstick of revenue per salesclerk.

In this light, Reichheld says that for a meaningful productivity ratio to work, the numerator of the ratio has to capture the *value* of output, not simply its volume. And just as disability combined with life expectancy ratios, provides a broader measure of the quality or value of life that a population may experience, the measure of business performance must essentially do the same thing. The qualitative must merge with the quantitative. This is the stuff of life, and perhaps the essential theme of this report.

The old definitions of productivity, therefore, may well be frayed, if not obsolete or perhaps even obstructive.

Another aspect of Dr. Reichheld's meditation merits comment. The revenue numerator of the productivity ratio must include price. And as the author of *The Loyalty Effect* has noted, in most industries real prices drop as competitors learn to deliver the product or service more effectively. Effectiveness must increase faster than prices decline if productivity is to improve.

The question, therefore, is what kind of productivity will differentiate one company from the next in the competitive global economy of the 21st Century? The differentiator is likely *not to be* investments in new technology, at least exclusively, because they can be copied. Even product redesign is fairly easy to duplicate. At the very least, both measures are transient.

The true distinction between the productivity indicators of the past and those of future could reside in the measurement of revenue, not just cost per unit of production. The qualitative numerator is expressed in Dr. Reichheld's example of measuring the output of a retail store on the basis of revenue, not cost per square foot. Advances along these lines have been made through quality control and piecework excellence standards.

As a competitive feature, improvements in employee loyalty are even harder to replicate company to company. Human resource systems built on intangibles such as trust and motivation, and subjective inducements such as career paths, training, compensation and measurement can be the source of a sustainable competitive advantage that is hard to duplicate.

The biggest enemy to this way of thinking is a failure to measure the contribution that employees make to the creation of value, value for the customer and value for the company. Another enemy is the mismatch between what employers pay as compensation from what they expect through productivity.

Dr. Reichheld says in his Harvard-published book that "productivity growth and revenue growth go hand in hand." He says we have entered an era when competitiveness will rest more and more on the problem-solving capacities, versatility and mobility of workers. At the same time, it will also hinge on learning how to motivate and give incentives to those employees.

A recent study by the Organization for Economic Cooperation and Development found that the median length of employment for U.S. workers is three years, compared to eight in Japan and Germany. Investment in formal training is also much lower in the U.S. and Canada. This is not surprising when the average worker stays for such a short period of time.

One CEO told *Fortune* magazine that, "for the U.S. to compete really well in the world, we have to put more thought content into our products. That's what we're really good at." Facing depressed earnings, the same CEO intends to do so by increasing productivity without reducing people. One reason for that is that in a highly competitive workplace environment, he can't afford to lose good people.

Some studies tell us that, typically, customers defect from companies at a rate between 10% and 30% a year. Employee turnover is similar. The average annual churn among employees in the United States can exceed 50%, prompting one economist to observe that "the most valuable inventory in U.S. business is vanishing without a trace from one company to the next.

Not Enough About Health
Sydney Taurel, President and Chief Executive Officer of Eli Lilly & Company, says much has been written about changes sweeping over organizations today, including globalization and successive waves of industry consolidation, but less has been said about the impact these forces are having upon workers and their families, and consequently, about the health of the organization.

Mr. Taurel calls for an all-out search for a philosophy of value in managing human resources. He endorses the concept of reciprocity as a basic plank in the contract between employer and employee and talks about a reciprocal ethical bond that ensures the needs of the company and employee are harmonized.

The Eli Lilly CEO talks about enabling people to do the things they do best in the company's best interests. We heard this theme earlier in this report. It resonates powerfully.

Eli Lilly has invested heavily in training. Mr. Taurel says, "our employees understand that they too must be flexible and they too must stretch to keep their knowledge and their skills relevant to our rapidly changing business." This is the reason Eli Lilly places an emphasis on career-long education, training and development.

The company has put in a child development centre at its corporate headquarters and introduced backup day-care, part-time work, work-at-home arrangements and flexible hours. So have other companies now awakening to the opportunity and the luminous challenge of adapting to the realities of human capitalization of business by competing in the global marketplace. Mr. Taurel says creating "an environment where people can do their best" is a core management responsibility.

He says efforts to support employees' own work/family priorities are simply good business. They are neither perks nor giveaways. They attract, motivate and retain people who will be more dedicated, more focused and, therefore, more productive.

He calls for comprehensive studies to draw a clearer link between productivity and work/family programs, between health, absenteeism and the financial results of the organization.

"More broadly, I think you can make a very persuasive case that one of the most important dynamics of the new global economy is a new way of understanding the value of people. The economies of the developed nations depend on a new kind of worker, one we call the knowledge worker, whose value lies not merely in what they can do with their hands but what they can do with their minds. And that is, more often than not, the value that appreciates over time."

Sydney Taurel makes an eloquent case for mental health as a business asset and mental illness as a business issue. He also implies a need for the kind of leadership that will see the world through the eyes of the employee, at least enough to better understand the balancing act that home and work pressures compel employees to perform just to get their job done and their family obligations met. In this, we see the spirit of empathy-based leadership.

Research tells us that emotions often determine how people do in life. Empathy is a way to see emotions as an insight into behaviours and work performances of others, especially those who have gone off track and drifted away from what is routinely expected of them.

The Search for Trust

In the search for trust and productivity ratios where human value can be measured, the capacity of the individual worker feeds the numerator (revenue) while helping to contain the denominator (costs). Employers will increasingly seek out employees who exhibit emotional maturity, dependability, empathy and perspective. Steven Covey, in his 1989 best-seller *The Seven Habits of Highly Effective People*, underscores the relevance of empathy to the capacity of leaders and followers to understand customer needs, and then to meet them.

Skill sets and mindsets go hand in hand in the global information economy. The common denominator of both is empathy. Interpersonal relationships will help produce a strong productivity numerator. Self-esteem is connected to this equation as well. The goal of the company is to facilitate the contribution of the employee to the creation of value by the company. Financial rewards must be matched by a clear and positive sense of self (the contribution 'I'm making') among working people. All of this emphasizes the importance of clear communications, relationships, tactfulness and expectation. Important underpinnings for a healthy and hospitable work environment.

Empathy for another, in fact, has been known to boost the coping ability of the person who receives it. Empathy is not sympathy (where objectivity is lost). It is the ability to sense reactions among other people, to pick up clues as to how they feel. It doesn't mean agreeing with another person's feelings, it means knowing they exist.

Responsive and empathetic awareness is known to facilitate and enhance many human activities. Empathy is a clinical skill. It is also a business tool. Consistently, management experts enumerate the principal skills of leaders in business as revolving around communication, vision and empathy, complementing financial skills as a major prerequisite.

The selection of employee candidates is influenced by a range of factors, obviously. But in the end, a match between the values of the person and the culture of the company, their predispositions, their capacity to enjoy productive working relationships that contribute to both the quality numerator (revenue) and quantity denominator (units of sale or production) are telling.

These are the currency values of human capital: adaptability, personal values and belief systems, an ability to focus and concentrate and get things done with integrity, a capacity for human follow-up and for listening to the next person, promoting a culture that is healthy and not political.

Dependability, accountability, self-confidence, emotional stamina, loyalty, tenacity, anticipation, trust, keeping one's cool, taking calculated risks, inviting dissent, perseverance and good communication skills — these are the skills that human capital buys and that financial capital can't get its hands on.

Yet, by and large, the ability of management people to sense out or underwrite ways to develop capacities of this nature, and deploy systems to do so, remains undeveloped.

For managers, three most often cited sources of stress are role conflict, role ambiguity and workload variance. Notably, the issue isn't always one of too much or too little work, but one of work flow. Where that is inconsistent, incongruous or disrespectful of the basic canons of valuing time, the effects on workers can be divisive.

In turn, each of these "sources of stress" is a crack in the strength of the human capital that a company possesses, just as a drain on cash flow erodes credit at the bank.

Role conflict stems in part from politically flavoured competition among employees and often from conflicting expectations from supervisors and managers and executives. They often derive from the employee's own perception that senior management itself is conflicted.

Role ambiguity, simply put, results from unclear expectations, vague goals or poorly written or absent job descriptions. It can also flow from inconsistency between the employee's job description and what he or she is actually asked to do. In some cases, role ambiguity stems from a person's own inner uncertainty about whether they wish to be part of the scene in which he works.

Fluctuations in workload are a source of distress, as is imbalance between home and work. Surviving an organizational downsizing, then facing more work for no greater reward in an atmosphere of uncertainty about what's going to "happen to me" produces the same undermining anxiety.

The mental resilience of employees is not a mysterious thing. The capacity to motivate people is not a mystery either. Both can be undermined when employees are mismatched with an inappropriate task; when responsibility exceeds authority and the person can't get their job done as a result; when tasks are unclear, sometimes in terms of setting priorities and sometimes in critical detail; when work goes on too long, one week to the next, without information being shared between the person doing the work and the person expecting the result. Delegation and deputizing do not mean "never hearing again" from the boss upstairs except when something goes wrong.

"The Art of Listening"*

The capacity to listen is crucial to the mental health of others. Managers often overestimate their listening skills, and they often listen poorly because they hear words without interpreting or searching for meaning. We hear managers say to their colleagues or subordinates, "get to the bottom line" — a dismissive expression of the concerns of the other person, and often too narrow a context to receive or impart useful information.

It implies efficiency, saving time, getting to the point, being effective, when in fact it may be none of these things — especially when industry must return to the top line in its search for new revenues, new ideas, creativity and a more productive, less exclusive relationship with employees.

Covey has brought his message of integrity and empathy to the process of sales training. His book has been described as "common sense organized well." Essentially, the message from Steven Covey is that business actions should be based on deeply held principles and not fleeting moods.

The effects of the downsizing era were described, in a 1996 article in *The Economist* magazine as "corporate amnesia." *The Economist* noted that many world corporations noticed that their processes may be "more perfect, their systems sleeker and their work forces leaner, but they are not noticeably more competitive." Even the reports of higher operating profits after the downsizing era were not accompanied by improved productivity.

* *The CorpWorld Group, 1986*

Costly Turf Wars

The CEO of Bank of America Corporation, David Coulter, took over his company in 1996. His first order, conveyed through the executives reporting directly to him was: "End the turf wars." End the office politics, which had been a major distraction at the second largest U.S. bank and were foreshadowing a further decline when he arrived.

Market analysts attributed the infighting and the Bank of America's ponderous bureaucracy to its competitive and productivity lag, and *vice versa*. These and other factors meant the Bank earned $1.15 for every $100 of assets, compared with $1.59 and $1.83 at its nearest competitors. Coulter was hired by the board of the Bank of America largely because of his people skills. His predecessor had been defeated, they said, by the "Balkan politics" practised in the bank.

Even former White House Press Secretary DeeDee Myers, now a television commentator, said office politics hurt her while she worked for the President, and she finally left.

In a study of managers in the United Kingdom, the two greatest causes of workplace stress were identified as unreasonable deadlines and office politics, coming even ahead of firing people.

In their book *The Four Levers of Corporate Change*, Peter Brill and Richard Worth say that corporate change must occur at the emotional level because this is where resistance to change usually occurs. They say the battle is on — for the hearts *and minds* of modern employees, not their backs and arms.

Could the distinction between the industrial and information eras be drawn more clearly than that?

The Self-Infliction of Hyper Competition

For almost two decades, managers have been learning to play by a new set of rules. "Companies must be flexible in order to respond rapidly to competitive markets. They must benchmark continuously to achieve best practice. They must outsource aggressively to gain efficiencies. And they must nurture a few core competencies in the race to stay ahead of rivals."

This proposition comes to us from Michael Porter, the C. Roland Christensen Professor of Business Administration at the Harvard Business School. He says new business dogma has evolved to the point where business executives jump from one competitive strategy to another, believing competitive advantage is transient and temporary.

He cautions: "Those beliefs are dangerous half-truths and they are leading more and more companies down the path of mutually-destructive competition" — as a result, a phenomenon he calls "hyper competition" has become, in some industries, "a self-inflicted wound, not an inevitable outcome of a changing paradigm of competition." Dr. Porter draws a link between the "hurried and worried society" discussed earlier in this report, and the leadership behaviour of business organizations intensifying their competitive efforts in a global economy and information-based society — creating, as a result, a state of permanent turmoil as they strive to define, sharpen and hold competitive advantage in supposedly ceaselessly changing conditions. Chaos theory at work. Dr. Porter:

The quest for productivity, quality and speed has spawned a remarkable number of new management tools and techniques — total quality management, benchmarking, time-based competition, outsourcing, partnership, re-engineering, and change management.

Acronyms multiply and the reflections of the curse of the "flavour of the month" has settled across a sea of employee faces as they greet each new management theory. While perception in these matters is accurate in emotional terms, there's no strong evidence the alleged curse is as widespread as employees who are introduced to "TQM" or "CI" may instinctively feel it is.

But what *has* happened, according to Michael Porter in a notable article in the 1996 year-end edition of the *Harvard Business Review*, is that the tactics of survival have largely replaced long-term strategic thinking — "management tools have taken the place of strategy, and as managers push to improve on all fronts, they move farther away from viable competitive positions."

At the same time, Dr. Porter fairly points out that the new ways to manage have produced often dramatic operational improvements. Still, "companies have been frustrated by their inability to translate those gains into sustainable profitability." Bit by bit, he says, "almost imperceptibly," the effects of hyper-competition take on the angry look of a self-inflicted wound.

Companies competing in a global world, like the society they are part of, have been rattled by change. Speed and the relentless downfield pursuit of a constantly shifting goal line push the company team toward what feels to many like ever receding performance demands.

In this competitive drive, there is no game clock, but something reminiscent of actor William Holden's comment as he crept up to the Bridge on the River Kwai, ticking explosives tucked under his arm:

"There is always, always, one more thing to do."

Always More to Do

Always, one more thing to do: in a workworld and workday where the job is over only when time runs out. The sense of achievement that we all need to nourish our energies of commitment and determination is more difficult, if not outright impossible when our day, our week, our year, our career have become one deadline replaced by two more and none of them sequentially spaced, all of them jammed together like a collector lane feeding Canada's busiest highway, the 401, across the top of Toronto on a Friday afternoon rush hour.

This is the environment in which companies look for competitive advantages in human capital as embodied in productive employees, suppliers and contracted knowledge workers.

Michael Porter once again: "A company can outperform rivals only if it can establish a difference it can reserve." And thus preserve. Mostly, as the Bank of Montreal and others have concluded, that difference is found in the people who work in the company, and not the shell that would exist if they weren't there.

Cost advantages are proving transient, according to speakers at a conference of the Washington Business Group on Health. The search is now on, as noted a few pages back, for a productivity model based on human health, which, in turn, is the heartbeat of human capital in the information economy.

Harvard and others are trying to do in business what astrophysicists are doing in their exploration of the limits of the universe — to discover a new frontier of performance behaviour and truth defining the global economy — and thus, eventually, to establish some kind of outer limit to the differentiation that competing corporations can realistically hope to reach.

Dr. Porter calls this the "productivity frontier", a time and place, he imagines, where the sum of all existing "best business practices" is present at any given time.

"When a company improves its operational effectiveness, it moves toward that frontier. Doing so may require capital investment, different personnel, or simply new ways of managing."

"The productivity frontier", he says, "is constantly shifting outward" as new inputs become available and new technologies and management approaches are developed.

Laptop computers, mobile communications, the Internet and software like Lotus Notes have redefined the productivity frontier for sales operations and have opened up possibilities of linking sales with critical back-office activities such as order-processing. This is what the Internet can do spectacularly well.

Dr. Porter's sales example illustrates in concrete and appropriately unglamorous terms the essence of functional integration in modern corporations — and what the so-called "health integration challenge," facilitated by new technology, is all about.

In healthcare, in business, in public service (where one-stop shopping is a strongly desired "end state" of municipal amalgamations in Ontario) and in retail services, the integration of computer-based functions is the path toward "mass customization" and the marvels of new-age industrial design such as the paperless creation of Boeing's 777 aircraft that author Thomas Stewart told us about earlier.

As companies move to Michael Porter's productivity frontier, they can often improve on many performance dimensions at the same time. Manufacturers who adopted the Japanese practice of rapid changeovers in the 1980s were able to lower costs while improving their differentiation in the marketplace.

For consumers, the benefit of this was noteworthy. In fact, it was the point at which business crossed a crucial threshold, and a myth was exploded. The legendary trade-offs between cost and product defects — if you cut costs, you increased product defects but you could also reduce prices — was found to be false, an illusion long fostered to cover up operational ineffectiveness.

The quality movement taught us that quality and lower costs could go hand-in-hand. In time, business also learned that environmentally sensitive production methods — requiring new capital expenditures — could also be at peace with making a profit.

We are now discovering, in business and in the wider community, that investments in health, requiring new dollar expenditures, can have a beneficial effect on productivity and are allies of profit-making as well.

In these two colourless words — productivity and profitability — we find the keys to open new doors of opportunity associated with the health of both our environment and our people.

The first Homewood Lecture at the 16th Congress of the Association of Social Psychiatry in Vancouver, B.C., in August, 1998, explored this "other" productivity frontier in some depth. Prepared by the authors of this report, the lecture carried a number of themes that seem relevant to our discussion here. The reader is invited to explore those themes with us. ❧

✺24✺
The Ultimate
Productivity Weapon

Homewood Lecture, August 17, 1998

THE GIVENS OF JOB SECURITY AND PLANNED RETIREMENT HAVE BEEN SHAKEN *by the economic quakes booming like sonic waves across an aging society. Our response to the issue of mid-life productivity — the middle-aged worker and the middle-aged corporation — may well define the times ahead.*

We are entering a time of merger and marriage among some of the largest corporations in the world. Not since the wave of industrial take-overs that created the great oil, steel and auto companies at the start of the 20th Century, has corporate life been reshaped by a sweep of merger activity as broad as the one taking place today.

From telecommunications to banking, from aerospace to entertainment, powerful new competitive blocs, free trade zones and massive market conglomerations like the ads for the movie Godzilla proclaim that size does count in the corporate run-up to the 21st Century. The New York Times:

> *What is happening at the end of the 20th Century is a reprise of the industrial upheavals that took place at the beginning of the century, when more than two dozen auto companies merged in 1908 to form General Motors, and J.P. Morgan created U.S. Steel out of a dozen different companies.*

Clearly, today's mergers are driven by the desire of corporations in a number of sectors to gain global reach. Perhaps the most telling implication of the world's globalization, in health terms, is the search now on for new forms of productivity and for a whole new approach to creating value and profitability in highly competitive industry sectors where, literally, the world is their marketplace.

We are entering the post-deficit era. The intensive — some say obsessive — efforts to cut business costs, slim down the midriff of corporations and reduce fat bureaucracies have probably run their course. From here on out, comparative advantages among competitors are increasingly unlikely to be found in pure cost-reduction.

This fact signals a return to the 'top line' as the principal source of nourishment for the bottom line (net income) and for shareholders in equity value (share price). The top line is the place not only where revenue and income are displayed on the balance sheet but a place of ideas, relationships, sales and new possibilities.

In the wake of the downsizing era, it is a more hopeful place, because it promotes real growth through expansion, not through cost contraction alone.

Metaphorically, the top line is the place where new employment is more likely to take root; it is the place where investment in training is more justified; where research and development become essential to success; where innovation is a determinant of the future; where people become the key business asset.

The top line is both the starting point and the finishing line for the race by corporations against smart and creative competition.

It is easier, no doubt, to get a dollar of profit growth by cutting costs than by raising revenue. But studies over the past two years have shown that investors know full well that those two dollars are very unlike each other in the message they deliver about the future of the companies in question.

Companies that simply cut costs, jobs and people to achieve bottom-line objectives without looking at revenue growth, had a far lower rate of success with investors — measured in share value — than those that combined prudent cost-cutting with new revenue — growth in the top line.

Corporations that are historically successful are those that consistently enhance the value of their workforce even in the face of difficult and necessary decisions to reduce costs.

A New Machine Age

As the impact of globalization and information technology take hold, and we explore the effects of mental illness on economic performance and corporate productivity, and the advantage of mental health as a productivity weapon, it is appropriate to consider the differences between the industrial age we are leaving and the information age we are entering.

The machine age, born at the start of the century, was about industrial relations. The information age is about human relations.

It will be about new models of leadership based on empathy, resilience and open communication. Information shared will be more powerful than information closely held. Office politicians beware.

Leaving the 20th Century, interestingly enough, our focus — for good business reasons — will be more and more on the mechanics and mysteries of being human. This may be a defining element of the information age.

Indeed, the search is on by corporations in the United States and Canada for new forms of productivity, value and profitability, seeking to achieve the right blend of incentives and conditions to define the productive workplace for the next 20 years — a blend of good health, fulfilling employment, a recognition of family and work linkages, and a new sense of employability without job guarantees.

This blend of incentives accents balance in work and personal lives, and our ability to adapt to non-exclusive relationships between employer and employee, a search for new compacts of trust in the workplace where human capital and motivation rank with financial capital and machinery as determinants of commercial success.

The commodity power of information — and most particularly its infusion into the institutions and nature of work — inherently places a premium on human behaviour and knowledge as factors of business success in a global world.

Human Return on Investment

The emergence of the knowledge economy pinpoints the inherent commercial value of the human factor. This, in turn, creates powerful economic incentives to invest in human health.

In the information age, corporations' return on their non-medical investments in human beings will be a more resilient, innovative and productive workforce. This is the embodiment of human capital.

In fact, human capital bridges human health and economic performance on the strength of two basic themes: one being the cost of investing in human health, and the other the cost of neglecting it.

In the information economy, human capital is a tangible asset and so an incentive to invest in human health — the underlying collateral of human capital — outside clinical settings as well as in them.

Organizations that promote their employees' mental and emotional wellbeing will brighten their own economic prospects, and achieve a new kind of competitive advantage.

Management practices can reduce mental disability or induce it. The definition of a healthy work environment in the post-deficit era means more than the absence of physical safety hazards.

It means fostering job fulfilment, and flexible work hours and job regimens. It means opportunities for personal growth in working populations, the reduction of social and economic distinctions between management and other employees, clear rights of access to due process, information and free speech inside the workplace and participation in the community which constitutes the place of work.

Mental Health Illiteracy

Why are we so illiterate about mental illness? Understanding is essential, particularly when we consider that four out of five cases of depression, a treatable problem, never get diagnosed or treated at all.

Harvard tells us that depressive patients suffer as much disability and dysfunction as patients with chronic medical disorders such as high blood pressure, diabetes, coronary artery disease and arthritis.

Business must listen, hard when we are warned by researchers at Harvard that in the next 20 years, disability or early death due to depression may cost more workdays than death by AIDS or violence.

The business laity must think about the fact that life expectancy is not only an incomplete measure of health, or the advances we have made in medical science, but a misleading one.

When we account for the very significant business cost of disability, and not just the number of years we are now expected to survive on this planet, we see a different picture of the quality of life of many.

In this daunting light, we see the lengthening shadow of psychiatric disorders. In their disabling effect, these constitute five of the 10 leading sources of disability and premature death as measured in the loss of productive working years in working populations.

The economic impact of disease and injury in Canada generally exceeds the total direct cost of public and private healthcare in this country by $13 billion a year, nearly 20%. Behind that statistic lies a striking reality: the behavioural component of disease and injury.

Studies tell us that 70% of early deaths in the United States and 80% of early disease relate to behaviour. Some 34% of the global burden of disease is estimated to be based in the behaviours of people. So much for destiny, fate or bad luck.

Sense of Urgency — Employee Health

The Ontario Institute of Work and Health in a national leadership roundtable on employee health concluded that Canadian businesses must look urgently for ways to improve the health of their employees. Disability prevention and management must become accepted business priorities.

Growing evidence suggests that psycho-social factors, like the amount of control a worker has over his or her job, have as much impact on health as physical and biochemical factors, and more impact than smoking, poor

diet, or other traditional lifestyle concerns.
Psychosocial factors have a very real impact on low back pain and the duration of disability. Duration, not the frequency of injury, is the main cost driver in workers' compensation in North America.

According to the Institute of Work and Health, workplace disabilities cost Canadian business between $10 and $12 billion annually — a conservative cost estimate, in that it reflects only those dollars expressed through payroll losses.

Workplace disabilities and illness are responsible for the loss of about 10 workdays per employee in Canada yearly, a jolting number.

A Global Crisis in Mental Health
Harvard cites an "unheralded crisis" in mental health worldwide. At the heart of this crisis lie demographic changes associated with aging populations and an increasing incidence and duration of depression.

In a global economy, there is nothing more important than the population base from which we draw the skilled workforce of the future, yet the National Association of Psychiatric Health Systems tells us mental disorders affect 22% of American workers each year.

For comparison purposes, respiratory problems affect about 50% of all American adults and cardiovascular disease, 20%.

At the start of the 1990s, 10% of what the U.S. spent on all forms of healthcare was applied to the treatment of mental disorders — in excess of $67 billion dollars.

When indirect costs, such as lost productivity, death, lost employment, car accidents, crime and welfare are included in this calculation, the total cost of mental-related disorders in the United States is about equal to the total annual cost of all cardiovascular diseases.

The Cost of Neglect
There are two formidable cost questions facing the economic and business community in dealing with human affairs. The cost of investing in human health and the cost of neglecting it.

Neglect is painful and expensive. In the U.S., studies found that 72% of people suffering from mental or addictive illnesses, or both, receive no treatment whatsoever. Homewood data tells us that 5% of all daily visits to a family physician in Canada are made by active alcoholics and drug addicts who are neither diagnosed nor offered treatment for their dependency.

On top of that, 30% of hospital beds in Ontario and other Canadian provinces are, at any given time, filled with active alcoholics and drug addicts and again, none are diagnosed or treated.

Some figures suggest that effective mental health treatment has could reduce the overall use of the healthcare system by over 50%. Even if those estimates were only half true, or a quarter true, the positive cost impact of not neglecting mental illness is dramatic.

The cost of mental illness materializes as a brake on the viability of business organizations in other ways. The weightiest part of that cost burden is indirect and economic in nature, including $7.5 billion in annual business costs in the U.S. resulting from employee suicide.

Nearly two thirds of the cost of depression in the U.S. takes the form of lowered productivity, replacement costs and disability. That's two thirds of $43 billion a year — or about $28 billion U.S.

The expanse of mental illness in society, and the economy, is visible from another perspective. It is estimated that a quarter of all medical out-patients in the United States and from one third to more than half of hospital in-patients suffer from diagnosable emotional disorders. This represents some 40% of all in-hospital days in the U.S.

Mental impairment often wears a mask. The symptoms of panic disorders can be confused with heart or brain problems. Eating disorders can appear as a chronic "something else" and are often linked to depression. Depression, in turn, is two to three times more common among general medical patients than among members of the community at large.

Mental Illness: a Business Issue and a Young Face

The fact that mental illness is a business issue may seem a long unrecognized statement of the obvious — but in one case study in the United States, the mere fact of recognizing the scale of the problem produced considerable results within one famous corporation — Chrysler Corporation — where psychiatric admissions of Chrysler's employees actually went down 12% in one year over another, and the length of stay in mental hospital facilities dropped 22%.

The company reported that the dollars saved stemmed from the introduction of new psychiatric benefits, and from employees and health professionals doing better at matching patients to the treatment they needed.

Mental illness as a business issue has another face — a young and troubling one. Mental illness is killing younger adults at a depressing rate. According to statistics we have reviewed, 37% of the deaths in the United States due to affective disorders occurred among 25 to 44 -year-old people, the heart of the working population.

Distinguished Canadian epidemiologist Dr. Roger Bland found that depression is increasingly a disease of the young. There are more depressed adolescents and young adults in Canada than ever before.

The line-up of employer concerns mounts. The growth of depression is fuelled by increasing numbers, by longer duration, greater likelihood of recurrence, delays in seeking and receiving treatment, diagnostic deficiency and inadequate treatment and follow-up.

These affect the basic strength of the economy, because this is the population that we will draw on for the work skills of the future.

The knowledge economy, it seems, will be faced not only with the unprecedented change and resonance of a technological revolution, but also a column of pressure building from rising emotional distress that must ultimately attract the attention of economic and business decision-makers.

The Crush of Stress
The financial worth of businesses is being hit and hit hard by the accumulation and intensification of negative stress.

A principal goal of the Homewood Centre for Organizational Health at Riverslea is to help make the impact of stress more understandable, and to shed light on the sources and characteristics of workplace stress itself.

One thing we do know is that the relationship between stress and employee performance is complex. Like it or not, it becomes the task of business managers to understand that this complexity exists and then do something about it. This entails a learning process.

The Corporate Leadership Council in the United States sets out a stress continuum for its corporate members as a guide to ensure their employees avoid the two extremes of by too little stress, which undermines motivation, and too much stress, which impairs performance, concentration, effectiveness and relationships.

Stress management strategies, then, are becoming more common at some of the world's largest employers. One of these, General reported a 40% drop in worker absences and a 60% reduction in health benefit payouts.

Another, The New York Telephone Company, reported savings of $2.7 million a year resulting from a reduction in sick days and employee health costs. The third, the U.K. Post Office, realized a 60% reduction in employee absenteeism, according to surveys recently announced.

Sick Work Environment
Business people can identify the indicators of a stressful environment by applyingcommon sense and available metrics to absenteeism and sick rates, employee satisfaction, excessive insurance premiums, excessive turnover rates and poor safety and accident records. The challenge is then to find the sources of those stressors and cultivate and support the necessary coping skills in individual employees.

One thing has become clear. There is no one solution for all companies The type of stress containment needed by an organization will vary according to the kinds of stressors that operate within it, the level of coping skills of its workers, and the organization's own culture. The pressures that create stress tend to multiply in the face of dramatic change and pervasive uncertainty in our transitional workplace. They manifest themselves in poor working conditions, long hours, work overload or underload, role ambiguity, role conflict, unclear mandates, ambiguous relationships, poor communication, job insecurity, mistrust, slow promotion, over-promotion and extremely vicious office politics. This is the soil where the seeds of unhealthy stress are sown.

Other external forces characteristic of the world we live in are also in play — dual careers among married couples and the pressures of maintaining a balance between family and working lives, financial difficulties, elder care and child care.

Increasing numbers of working adults must provide care and support for their children and their elderly parents, uncle and aunts, or even friends, for whom they feel a responsibility.

Stress and Biology
Severe stress can affect our biological functions. As scientific knowledge of the brain grows, we know that mental illness is tied not only to behaviour but to the functioning of our immune and cardiac systems.   S t r e s s can alter the functioning of the brain and turn on our body in a response by the biochemicals our body produces to combat it.

In many respects, companies are being drained of both financial and human capital by the effects of stress-related disorders. Disability benefit claims are on the rise across North America. In Canada, the average rate of long-term disability claims climbed 33% per 1,000 employees between 1981 and 1994.

This fact is perhaps singularly responsible for the trend among business organizations to curtail these escalating disability costs.

Even so, one survey revealed that six out of ten Canadian employers do not intervene directly with disabled employees during disability leaves. But the task of containing disability will become increasingly important as the workforce ages and faces a growing incidence of chronic disease.

Disability management has been defined as a cohesive or systematic process to minimize the impact of impaired capacity on an individual's social and work roles, and to maximize employee health, prevent disability and rein in deterioration when disability does strike.

Efforts to enhance employee health and control disability costs date *back to the early 1970s. At the start, they focused on drug and alcohol problems. Efforts were piecemeal, applying a limited range of employee health problems with a variety of unco-ordinated strategies.*

Current models are more comprehensive and systematic. They are the threshold from which the next generation of disability management — called organizational health — will unfold.

Early Interventions Save Money

There clearly are significant dollar savings to be realized from the disability management process with generally accepted estimates of $5 of savings and $3 of productivity returns for every $1 invested in EAP services to prevent and manage disability.

One analysis of a large Fortune 500 company's health expenditures revealed that 80% of total benefit costs were consumed by only 14% of its employees. This is broadly consistent with findings of a study in 1995 of Canada's workers' compensation system which found that 20% of the claimants drove 80% of the costs.

In another Fortune 500 study, with 60% of the surveyed employees eligible for health promotion and safety education programs, their employers estimated a $5 return in reduced disability costs and increased productivity for every $1 invested in the promotion of health in the workplace.

Agony of Re-Entry

Studies have demonstrated that psychological distress is a serious problem afflicting many in the workforce. It is responsible for a significant number of disability claims, and this is rising every year.

Data from one survey of 1,300 employees and 37 organizations between 1990 and 1992 found that overall, 40% of the workers described their jobs as very stressful. Thirty-four per cent stated that having too little time to finish their work was problem one.

Half the respondents admitted that stress reduces productivity. Another third reported stress-related physical or mental conditions.

Stress-related disability in the United States more than doubled from six to 13% of all disabilities in the 10 years after the previous study. Research is establishing links between psycho-social stress and serious medical illness such as cancer, and suggests that stress-related ailments may be even more prevalent than these statistics indicate.

Business decision-makers must recognize that psychological trauma accompanying a physically disabling injury or illness must be given proper attention. Too often, these secondary injuries are obscured by the physical manifestations of disability and are only recognized after the individual responds fully to treatment for that but still seems unable to return to work. The risk, of course, is this failure to see the psychological factor can bring on chronic, long-term mental disability.

The case for early intervention in such circumstances was made through a recent study of 200,000 workers' compensation claims by ITT Hartford Insurance. This showed that injuries reported to the insurer within 10 days were 47% less costly than those reported one month later.

Meanwhile, the anxiety associated with returning to work after suffering from a mental illness is such that 75% of employers in one recent survey said that it was the biggest obstacle facing their mentally disabled employees.

William Mercer Company, a consulting firm, said the stigma associated with these problems makes people want to conceal them. They affect self esteem. People are concerned with how they will be viewed when they return. We call this the agony of re-entry. It is one focus for the work we propose to do at the Centre for Organizational Health at Riverslea.

Indeed, according to surveys, 53% of employers contacted by Mercer claimed to have more difficulty returning an employee to work following a behavioural health disability than after a physical disability.

Seventy-four per cent cited the employee's own reluctance to return to the job and fully a third cited other problems, including uncertainty about how to create a supportive environment in the workplace for the returning employee, resistence by supervisors to facilitating re-entry and by managers to having the employee back in the first place. This last point was cited by fully one fourth of those surveyed.

The Co-Morbidity Challenge

The challenges of returning to work as part of the process of recovering from mental illness are complicated — the underlying emotional health problems are often masked by concurrent physical problems. This is the co-morbidity challenge.

The changing nature of the workplace is partly to blame for the rise in these illnesses — downsizings, reorganizations, more stress in the workplace, people having to do more with less and layoffs in the ranks of the white-collar employees.

Recent studies show that back pain and heart disease can be influenced by psycho-social factors. Research done last year at a General Motors of Canada plant in Oshawa, Ontario, according to a news report in the Globe and Mail, found that workers who had little control over their jobs or lacked support from co-workers and supervisors were significantly more likely to report lower back pain.

A study of British civil servants revealed more coronary heart disease in lower level positions than among senior managers. In fact, the U.K. study found low job control was a better predictor of cardiovascular disease than smoking, exercise, weigh or cholesterol levels.

The research shows social and psychological factors have as much effect as physical ones in influencing workplace illness. This comes from no less a distinguished a source than the former Chairman of the Manufacturers Life Insurance Company, William Blundell.

At a Toronto conference, held by the Ontario Institute for Work and Health, he pointed to the need to broaden the focus of workplace health programs. Mr. Blundell's proposition is a welcome one. Eventually it would lead to considering overall company performance and employee health as a unified proposition.

The Chief Executive Officer of Algoma Steel, Sandy Adam, says he believes "we shouldn't sacrifice the health and safety of employees to achieve cost reductions."

Mental Health: A Business Asset

It is becoming obvious that mental illness is a business issue, and that mental health is a business asset. We must learn to talk about it in practical, constructive ways.

Fundamentally, non-medical health strategies are best united around economic and social change where human health is seen as the principal currency underwriting the company's human capital base. There are different and powerful economic incentives to tackle mental illness as a threat to productivity — different from the incentives found in the healthcare system and powerful as a prevention tool.

Notably, companies that have been researched as a "great place to work", are financially profitable in addition to having formally integrated "people plans" in parallel with their business plan.

Core Values and Human Capital

The healthy organization embraces core values that are fundamental to effective working relationships — values such as mutual respect, trust, confidence, reliability, fairness and justice.

When business people take into account the style or culture of their organization and not just the individual lifestyle of their employees, they get a clearer perspective of the conditions that must exist not only to resolve human health problems in the workplace, but to prevent them, and in addition to underwrite human capital as a precious and non-renewable business resource.

There is a growing range of incentives for business people to learn more about mental health. The most telling may be found in the truism that psychologically healthy people do more for less, and they do a better job with less time away from work.

Total Quality Management, which took root in the early 1980s depends on the mental health of working people. In the "quality" context, mental health becomes the ultimate productivity weapon.

Economic Behaviour — Questions of Health and Illness

Dysfunctional work environments cause illness and disease, as do social and economic issues such as unemployment, poverty and hopelessness. They are well beyond the ability of the healthcare system, or even the most dedicated medical practitioners, to resolve alone.

The industrial age was about machines that could do things faster and cheaper than people. The information age is about machines that depend on the adequacy, skill and emotional intelligence of people not only to do things quicker — certainly computers can do that — but to create value that defines the competitiveness of the company itself.

In 1991, world industry crossed a divide. For the first time since the industrial age dawned, corporations spent more on information technology than on traditional industrial production equipment — $112 billion versus $103 billion.

Industry has crossed a threshold where skillforces are increasingly replacing workforces, where technology is deployed in the form of information, not only to do things faster, or calculate data quicker, but to alter the way we approach the conduct of commercial enterprise.

Health-Based Productivity

Some of the world's largest corporations — Pepsico, AT&T and Eli Lilly — are investigating ways to optimize the health of working people as a new competitive advantage.

It is fair to say that the industrial world has probably done as much as it can do through cost reduction to create competitive advantage and ensure profitability. Certainly, industrial consolidation will produce restructuring and downsizing. But underwriting success simply by reducing cost and head count will be a less likely vehicle of comparative advantage in the next five years than during the past 10.

So where will competitive advantage come from in future if not from cutting straight line costs? It will come from the top line, where we generate cash flow, sales revenue, customer relationships and innovative thinking.

Even as the stock market soars, business experts warn that the "low-hanging fruit of business cost cutting and restructuring have already been picked." Indeed, business productivity gains have been marginal in North America over the past three bull market years, certainly not enough to offset much larger increases in wages as the labour market has tightened. In Canada, we face a productivity challenge, if not a crisis. We have the worst productivity rates among G-7 countries. Some see improved productivity as the only real way to support the falling Canadian dollar in the face of very high long-term foreign debt.

In these terms, productivity is a function of human capital, and thus a health issue. In that context, human health — the collateral of human capital — is a business and economic imperative.

Global Access to Needed Skills

The globalization of markets has made it absolutely essential for companies to gain access to people, ideas and products from around the world to meet customer needs.

A brand new consumer market has opened up in Eastern Europe with the collapse of the Communist Empire. It has a huge appetite for products of all sorts, without reference to country of origin.

From all this, we can take a hint about what will characterize the employer-employee relationship in the 21st Century. There will be a growing demand for knowledge-based systems and a capacity among resilient, adaptable workers for self-initiated change.

There will be greater reliance on equity compensation, particularly stock options, to provide the necessary incentives and behaviours from corporations and employees in a non-exclusive environment.

There will be new metrics to value the worth of companies which will not rely exclusively on historical accounting. These "health metrics" will measure the financial impact of so-called intangibles such as human capital, employee health, training and the mid-life renewal of experienced workers, managers and executives.

A link will be made between workers and earnings through new metrics defining revenue per employee. This feature of the top-line environment in turn has implications for the structure of the corporate balance sheet. Visualize, on the left of the balance sheet, the assets of the company, things to invest in long term and capitalize to receive tax advantages. On the right side, company liabilities, expense items and costs which much be recognized in the current year.

People are essentially on the right of the standard balance sheet. Investing in them is a current year expense. **Things** are on the left, an asset. Investing in **things** can be capitalized. That is, the anticipated value of plants or equipment can be financially accounted for. Not so for human *effort. Current accounting practices cannot yet quantify an intangible and the mind, flesh and blood of people are intangible.*

This basic dichotomy must be resolved before human capital can take hold in a global information economy.

Nonetheless, it is clear that we have entered an era in which health can become a corporate investment if human beings can, financially, be reported as an asset. It is one step toward the formulation of a health-based economy.

Impact of Work Climate

The Washington Business Group tells us that a *"greater understanding of the impact of the work climate on health-related outcomes and workforce performance is driving business interests in the concepts of corporate health".*

A Michigan State University study found that a corporate climate promoting teamwork, open communications, and profit-sharing with employees correlated with lower per employee disability costs.

In another study of 30 business units by Solution Point Inc., a health technology company in the United States, work climate factors such as employees' understanding of company goals and objectives, evidence of respect, and employee satisfaction predicted reductions in disability, on-the-job accidents, and sickness absence rates.

These insights reach us at a time when the field of human resource management itself is undergoing dramatic change.

The University of Michigan study: "There is an entirely new role for the field that focuses not on traditional HR policies such as staffing and compensation, but on business results that enrich the company's value to customers, investors and employees."

Corporate Self-Interest

The fact is that we need new ways to show how people contribute to the success of the company. We will then find the corporate self-interest in investing in human health broadly and mental resilience particularly. For this, we need to reconcile a battery of perspectives held by the different players who can make or break the attempt. Accountants, for example, view a corporation's human capital as an intangible, an asset for which it is difficult to specify a value.

The fact is, if it's an intangible asset, in accounting terms, it becomes a liability, a current year expense, a vulnerable item when it comes to cost-cutting, and not a large incentive when it comes to making investment decisions in one direction or another.

The accountant measures corporate performance in terms of profit and loss and all of the variables that go into that bottom line.

At the same time, the economist's point of view is broader. Corporate performance is seen in terms of the rate of return realized from assets dedicated to production. "People value" is likely to be more measurable or accepted as part of this equation.

Nonetheless, beyond either of these, a new metric is needed to relate the human factor to economic value added and other measures guiding investor expectations. Such a metric would emphasize value creation and may point the way in quantifying the economic value of human health.

Revenue generation and customer relations are "value drivers." The challenge for business is to develop reliable metrics to measure the impact of employee competence, attitude and wellbeing on them.

Critical to drawing links between human health and economic performance is connecting employee health to other proven measures such as margins of operating profits or earnings per share as indicators to shareholders that there is a defensible or attractive return on the investment in human health and well-being.

Other business results with which to qualify the investment in human capital and therefore human health as indications of "value" might include market share as a measure of competitive strength, customer loyalty as a measure of future stability, and cash flow growth as a critical function of a healthy company.

These are the ties that will bind human health and mental resilience to the design of health-based productivity strategies in business terms, not as ancillary expressions of idealistic management styles.

The Washington Business Group — which includes representatives of many of the exclusive "Fortune 500 Club" — maintains that successful companies in the 21st Century will make investments in people like health management part of their productivity efforts.

A Free Trade Issue

Mental illness has an intense grip on the lives of millions of Canadians and hundreds of millions of working people worldwide, who constitute the labour markets and consumer populations of Canada and its trading partners, including those in present and future free trade zones.

In the age of free trade and human capital, business must depend more than ever on the proficiency and resilience of skilled information workers critical to the operating integrity of the so-called information economy.

Healthy employees are also healthy, active consumers. It makes profound good business sense to "defang" mental illness as a deterrent to productivity and consumption.

Governments and corporations would do well to hear the call by

Harvard University and the World Bank, to the international community to take action on containing a clearly underestimated threat to public health and economic progress — psychiatric illness.

If current trends continue, depression will cause more workdays lost in richer developed economies in the early part of the 21st Century than AIDS, violence, suicide, heart disease, cancer or smoking. And as we noted earlier, the average age of onset of this treacherous disease is getting lower.

Is mental illness a business issue? We believe it is, and we also believe there are eight principles or statements which can anchor business practices in the non-medical fight against the cost and suffering of mental disorders in the workplace — in defence of corporate equity values, productivity standards and income:

- Employees are a quantifiable capital asset, not a liability as they currently show on a balance sheet, in contrast to machines.
- Health is a strategic issue, not a tactical cost, and health should have a place in organizational and asset planning.
- Jobs are not just what people go to, they are the community they belong to. Research tells us that work is the thing Canadians most identify with and the place that makes them sick most.
- In business terms, the stigma of mental illness is expensive and counterproductive.
- The structure, culture and governing processes of organizations can cause or reduce affective disorders to an extent rivaling or surpassing employee lifestyle behaviours.
- Non-medical investments in health are necessary to complement cost-effective expenditure of dollars on healthcare, but without this complementarity, the health status of our working population will not be enhanced sufficiently or at all.
- Human capital — the skills and output of people — is the most important form of capital in the world today — more important than money, and is fundamental to economic growth.
- Strategic commitment to organizational health is a common sense imperative involving a variety of non-medical health management strategies. Among them are:
- Non-medical investments in organizational design, in training and development and middle-age renewal.
- Non-medical investments in disability management and prevention, and new concepts of employee assistance and education.
- Supplementary health strategies and the promotion of fairness, honesty and open communications in the contemporary workplace.

In disability dollars alone, the organizational health market in this country is $12 billion, which is probably an underestimate. By and large, these are dollars of reaction and waste — not because they are insufficient, although some are, but rather, because they are driven by preventable ailments, including stress-related disorders, depression, prolonged soft-tissue injury and drug interactions, the last item representing one of the fastest growing emergency hospital costs.

❧25❧
Lessons of History

In 1970, the government of Canada introduced the Canada Water Act, a pollution control statute containing longer-term provisions for management of Canada's water resources.

Then, and for years to come, the question of industrial compliance, and eventually, support, was centred on the issue of cost — on the number of business facility improvements, plant design changes and future investment requirements — needed to reduce the level of waste that companies dumped into Canada's rivers and lakes.

In those days, the trade-off was between cost and profitability in the first instance, and then between preserving jobs or sacrificing them on the altar of *new costs in* (new pollution abatement expenses) and *old costs out* (fixed overhead in the form, mainly, of wages paid to employees).

The quality movement in the 80s combined with the continuous improvement model have served to expose the obsolescence of that kind of rigid "cost in, cost out" thinking.

Then all hell broke loose, so to speak.

First, the Berlin Wall collapsed. The microprocessor began to take over our lives. A billion new consumers were born. A deep recession fell across the world. Global real estate markets collapsed. Share values of some of the most august Canadian and U.S. companies plummeted. The stilts supporting the Asian economies (the "Five Tigers") were found to be fragile. We drove in one end of a dark economic tunnel — and came out the other end to a global economy characterized not only by freer movement of goods and services but, more important, by liberalized movement of ideas and capital, compliments of new technology.

Capitalist George Soros says, "The globalization of financial markets in particular has accelerated in recent years to the point where movement in exchange rates, interest rates and stock prices in various countries are ultimately connected."

"In this respect," Mr. Soros says, "the character of the financial markets has changed out of all recognition over the past 40 years."

In George Soros' view, the so-called global economy "should really be thought of as the global capitalist system." He refers to "global integration," a development which has produced significant benefits.

One is the international division of labour, producing comparative advantages in cost production between one country and another. This is at the heart of U.S. labour's resistance to free trade, and concerns among environmentalists and nationalists about the emergence of lowest common denominator cost structures.

A second benefit of global integration, Mr. Soros tells us, is economies of scale and the rapid spread of innovations from one country to another. A third is the greater "freedom of choice associated with the international movement of goods, capital and people; and the fourth, freedom of thought associated with the international movement of ideas."

Inherent Instability of Competition

Mr. Soros reminds us of the findings of sociologist Michael Adams, who earlier in this report was quoted seeing a whole new era defined less and less by demographics — a new information technology facilitating the transportation, exploitation and importation of ideas and perceptions without deference to the conventions of culture and community we have lived by up to now.

George Soros also travels Michael Porter's new productivity frontier of hyper competition when he rejects laissez-faire ideology that contends that free markets are self-sustaining, that market excesses will necessarily correct themselves and that they should be left to do so.

He says the benefits of global capitalism are unevenly distributed, and he worries that financial markets are inherently unstable, especially international money markets. In fact, he says, "our theoretical understanding of how financial markets operate is fundamentally flawed." The concept of equilibrium, where investors and other participants in the financial markets discount (that is, predict) the future is "misleading."

Mr. Soros says that "instability is not confined to the financial system. The goal of competitors is to prevail, not to preserve consolidation in the marketplace."

The global market that George Soros refers to is characterized by the condensed dynamics of financial capital traded on a world scale. In that taut environment — where levels of cost management become paramount in determining the competitiveness of companies facing change on every front — the way an organization operates from day to day becomes all important.

But operational effectiveness is not sufficient when competitors, as in the intense commercial printing market, invest capital, reduce crew sizes, and hold the line on prices — and preserve or improve their market share, only to see their profit margins narrow.

In his *Harvard Business Review* article, Michael Porter makes a definitive point in that light. Sameness of the kind generated by rapid advances by competitors across a productivity frontier — the outer perimeter keeps shifting like a desert mirage — is not enough to sustain the performance of companies trapped in the constant shifts of that frontier.

"Competitive strategy," he says, "is about being different. It means deliberately choosing a different set of activities to deliver a unique mix of value." He cites Southwest Airlines in the U.S., which tailors all of its activities to deliver low cost and customer convenience. Ikea, the global retailer based in Sweden, targets young furniture buyers. Some companies consciously offer choice in great variety and other companies aim at the needs of particular groups of customers. All of these examples produce sharply focused companies that have a clear picture of the skills and outlooks of the employees they need to recruit and retain.

Productivity can improve when employees have a clear idea of what is expected of them, and believe that once met, the fulfilled expectation will produce recognition and reward.

From a global perspective to a very local one, Debra DeMonte, a Toronto business owner and restaurateur, says it is important "to mandate your people clearly — not only should they recall and explain what the lunch specials are, they should personally relate to the local neighbourhood, attend street fairs and by doing so, promote not just the success of the merchant they work for, but the entire commercial area." A retail strip is a community in its own right. Knowing that, employees will have a rewarding job and be appropriately recognized for their total effort. Employee productivity becomes more predictable.

Built to Last

Clear employee mandates mean that increasingly, companies can't be all things to all people. Thus the general retreat from diversification strategies over the past decade. The ITT experience is the most dramatic evidence of that. From one of the world's most diversified multi-nationals, to a mere hotel and casino owner. According to Michael Porter, the essence of strategy is "choosing what not to do."

Having said that — once a company has decided what its core business strengths and competencies are — within that, as at Southwest Airlines, "everything matters."

"The strategy then involves a whole system of activities, not a collection of parts." Competitive advantage comes from the way a company's activities fit and reinforce one another — and while technology can *help* this happen, people *make* it happen.

This kind of competitive advantage requires leadership.

Dr. Porter: "In many companies, leadership has degenerated into orchestrating operational improvements. Strategy is making choices, avoiding organizational distractions, guiding employees in making choices that arise because of trade-offs in their individual activities and day-to-day decisions."

"The strategic agenda (of a company) demands discipline and continuity: its enemies are distraction and compromise."

In a separate commentary, the *Harvard Business Review* says "the dynamic of preserving the core business of the company while stimulating progress is the reason that companies such as Hewlett-Packard, 3M, Johnson & Johnson, Proctor and Gamble, Merck, Sony, Motorola and Nordstrom became elite institutions."

In each case, the companies navigated enormous change but stayed focused "on core values. In 1996, 3M sold off several of its large business units, which surprised a lot of people, in order to focus on its enduring core of solving unsolved problems innovatively." The EdperBrascan Corporation, one of Canada's most successful business institutions, did some of the same.

In *Built to Last*, chronicling the habits of successful companies, James Collins and Jerry Porras, professors at the University of Virginia and Stanford respectively, found that visionary, disciplined companies — receptive to change, often inducing it themselves — have outperformed the general stock market by a factor of 12 since 1925.

The Value of Values

Core values are the glue binding a company's history to its future.

Walt Disney's core values of imagination and wholesomeness are rooted in a belief system, not in market surveys.

William Proctor and James Gamble, the *Harvard Business Review* tells us, embraced excellence almost as a religious tenet. That respect has been handed down from one P & G generation to another for 15 decades. Bill Hewlett and David Packard wrote business history because "respect for the individual was first and foremost a deep personal value".

The CEO of Johnson & Johnson, Ralph Larsen, is quoted on the subject this way: "The core values embodied in our credo might be a competitive advantage, but that is not why we have them. We have them because they define for us what we stand for, and we would hold them even if they became a competitive disadvantage in some situations."

The *Harvard Business Review*: "The point is that a great company decides for itself what values it holds to be the core, largely independent of the current environment, competitive requirements or management fads."

Describing "core values as a company's essential tenets," the HBR examined several of the most successful corporations. We might sample these briefly.

Merck espouses honesty and integrity; Nordstrom, being part of something special; Sony encourages individual ability and creativity; Walt Disney, no cynicism, imagination, consistency, and attention to detail.

The original Henry Ford said, "When I'm through... everyone will have one and the horse will have disappeared from our highways." He was motivated, obviously, by a lot more than an income statement.

Other pioneers stood in a similar self-casting light. HBR once again: "Company builders such as David Packard of Hewlett-Packard, Masaru Ibuka of Sony, George Merck of Merck, William McKnight of 3M, and Paul Galvin of Motorola, understood that it is more important to know who you are than where you are going — because where you are going will change as the world changes around you.

This differentiates leaders and managers, strategy and tactics — in Michael Porter's terms anyway. These leaders make choices in life and business on the basis personal and strongly held beliefs. In this context, the original roots of business are dug deep in the hearts of remarkable people.

Noting a range of core values espoused by some of the most successful corporations in the world, none of them fall into the category of maximizing shareholder wealth.

"When people in great organizations talk about their achievements, they say very little about earnings per share. Motorola people talk about impressive quality improvements and the effect they create on the world."

"When a Boeing engineer talks about launching an exciting and revolutionary new aircraft, she does not say "I put my heart and soul into this project because it would add 37 cents to our earnings per share."

As we approach the 21st Century, inspiration needs to catch up to perspiration.

In the downsized global economy, people have to work longer and harder with a perceived widening gap in the rewards some are receiving from the global economy compared to others.

Core values provide the inspiration and they are a proven commodity. Companies with those values are producing wealth, without romanticizing it, consistently and in great abundance.

The dawning of the era of human capital means core values will have even greater currency. As companies move into the 21st Century, they will need to draw on the full creative energy and talent of their people.

But how and why will the survivors of an age of brutal restructuring respond? Can they trust the signs? They probably can if they are given enough reasons to believe in themselves and in their company. That is both a goal and a challenge for corporations in the post-deficit society. The HBR again:

"Confronted with an increasingly mobile society, cynicism about corporate life, and an expanding entrepreneurial segment of the economy, companies more than ever need to have a clear understanding of their purpose in order to make work meaningful and thus attract, motivate and retain outstanding people."

The outstanding qualities of outstanding people are resilience, values, outlook and mindset, all of which contribute to emotional wellbeing and generate human capital. And all of which define mental health as the ultimate productivity weapon of the 21st Century.

❦

Part V
Conclusion

Scouting the
Way Ahead

❧26❧
Billions and Millions:
The High Stakes of Mental Disability

THROUGHOUT THIS REPORT, WE HAVE USED A CONSIDERABLE AMOUNT of statistical data. Understandably, and correctly, most of us have a healthy skepticism about taking statistics at face value. Or blindly marching off to war — or even to a movie — based on statistical evidence alone.

Whether depression, as one study claims, costs North American business in excess of $50 billion or whether it is only $25 billion, does it really matter? The order of magnitude is established.

The fact is, mental illness is measurable in the billions and millions. Billions of dollars. Millions of people. That much the data tells us indisputably. And surely that's enough to get our attention.

Especially when each and every one of those dollars — whether expressed in U.S., Canadian, British or Japanese currency — is spent through (and on) personal suffering, economic dislocation and corporate dysfunction.

Mental illness is, in many heartbreaking ways, a voice of our times. We live in an emotionally unsafe and conflicted society. A place where the future has been overtaken for many by unremitting uncertainty. Fundamental givens — once basic — homes, funded retirement, a job after university — are now unanchored for millions.

The average age of depression for 40% of the one in four women, and one in 10 men who contract the disorder, is 20 years of age. There is irony in this: as the world gets older, depression gets younger.

Truly money can't buy happiness. Which may be one reason why depression will go from fourth place to first in *developed* economies and from fourth to second in developing ones as the source of global work days lost through disability and early death. The rate of depression escalated in Taiwan as the country went from a hand-out to a leg-up country.

A Communicable Disease

Mental disorders are some kind of plague — not infectious in a molecular sense, but communicable just the same. From depressed mother to infant. From troubled boss to employee. From office politician to idealistic co-worker.

If unsafe sex transmits disease and risk, so does unsafe emotional behaviour — the kind that pollutes a work climate, blurs job and work performance expectations, cheats working people and senior executives alike out of their potential, proliferates stress among those most vulnerable to it, and generally creates emotional work hazards that are as dangerous as defective production equipment.

Mental illness is not a healthcare issue. It is a health issue. It is not just a medical matter. It is also a non-medical one. Consider this:

- Companies that people enjoy working at are the most profitable. Those same companies have a "people plan" integrated into their business plan.
- Healthy organizations have core values that their employees discern as real, not rhetorical.
- Success in the so-called knowledge economy will be defined — and realized — not only by production output (statistically quantified) but by employee competence, commitment and "their match" with the jobs they perform. This produces mental health.
- The global economy is unplanned.
- The balance sheet of the future will define organizational and mental health as quantifiable assets.

Human capital is in danger of becoming a buzzword. Let's not let that happen. Let's define it as a powerful mix of human values and human capacity for innovation and sustainable productive output. Human capital will generate growth through relationships, ideas, and trust. Has anyone ever purchased a product at the same place — twice — if one of these was really missing?

The Internet is Not a Person

Even the CEO of Canada's biggest company, BCE Inc. warns us that the trust of consumers (in the technology) is key to fulfiling the Internet's promise as a medium for commercial transactions.

But let's be cautious. The Internet is not a person. It isn't a thing.

It is a place. As such it will reflect and propagate values of some kind. It is already a community centre — of sorts.

The vision of Bill Gates sees the Internet becoming the ultimate 21st-Century marketplace. What happens, in that case, to sales clerks, mall managers, show window designers — what world of uncertainty will they find themselves in?

Toronto columnist David Crane says human capital is more important than money. That being the case, let's ask the question again: what will the capitalization of business organizations really look like in the 21st Century?

Experts tell us again and again — and we recorded their admonitions quite extensively in this report — knowledge in the information economy is more important than raw materials, more important than oil and steel.

Mental health is the underpinning of human capital, the animator of human knowledge and the indisputable expression of our receptor capacity to deploy new information to productive ends. Mental health makes money. Mental illness loses money.

If human capital is more important than money, if information about money is more important than money itself, then mental health is more important than financial capital, cash reserves and credit lines. At least in the global information economy.

Columnist Crane again: "Knowledge and ideas now have a bigger part to play in economic affairs than monetary capital."

If that's true, then the mental health of working populations — not just specific employee groups — is a dominatingly important economic consideration for corporations and the country at large. Fiscal policy, business practices and health policy are intimate correspondents. The Minister of Finance has more to do with our health than the Minister of Health.

As assets, people will *appreciate* if we prevent disability. Which is preventable. Confronting disability means confronting the non-medical conditions which contribute to mental illness.

When disability, not life expectancy alone, is measured as a weight in the global burden of disease, mental disorders occupy five of the 10 leading causes of work days lost through premature death and disability. And the top two — depression and ischemic heart disease — are interconnected.

Life expectancy is an abstraction. A law of averages. Disability is an equalizer. Mental illness — in economic and human terms — is a powerful cause of disability. A force gaining steam. A crisis unheralded because, by and large, society doesn't know how to greet and understand it. The illiteracy of mental health is the stepmother of stigma. Both are enormously expensive.

Education creates mental health. According to one study, a 10% rise in employee education can produce nearly that much in productivity gains, while a 10% increase in capital stock — which values fixed assets — can't do half that. Mental health already appears on the balance sheet — implicitly. It just isn't valued. It needs to be treated as an asset. Corporate strategist Gwyn Williams notes that we can financially quantify disability, but not ability in a business context.

Principal Business Asset

The human mind is the principal business asset of the information age. Emotions are the principal underlying feature of that asset. Mental health is a commodity.

Disability, like bad weather, can be forecast by the way employees perceive the values the company is operating by. Disability rates are tied to the personal opportunity working people perceive themselves having access to. Opportunities for recognition and fulfilment are strategic health measures with significant economic repercussions.

Best management practices are a crucial dimension of disability management. Profitability stems directly from revenues minus cost and taxes. It stems too from human resilience, skill, talent, commitment and capacity minus the incidence of disability, quotients of perceived unfairness and stress pollution levels within the work environment itself.

Hope produces profit. "No end in sight" deadlines and relentlessly changing operating priorities undermine employee hope and productivity.

Global Tragedy

Pervasive uncertainty at work is a source of grief. Explained uncertainty is less so.

The dawn of corporate "life and work" strategies is a bright light on the horizon.

Fairness is a corporate value when expressed in the manner by which supervisors recognize and assess the work of those they are responsible for. It is more important than wages for large numbers of surveyed workers as a measure of job satisfaction.

Stress-related disorders are propelling disability insurance claims skyward. Some corporations are reaching annual levels of expenses in July. Prescription drugs are the fastest growing health cost of all. Prozac is a household name.

One of the world's largest corporations, Chrysler, reduced mental disability by 22% by seeing the problem as an investment.

The Ontario Psychological Association reports that 60% of annual employee absenteeism experienced by one company was attributed to "psychological problems." One Homewood study revealed that in 1996, Canadian workers reported anxiety and stress-related disorders more frequently as a reason for their absence from the job than physical injuries and disorders. Mental illness is a global tragedy. Harvard University:

> Unless we act now, the unprecedented gains over the past 40 years is reducing child mortality, improving physical health and increasing life expectancy, worldwide, are in jeopardy, offset by a steady growth in mental and behavioural problems.

We are well advised to consider the implications of this warning.

Strikes at The Essence of Humankind

Mental illness strikes at the very essence of humankind's nature. The struggle to understand and deal with mental illness has stretched across broad spans of civilization.

All mental illnesses, it seems, revolve around one common theme — the activity of the mind, which is the principal tool of knowledge workers and the defining qualities of human capital — memory, mood and emotion, perception, judgment, impulse control, willed actions, executional functions, the ability to think in representative ways, language and consciousness.

Neurologists, psychiatrists and biologists are keying in on the physics of mental illness. Mental illness has a physical face. A physical reach. A physical touch.

For example, a layman might conclude that mental illness is a blood disorder when he learns that it can increase levels of clotting and exacerbate risk of heart attack.

A lay person might conclude that mental illness is a biological and chemical disorder when she learns that the alteration of the levels of brain fluids can trigger depression. Science tells us that our immune and nervous systems are linked. Emotional stress, among some of us, will suppress our capacity to ward off physical infection.

Similarly, mental illness is a thyroid problem — doctors point to links between depression and hypothyroidism.

Mental illness has implications for our cardiovascular system. Cardiac arterial disease and depression can play off each other. The risk of one complication born of that interplay (sudden death) is increased four to five times. In fact, the functional impairment of the disorders together is about twice that caused by either one alone.

Depression can have an adverse psychological effect on the course of chronic disease, and it is possible 85% to 90% of all cases of depression are badly treated, according to one high-level estimate we have received. And that's a shame.

Arthritis, cancer, lung disease and cardiac disease are associated with mental disorders. Medical in-patients with mental disabilities stay in hospital longer, use emergency rooms more and re-enter hospital more frequently.

Stroke is a "brain attack," the Heart and Stroke Foundation of Ontario tells us. Addictions and depression are brain disorders too.

A Social Question
Mental illness is a social and economic issue. And while science has yet to nail down the precise way that social experience is transformed into mental illness — and while we have yet to discover the specific links between social and economic change *and* rates of depression, those links most certainly exist.

There is also a blood line between job loss and recession, on the one hand, and rates of suicide and psychiatric hospitalization on the other. Similar ties have been documented between depression *and* social uprooting and refugee status.

In other words, losing the identity and usefulness of gainful employment, experiencing the deep cuts of economic diminishment, losing one's home and family and even school chums by moving away from them, or falling into a country-less limbo — all of these things can produce the conditions which breed mental illness and the body joins the mind in reacting to them.

If the term "mental health" is not obsolete — and one might argue that it is — then certainly the notion that mental health and physical health are separate entities is obsolete.

A Single Entity
The Homewood Health Group wishes to erase the line between mental and physical health — not to blur the distinction between different disorders, obviously, but to underscore the basic proposition that the body and the mind — unified by the functions of the brain, the indi-

viduality and psychology of the person and the spiritual premise of human existence — are a single entity touching, and touched by the environments we create, the relationships we have, the jobs we go to, the fairness we offer and receive from others, the progress and prosperity we aspire to, share in or get left out of.

In this context, what we feel about ourselves, about others, about our prospects, is as important as what we know and what we think to be fact. A concept worth noting in business circles. Purely rational thought is not the sole standard of human effectiveness. Corporate pressures that confuse, challenge or assault the belief systems of people working in the company are as destructive emotionally as those that threaten to separate them from their job.

Treating the Soul

Dr. Albert Cheskes is a leading Canadian ophthalmologist and a pioneer in corrective eye surgery. He says that physicians engage in an "incomplete treatment" of their patients unless they "treat the soul and not just the disease."

In these words, a man of enormous scientific skill and reputation sets the table for understanding the interdependence of the body and the mind. In this case, the source in one field deepens the integrity of the concept. As does the source in another. Baseball hero Mark McGwire says the mind is the "greatest muscle we have if only we know how to use it."

In this light, let us turn to the arena of business management where we see so-called "soft" concerns of people replacing the foundations of concrete that have metaphorically and physically supported business and commerce since the industrial revolution began.

The three most frequently cited sources of distress in the workplace are soft issues — role conflict, role ambiguity and workload variance.

These are non-medical determinants of mental health. So are deadline-stacking, no control, rigid behaviours, lack of trust, no personal involvement in the things that affect your job, flawed two-way communication, a sense of being underappreciated, inequity, and leaderlessness.

They are sources of "work and life" stress — and one of the reasons the University of Guelph has created an interdisciplinary Centre for Families, Work and Wellbeing.

The University — across its entire academic regime — will use research and teaching to promote individual and family accord, productive work and hospitable work environments — and sustainable healthy communities. A sign of the times. And a welcome one.

Management Creates Health

Effective management can prevent disability. Dr. Len Sperry, in this report, calls not only for "population health" studies of corporations, he believes early warning systems can be built into companies in order to diminish the impact of emotional disorders — and to reduce the incidence of those disorders themselves, a point Dr. Joffe also registered earlier.

Dr. Sperry believes that dysfunctional companies develop behaviours akin to a dysfunctional person or family — which it is a version of.

Organizations can become diseased. Financial results can be high and morale low. Share value can increase while the emotional hardiness of employee groups recedes.

In this we find a particular challenge in managing the health of the organization and the people in it.

One part of that challenge is how to identify and reverse trends inside corporations that portend dysfunction. Dr. Sperry calls for research.

Corporate strategist Gwyn Williams strikes this ironic note on the point we visited a moment ago. Disability, he says, can be measured in dollars, but "ability" can't. In the context of the subject of this report, he puts the provocative question whether society can measure gross domestic product in terms of unhappiness, grief, and love.

Perhaps they can be measured only by their effect or implication — and perhaps somewhere in them, we find the essence of the World Bank's innovative concept known as a genuine progress indicator.

How do we quantify other fluid and elusive influences that have a material impact on physical and emotional health? The impact of hassle, for example. This is not an idle question — in fact, "daily hassles" are predictors of negative health outcomes, one study found.

Small things can drive us crazy and make us sick. And we can do that *same thing* to each other.

The same study cited "troubled relationships" at work as a principal predictor of ill health.

Hassles are a public health risk that generate stress which spears the emotional and cardiac health of many of those beset by them.

Work Climate and Health

The psychological demands of work are telling. It is high time that after decades of focusing on individual lifestyles as the principal source of organizational bad health, societally we now widen that frame of reference.

Organizational health must also come to define the effects of the cultural influences inside companies and the quality and style of leadership which its senior-most executives exhibit.

The Ontario Institute of Work and Health told us earlier that most health indicators (absenteeism, sick leave, excessive prescription drug use) are not pure indicators of worker health because they also reflect non-worksite factors and fail to give sufficient consideration to the indigenous conditions at work which shape behaviours.

The Bank of Montreal says organizational health and work climate are synonymous.

As we consider next steps in managing the quantifiable impact of mental health and mental illness in cyberspace, the workplace or the space we call home, clearly the defeat of depression assumes premiere status.

Dr. Brian Hoffman, Director of the Centre for Occupational and Organizational Psychiatry at North York General Hospital:

Emotional and mood disorders account for more disability claims than all physical complaints combined and while physical illness tends to be concentrated in the older sections of the population, mental illness starts young and can last a long time.

To greet this challenge, we applaud initiatives designed to bring psychiatrists and family doctors together and thus improve the quality of mental health care. A new Community Mental Health Clinic in Hamilton, Ontario, for example, is designed to be more "user-friendly" to family doctors.

Further, a plan sponsored by the Canadian Psychiatric Association and the College of Family Physicians involves the creation of mental health teams consisting of a family physician, social worker or psychologist. The teams will be deployed in family practice settings.

We note the leadership of Dr. Pierre Beauséjour in this matter. He is the outgoing President of the country's 3,500-member national association of psychiatrists.

Against the backdrop of a new push for professional unity in the fight against mental illness, Dr. Beauséjour deplores, however, "the erratic patterns of inclusion and rejection of newer antidepressant medications" among the province's approved drug lists. Another front of the "other drug war" we discussed earlier in this commentary.

Business Goal Is the Same

Early detection of mental disorders is a principal goal of the newly formed Canadian Business and Economic Roundtable on Mental Health, an example of another kind of alliance, this one bringing corporate leaders onto common ground with health professionals.

The Roundtable's premises statement is offered as an appendix to this commentary. Three highlights are worth visiting here:
* Mental illness and physical illness, when they play off each other, are a source of growing disability, but are under-covered as a business and health issue
* Workplace stress is a "hot" topic, but not a very well understood one
* The role of the Roundtable is, among other things, to make mental health more intelligible as a business issue, and to fight stigma

A Premise of Co-operation

The co-operative venture embodied by the Business Roundtable and the physician-psychiatrist initiative creates platforms on which to tackle the medical and non-medical determinants of mental health.

The Homewood Centre for Organizational Health at Riverslea will keenly support these initiatives. It will:
* Seek to define and understand the dynamics affecting mental health in cyberspace
* Seek to define and understand the implications of human capital, mental health and economic performance as three converging parts of one business, healthcare, and social entity, fundamentally germane to functioning in the knowledge economy.
* Seek to define and understand organizational health, emotional intelligence and corporate productivity as a vital interconnection of the knowledge economy.
* Seek to define and understand the formidable powers of empathy as an instrument of corporate and public-sector leadership suited to the new economy of change and the era of pulsating transformation we are going through in almost all aspects of our lives.
* Seek to define, as part of the equation between human (mental) health and human capital, the relevance of the emotional and economic power of women in the management of the information economy.

- Seek to define a new literacy among decision-makers, healthcare professionals and broader comminities about mental illness and its patron, mental health. In this, the Centre at Riverslea will support the Business Roundtable's focus on co-morbidity as a principal ingredient in this new literacy.
- Seek in all of this a new plain of acceptance, detection and resolution of mental disorders as uninvited intruders, which discriminate against none and threaten all.

Exploring, not Defining the Subject

We noted earlier that in travelling the topic of mental health and economic performance, we are exploring, not defining, our subject. In the months ahead, we will join others to continue this process. A number of the themes and interpretations offered by our sources will be examined as we attempt to more precisely define the indigenous economic impact of mental health, particularly so in the face of the dynamics of an information and knowledge economy.

In this context, we see a number of over-arching themes forming above the horizon of the 21st Century.

One is mental health in cyberspace. The pace of change, the intensity of change, the sheer magnitude of change in the digital society is assaulting, or at least challenging the emotional equilibrium and mental resilience of large segments of the working population.

Don Tapscott, President and Chief Executive of the New Paradigm Learning Corporation, one of the world's leading experts in "networked intelligence" and best-selling author of *The Paradigm Shift*, discusses this phenomenon of discontinuous change in his other *New York Times* bestseller, *The Digital Economy*. We listen in:

Unlike revolutions of the past, the opportunity to share more fully in the *largesse* of this revolution is huge… and apparent rhythms are at work and are beginning to appear.

[But] a looming dark side holds the possibility for severe social stratification, an unprecedented invasion of privacy and other rights, structural unemployment, massive dislocation and conflict…

From Process to Behaviour

The 1990s were characterized by an emphasis on process reform in business. "Process re-engineering," they called it, adapting business systems and methods to the changing times. But re-engineering stumbled. The resistance to it was found in fact at the top, Mr. Tapscott says, the lack of executive consensus, leadership or championing, the prevalence of unrealistic expectations.

CEOs' attention is shifting, in terms of where they spend their own time anyway, from questions of business process to ones of human behaviour. A good thing, too. Behaviour, in the form of human capital, knowledge and innovation, will be a defining competitive issue of the early 21st Century.

Mr. Tapscott, a member of the Canadian Business and Economic Roundtable on Mental Health, and patron of the Tapscott Chair in Schizophrenic Studies at the famed Clarke Institute, comments on this new dimension of the cyberspace frontier:

> For the next millennium, corporations need to get beyond re-engineering to the transformation of the corporation enabled by information technology. The goal should not just be cost control but the dramatic and profound transformation of customer service, responsiveness and innovation.

The stuff of human capital

He adds this: "In the New Economy, adding ideas to products and turning new ideas into new products is what the future is all about."

This future will rest, in these terms, on the health and resilience of skillforces that will increasingly dominate the composition of the working population of this country and the developed world generally.

Small wonder, then, that we are seeing the emergence of the "CEO as Psychologist" — the theme of a book by two principals of the prominent management consulting and accounting firm PricewaterhouseCoopers, William Dauphinais and Colin Price.

Straight from the CEO tells us, "nowadays CEOs are spending much more time on people issues, and in that sense, they are getting into applied psychology."

The authors of this remarkable treatise draw their conclusions from CEO surveys done by the former Price Waterhouse in North America and Europe. They say, "CEOs have become more curious about issues of psychology" — taking a critical look at how people can do their tasks better.

An "eyepopping discovery," is how they describe this apparent shift in the thinking of corporate leadership of the Western World. In fact, 47% of the CEOs surveyed said reshaping corporate culture and employee behaviour both rank on a par in priority-setting with monitoring financial results.

CEOs, in this context, are not travelling a road of conversion to "touchy-feely" corporate dogmas, as these issues would have been known just a few years ago. They are seeking to synchronize employee behaviour and corporate goals in the face of enormous social and economic change.

The Depression of the Internet

Mental health in cyberspace is not a given. It is an emotionally ill defined place and time.

A $2 million study just released in the United States turned the tables on conventional thinking about the "less passive" medium called the Internet. Acclaimed as superior to the "more passive" properties of television because users have the options to act on the information they receive from it, the Internet, it seems, has a dark side.

It represents, for large numbers of dedicated users, a sad, lonely, entrancing and isolating world. The study, funded by microprocessing and communications giants, Intel, AT&T, Hewlett-Packard and Apple Computers, with the U.S. National Science Foundation, found that one hour a week on the Internet, on average, led to a one per cent increase in the rate of incidence of clinical depression; a loss of an average of three friends in the user's social circle, and a measurable jump on the "loneliness scale." According to a New York Times account of the study:

> Based on these data, the researchers hypothesize that relationships maintained over long distance without face-to-face contact ultimately do not provide the kind of support and reciprocity that typically contribute to a sense of psychological security and happiness.

One of the researchers added:

> Our hypothesis is that there are more cases where some people are building shallow relationships, leading to an overall decline in feeling of connection to other people.

The findings touch upon the mental health implications of cyberspace. Developments at Canada's Nortel reflect another: a layoff due to the expanded use of the Internet as a vehicle of sales and commerce, a general point we discussed earlier.

Nearly 80 million people in Canada and the United States are "on line." Similar numbers materialize in characterizing the use of computer technology to redefine work, such as telecommuting, home offices and virtual reality relationships described as "chats." All these may increase disparities in the nature of human relationships, isolate numbers of middle-aged workers, and raise the spectre of social isolation, a known source of depression and anxiety.

The magnetic draw of depersonalization that becomes manifest in the destiny of cyberspace may spring from the deep wells of hassle and irritation that growing numbers of people are sensing, perceiving or experiencing in their daily lives.

Results from one study show that subjective job stress is a pervasive distraction for working people. Its source, we understand, is "too much trouble at work," too many things to juggle, and poor relationships with superiors. Subjective job stress has implications for mental health, a point we have examined extensively in this commentary.

Cyberspace is one context in which to assess and quantify the issues bearing on the mental wellbeing of the working population in the information economy. There are other issues that merit our attention as determinants of human health. A brief final word on them:

- The defeat of depression. It *is* beatable, because it is treatable, yet it continues to reach into too many lives.
- The de-hassling of modern society, relationships, bureaucratic processes and personal interaction. This is a commercial and health priority. It is costing us lives and money.
- The repositioning of mental disability as a health "policy" priority and as an economic issue affecting the competitiveness of our economy and the prospects of corporations with assets in the hundreds of billions of dollars.
- A re-examination of physician training and professional development to equip practicing family physicians and new graduates in medicine to more effectively diagnose and treat depression, anxiety disorders and addictions. We applaud Dr. Rosser's particular leadership in this area. In the same sense, a greater focus on the "physician-ness" of psychiatrists merits the attention of that discipline.
- The articulation of a new health management "business agenda" incorporating specific dollar targets to reduce mental disability in Canada particularly where it implicates productivity rates and the incidence of long-term disability. Tens of billions of dollars are currently being drained out of the economy to pay for disabilities which are otherwise preventable, detectable and treatable. Mental disorders, low back pain and stress-related absenteeism prominently among them.

- The role of complementary medicine in the management of mental disorders. The work of Dr. Mary Wu, founder of the Toronto School of Traditional Chinese Medicine, stands out.

The mental disability market is calculable in the tens of billions in Canada alone. In terms of those who deliver health and disability services, it is virtually an untapped market. It is sizeable, and it is scandalous. Thirty to 35 million women in the North American free trade zone suffer depression. Gender specific research — except when it involves men — continues to lag although Drs. Barbara Dorian, Susan Abbey and Donna Stewart are leading a courageous charge.

In Volume Two of this commentary, we will discuss many of the questions raised in Volume One and will offer an Agenda for Action in organizational health, a term we gratefully borrow from the University of Toronto's Dr. Harvey Skinner. For the moment, however, we stop here, having explored, not defined, our topic.

May we close on this thought. It was written once that "he who troubleth his own house shall inherit the wind." In the terms set out in this report, our house is troubled. As are growing numbers of people who can't get work or who don't have enough time to do the work they do get.

As an inheritance, a gust of wind lacks something. Yet that is what we risk leaving future generations if we fail to assess the terrific costs of neglect associated with failing to tame the unheralded crisis in mental health.

With good sense, good professional care, strong fiscal policies, a sensible investment in research, wise business management practices and a more understandable portrayal in our personal and institutional minds as to what mental illness is — and isn't — we *can* replace the wind with hope and transform neglect into wisdom — producing, as a result, a future of possibility we can see with a clear mind's eye.

Appendices

Appendix I

Canadian Business and Economic Roundtable on Mental Health 1998

Chairman of the Roundtable
Tim Price, Chairman of the Board,
Trilon Financial Corporation

Co-Medical Advisors
Dr. Edgardo Pérez, Chief Executive and
Chief of Staff, Homewood Health Centre
&
Dr. Walter Rosser, Chair, Department of
Family and Community Medicine,
University of Toronto

President of the Roundtable
Bill Wilkerson
Co-Director of the Homewood
Centre for Organizational Health at Riverslea

Purpose and Background

THE BUSINESS AND ECONOMIC ROUNDTABLE ON MENTAL HEALTH IS A vehicle or channel of information among senior executives, physicians, mental health professionals and educators.

It does not have funding or fundraising purposes, but will serve to develop and disseminate information of strategic relevance to the business and health communities in a context provided by the links which we know to exist between human health and economic performance.

Roundtable members will be drawn from the communities of business, health and education. The term Roundtable is intended to convey the sense of information exchange and dialogue. The focus on mental health is based on a number of considerations:

- Mental and physical illness are cohorts in the disabling of otherwise productive Canadians. Disorders of the mind, in this context, are certainly "under-covered" as a business and health issue.
- Psychiatric illness is growing faster, as a percentage of the global burden of disease and injury, than cardiovascular disorders. Depression, itself, inside 20 years, is projected to be the leading source of work days lost through early death and disability in the developed world. It is costing business in the United States an estimated $50 billion (U.S.) a year.
- Workplace stress is a "hot topic" but not a very well-understood one. There are factors endemic to the organization of work which create stress and there are predetermined characteristics of people that science is only beginning to understand that make some individuals more vulnerable to stress and the disease it triggers. This is germane to younger and older adults particularly.
- The world is experiencing enormous change. This has a bearing on the performance of business organizations in a global economy and the sense or fact of emotional well-being people enjoy or lack in their lives. The impact of change, in these terms, must be better understood in order to be managed more effectively.
- In the U.S., depression alone is estimated to cost the economy $50 billion a year in direct expenditure for treatment and indirectly through lost productivity. That number climbs to a quarter of a trillion dollars when you consider all forms of mental illness including addictions.

- The contribution of mental illness to the cost and disability of the working population of this country may also be observed in this context: the Canadian health care system, by and large, embodies three groups of spending and cost.
- One is an estimated $48–$50 billion a year through federal and provincial tax expenditures on the "medically necessary" components of the health care system.
- The second is an estimated $24–$26 billion a year through private insurance and personal fees for supplementary health services.
- The third is the economic burden of disease, estimated in 1993 by Health Canada to be in excess of $85.1 billion. Almost half of that amount was attributed (five years ago) to loss of productivity resulting from long-term disability.

The role of mental illness in the economic affaairs of Canada has not been well documented. It is fair to assume its impact goes beyond the direct costs attributable to mental health services and is both a medical and economic burden. The issue can be usefully explored.

The Goals and Objectives of the Roundtable

Broad Goals
- To contribute to efforts to contain the economic cost and human suffering associated with mental illness.
- To help make mental health more intelligible to business executives, physicians and the wider community as a source of or deterrent to economic performance including productivity as a key tenet of the global economy.

Working Objectives in 1998–99
- To help shed light on the cohort effect of mental illness and chronic physical disease as the cause of severe, costly and potentially lethal disability among working Canadians.
- To help shed light on the economic, social and workplace effects of depression which afflict a broad and encompassing range of the Canadian population — possibly one in five.
- To help pool and communicate information on non-medical strategies and models that will support efforts to detect depression in the workplace earlier and to reverse trends that indicate growth in the incidence and prevalence of this treatable disease.

- To help draw business attention to the results and challenges being realized and met within the scientific community to understand and resolve the neurological, chemical and biological aspects of mental illness.
- Where possible, through open discussion and information, to help combat stigma to the extent that it impairs the detection and treatment of disabling mental disorders.

Themes
The Roundtable will concentrate on two themes. They both relate to the goals of sustainable human health and sustainable business and economic performance. The themes are:
- *Accelerating Change and Stress*
  · Through information, awareness and detection, to help contain the effects of depression and mental anxiety as a source of disability and work days lost.
  · Through information, awareness and detection, to help encourage a greater understanding of cardiac illness and depression as affiliated disorders. Independently, they are leading causes of death and disability and, together, comorbidly, they constitute a major risk to public health.
- *Mental Health and Human Capital*
  · Through information and awareness, to help define the nature of business and organizational strategies that will be necessary to ensure that mental health is a sustainable asset and source of human well-being in the global information economy that is now unfolding.

Roundtable Partners

In effect, the Roundtable is an informal partnership, an unstructured network through which information on the themes noted above will be distributed, examined and shared inside and outside the list of participating members. The work will be done on an entirely voluntary basis.

The efforts of the Homewood Health Centre at Guelph, Ontario and its affiliate, the Homewood Centre for Organizational Health, have been particularly dedicated in encouraging the creation of the Roundtable and in directing its own resources to the effort.

Mr. Tim Price, Chairman of the Board of Directors of Trilon

Financial Corporation and a principal of the EdperBrascan Corporation will chair the Roundtable in 1998 and represent it at a number of events.

Bill Wilkerson, Co-Director of the Homewood Centre for Organizational Health, will serve as President of the Roundtable and will perform the principal executive functions and will serve as public spokesperson for the Roundtable.

Dr. Walter Rosser, Chairperson of the Department of Family and Community Medicine at the University of Toronto and **Dr. Edgardo Pérez**, CEO and Chief of Staff of the Homewood Health Centre, have agreed to serve as medical advisors to the Roundtable.

The membership of the Roundtable reflects a wide range of corporations with assets in the tens of billions of dollars, as well as leading universities and health organizations. The first list of participating members is attached and will be updated as new members join the Roundtable.

Roundtable Projects

The Canadian Business and Economic Roundtable on Mental Health will support and participate in information projects in 1998 and will develop and transmit data on the themes described in this paper. Among those initiatives:

- Supporting the leadership of Mayor Don Cousens of Markham, Ontario and other Canadian mayors in recognizing World Mental Health Day Canada in 1998.
- Participating in two creative events next fall centering on disability and health issues associated with the comorbidity of heart disease and depression and, more broadly, health and economic performance. These events will involve researchers, physicians and business people from teaching hospitals, research centres, universities and corporations based in Canada with strong international dimensions.
- In partnership with the Homewood Centre for Organizational Health, participating in the World Congress on Social Psychiatry being held in Vancouver in August.

In each case above — and in other projects now in the latter stages of planning — the Roundtable's fundamental purpose will be to generate, interpret and produce information of strategic value to business and economic decision-makers through the efforts of the Roundtable's interdisciplinary membership.

Postscript

The Canadian Business and Economic Roundtable on Mental Health is a concept which developed, gradually, from a "one off" discussion meeting of business executives and physicians hosted by Mr. Price last fall. The meeting focused on depression and the workplace and the business participants expressed a need for analysis of stress as a trigger of depression and source of absenteeism.

In the months following, the Homewood Health Group, well represented at the meeting, undertook to do such an analysis, created the Centre for Organizational Health at Riverslea and commissioned the Canada Health Monitor to evaluate workplace stress data as a source of absenteeism from work.

This produced a report which was then published, attracting attention from major daily newspapers, radio and television outlets, trade journals and health, workplace and educational organizations across the country. In addition, attendees of the original meeting have received information regularly on these topics.

It should be noted that the value of the Roundtable as a concept and virtual network will be assessed from time to time. It will function as long as it seems to be serving a useful purpose. Those behind it have no growth ambitions in the form of structure and not only will *not* duplicate what others are already capably doing in the mental health/information field, but will celebrate and publicize it.

For information or to comment, contact:
Bill Wilkerson
President of the Roundtable and
Co-Director of the Homewood Centre
for Organizational Health at Riverslea

Tel: 416-481-8514
Fax: 416-481-4389

Appendix II

World Mental Health Day
in Canada
1998

Depression:
The Heart of the Matter

The Mayors' National Initiative on Mental Health

in association with

The Homewood Centre for Organizational Health at Riverslea
The World Federation for Mental Health
The Canadian Business
and Economic Roundtable on Mental Health
The Canadian Mental Health Association
The Canadian Psychiatric Association
The Heart and Stroke Foundation of Ontario
&
The Ontario Psychological Association

October 8, 1998
Markham, Ontario

World Mental Health Day in Canada
1998

Mayors' National Initiative on Mental Health
His Worship Don Cousens
Mayor, Town of Markham, Ontario
Chairperson

Roundtable Discussion
"Depression: The Heart of the Matter"

Markham Civic Centre
Council Chambers
October 8th, 1998
10:00 a.m. to 1:00 p.m.

Honoured Guest
Her Excellency Diana Fowler LeBlanc

Honorary Co-Chairs
Dr. Paul Garfinkel
President and Chief Executive
Centre for Addiction and Mental Health
&
Tim Price
Chairman of the Board, Trilon Financial Corporation and
Chairman, Canadian Business and Economic Roundtable on
Mental Health

Introduction by Dr. Edgardo Pérez,
CEO and Chief of Staff, Homewood Health Centre and
Co-Director of the Centre for Organizational Health at Riverslea

Opening Remarks by Dr. Rodrigo Muñoz, President
American Psychiatric Association
Moderator - Bill Wilkerson, Co-Director of the Homewood
Centre for Organizational Health, Vice-Chair of the Mayors'
National Intiative on Mental Health and
President of the Canadian
Business and Economic Roundtable on Mental Health

Presenters and Discussants

Dr. Susan Abbey, Director, Program in Medical Psychiatry, Toronto Hospital

Dr. Pierre Beauséjour, Chairman of the Canadian Psychiatric Association and Clinical Director of Psychiatry at Royal Ottawa Hospital, Ottawa, Ontario

Dr. Earl Berger, Managing Director of the Canada Health Monitor, Toronto, Ontario

Dr. Vincenzo Di Nicola, Chief of Child Psychiatry, University of Montreal

Dr. Barbara Dorian, Psychiatrist-in-Chief, Women's College Hospital and Director of the Women and Society Program at WCH, Toronto, Ontario

Dr. Paul Dorian, Terrence Donnelly Heart Centre, St. Michael's Hospital, Toronto, Ontario, and Associate Professor of Cardiology, University of Toronto

Dr. Russell Joffe, Dean of the School of Health Sciences, and Vice President, McMaster University, Hamilton, Ontario

Dr. David Koczerginski, Psychiatrist-in-Chief, Markham Stouffville Hospital

Dr. François Lespérance, Department of Psychiatry, Montreal Heart Institute; Adjunct Professor of Psychiatry, McGill University; and Clinical Adjunct Professor, Department of Psychiatry, Université de Montreal

Tom Reynolds, International Director, Employee Assistance Programs, Bank of Montreal

Dr. Walter Rosser, Chair, Department of Family and Community Medicine at the University of Toronto

Dr. Terry Sullivan, President, Institute of Work and Health, Toronto, Ontario

Dr. Robert Swenson, Director, Medical Psychiatric Unit, Ottawa General Hospital; Associate Professor of Psychiatry, University of Ottawa; and Consultant Psychiatrist, Ottawa Heart Institute, Ottawa, Ontario

Themes and Implications Panel
(Input for International Report on the Dialogue)

Dr. Graeme Cunningham, Director of Addiction Medicine, Homewood Health Centre and President of the Canadian Addiction Institute

Maria Gonzalez, Vice-President, Strategic Initiatives, Bank of Montreal

Dr. Beth Reade, Psychiatrist, Homewood Health Centre

Dr. Pierre Ritchie, Past President, Ontario Psychological Association, Professor of Psychology, University of Ottawa, and Executive Director, Canadian Register of Health Service Providers in Psychology

Dr. Jack Santa-Barbara, President and Chief Executive Officer, CHC - Working Well

Neil Seeman, lawyer, health policy analyst and Editorial Board, *The National Post*, Southam Inc.

Homewood

Acknowledgement

THE SUPPORT OF KEY PEOPLE IS ALWAYS ESSENTIAL TO A PROJECT LIKE *Mindsets*.

For their unwavering interest in, and commitment to, this initiative and the broader purposes of the Centre for Organizational Health at Riverslea, the authors wish to express our most genuine appreciation to Ken Murray and Bill Hamilton, Chairman and President respectively of the Homewood Corporation; David Sands, Homewood's Vice-President and Chief Financial Officer, and CEO of Orangewood Properties Limited; and Colin Ferguson, the company's General Manager of Hotel Services.

We thank as well Dr. Graeme Cunningham, Dr. David Wright, Dr. Diane Whitney and Dr. Wilson Lit for the benefit of their clinical knowledge and direction through this process. We are grateful to Dr. Beth Reade for all of that plus her resolute contribution to the research and judgment process.

To the entire Homewood community, too many to mention by name, simply, our gratitude to each of you — you are the essence of purpose behind the landmark in mental health care that Homewood has become.

Homewood
and Guelph, Ontario

THE HOMEWOOD HEALTH CENTRE SITS ON THE CREST OF ROLLING GROUNDS that meet the Speed River in a delicate intersection of nature's best. Its porticos reflect the history that Homewood embodies.

Founded 115 years ago, Homewood is one representative of how private enterprise and public medicare can work together. Homewood is privately owned, but provides a public service, treating people with mental, behavioural and emotional disorders with a mix of modern science and spiritual safety.

Homewood's legacy has been penned by the dedication of pioneers like Stephen Lett, its first superintendent, who projected a vision of holistic and outcomes-based care well ahead of his time. The progression continues.

Homewood today is an internationally known specialist in addiction medicine, trauma care and the treatment of depression, eating disorders and other forms of psychiatric and emotional illness.

Ken Murray and Bill Hamilton lead the Homewood Corporation, Mr. Murray as Chairman, and Mr. Hamilton as President. Both hold strong beliefs in the parallel courses of clinical and community service that Homewood has come to represent.

The Homewood Corporation is the holding company for the Health Centre, the Homewood Behavioural Corporation and Orangewood Properties Ltd., a property management and retirement home investment company. Two million shares of the Homewood Corporation are traded publicly and distributed widely.

Guelph, Ontario, is Homewood's home town. A city with a population of 84,000, a strong manufacturing base, a professional and university community, and a well run local economy, Guelph represents a classic blend of aesthetics, history and planned growth. It is a smaller Canadian city with a clear sense of place, nestled between bigger communities to the west and Canada's biggest metropolis, Toronto, an hour to the east.

This book was designed by
Douglas McKercher, Book Designer

*The body type and chapter headings are
Bitstream Goudy OldStyle. Chapter numbers
are Goudy Handtooled, and the fleurons are
by Hermann Zapf.* ❧